Kovels'
Know Your
Collectibles

Kovels' Know Your Collectibles

Ralph and Terry Kovel

Crown Trade Paperbacks
New York

To ADRIAN SHAPIRO
whose smile, encouragement, knowledge,
help, dedication, and friendship have made our books
possible these past 28 years—
thank you—
and, of course, to
Kim and Lee

Copyright © 1981 by Crown Publishers, Inc.

Published by Crown Publishers, Inc.,
201 East 50th Street, New York, New York 10022.
Member of the Crown Publishing Group.

Crown Trade Paperbacks™ and colophon are trademarks of Crown Publishers, Inc.

Manufactured in the United States of America

Library of Congress Cataloging-in-Publication Data
Kovel, Ralph M.
Kovels' know your collectibles.
1. Antiques. I. Kovel, Terry H. II. Title.
III. Title: Know your collectibles.
NK1125.K653   1981   745.1   81-5515
                                   AACR2
ISBN 0-517-58840-4

10 9 8 7 6 5 4 3 2 1

First Paperback Edition

Kovels' Know Your Collectibles

Ralph and Terry Kovel

Crown Trade Paperbacks
New York

To ADRIAN SHAPIRO
whose smile, encouragement, knowledge,
help, dedication, and friendship have made our books
possible these past 28 years—
thank you—
and, of course, to
Kim and Lee

Published by Crown Publishers, Inc.,
201 East 50th Street, New York, New York 10022.
Member of the Crown Publishing Group.

Crown Trade Paperbacks™ and colophon are trademarks of Crown Publishers, Inc.

Manufactured in the United States of America

Library of Congress Cataloging-in-Publication Data
Kovel, Ralph M.
Kovels' know your collectibles.
1. Antiques. I. Kovel, Terry H. II. Title.
III. Title: Know your collectibles.
NK1125.K653   1981   745.1   81-5515
                                   AACR2
ISBN 0-517-58840-4

10 9 8 7 6 5 4 3 2 1

First Paperback Edition

Contents

Illustration Acknowledgments

Illustrations for this book appear by courtesy of the people, museums, companies, and shops listed below:

Adirondack Museum, Blue Mountain Lake, New York (pages 43, 44 47); Auctions by Theriault, Annapolis, Maryland (pages 314, 315, 388); Joan Bogart, Rockville Centre, New York (page 45); Richard A. Bourne Co., Inc., Hyannis, Massachusetts (page 171); Brown Group, Inc. (page 335); Christie's, New York City (pages 37, 125, 127, 265, 266); Coca-Cola Company, Atlanta, Georgia (pages 335, 336); Robert C. Eldred Co., Inc., East Dennis, Massachusetts (page 51); The Farmers' Museum, Cooperstown, New York (page 135); Greenfield Village and The Henry Ford Museum, Dearborn, Michigan (pages 40, 41, 113, 324, 388); Betty Grissom, Peoria, Illinois (page 150); Malcolm Halsam, Heisey Museum, Newark, Ohio (pages 221, 222); Index of American Design, Washington, D.C. (page 59); The Magnificent Doll, New York City (page 319); Margaret Woodbury Strong Museum, Rochester, New York (pages 319, 320); Mattel, Inc. (page

317); Morton-Norwich, Morton Salt Division (page 346); Moxie Industries, Inc., Atlanta, Georgia (page 347); Nabisco, Inc., East Hanover, New Jersey (page 347); Museum of Our National Heritage, Lexington, Massachusetts (page 45); Newark Museum, Newark, New Jersey (page 120); Pepsico, Inc., Purchase, New York (page 348); Phillips, New York City (pages 247, 268, 269, 312); Standard Brands Incorporated (page 349); The Procter & Gamble Company (pages 344–345); Lloyd Ralston Auction, Fairfield, Connecticut (page 289); Robert W. Skinner, Inc., Bolton, Massachusetts (pages 93, 231, 252); Sotheby's Los Angeles (pages 287, 308, 316, 318); Sotheby's New York (pages 27, 28, 29, 38, 45, 63, 64, 67, 78, 168, 174, 246, 249, 250, 256, 257, 267, 269, 276, 278, 291, 297, 302, 305, 306, 311, 380, 381); David Stockwell, Inc., Wilmington, Delaware (page 33); White House Collection, Washington, D.C. (page 112); Woody Auction Company, Douglass, Kansas (pages 232, 233, 234); Yale University Art Gallery, New Haven, Connecticut (page 40).

Authors' Note

Know Your Antiques was written in 1967. Our newspaper column had been running nationally for fifteen years and the book was the result of the questions received from readers through the years. Now, fourteen years later, we have decided another book is needed. Collecting and collectors have changed during those years. Collectors are often younger, buying old furniture or glass because they like the quality of workmanship of the old compared to the new, or simply because they want something not readily available to everyone. *Collectibles* is a term that was not even in existence in 1967. It seems to mean anything collected that isn't really antique or one hundred years old. Just as *Know Your Antiques* included some pieces now called collectibles, such as bottles, *Kovels' Know Your Collectibles* includes some antiques, such as one hundred-year-old furniture. The objects included in this book were chosen to reflect the interests of our readers and ourselves. Do not interpret this as anything but random selection. Some important collectibles may have been omitted. The amount of space given the subject does not necessarily indicate its importance. Some things you might expect to see are included in *Kovels' Know Your Antiques* and have not been repeated. Some things, like wicker furniture, are included here because they were not in our other book. Thus, the pair of books should cover most of the interests of today's collectors.

We have stressed the easy identification features and the history of the objects. Marks, factory dates, and pictures of many pieces are included. We have omitted some categories such as oil paintings or folk art that are always unique examples. There are expensive items such as Handel lamps and inexpensive items such as 1950s toys. In most chapters we have followed the interest of the collector to the 1950s or after.

We have tried to be accurate but sometimes it is more difficult to check the dates of a twentieth-century company than those of a nineteenth-century firm. As the explorers in a largely uncharted sea of collectibles we have found contradictions, errors, and confusion. To help you decide what is right, we have added an extensive bibliography of publications on each subject. It has taken ten years to write this book and a few of these publications are now out of print but can be found in many good libraries.

Many of the companies mentioned have aided in the preparation of the material about the firm. Trademarks, early advertising leaflets, and general history were sent. In some cases the original material was totally changed by the company a few years later. If any errors still remain we welcome corrections.

We thank the many commercial companies, the auction houses, the museums, and the authors who have helped with the research and selection of pictures. We thank the readers of our other books, such as *The Kovels' Antiques Price List,* who have asked about areas of collecting every year since 1967. It is these questions and the research required that led to this book.

RALPH M. KOVEL, senior member ASA
TERRY H. KOVEL, senior member ASA

September 1981

Kovels'
Know Your
Collectibles

1

How to Collect, Protect, and Sell Your Antiques

Sooner or later everybody seems to own an antique or collectible. Maybe it was part of an inheritance, maybe it was a bottle that was under the floorboards in the attic or porch of an old house, maybe it was a vase that captured your imagination at a house sale. Whatever the reason, antiques are found everywhere and they seem to be appreciated by almost everyone.

If you decide to look up your "find," you need some basic information before you start. What is gutta-percha? Egyptian Revival? Or a splat? Unfortunately, almost everyone starts with little knowledge, and often it is impossible to look up an antique without help from someone who knows the vocabulary. You may be an expert in American silver but know little about old toys. There are special features, marks, and hints that go with each field of collecting. We hope that *Kovels' Know Your Collectibles* will furnish the extra knowledge that will help you to recognize the good from the bad, the rarity, or the best example.

How to Look Up Your Antiques

The most obvious place to do research is in a library. You can try the encyclopedias, books about antiques, price guides to antiques, and any one of the hundreds of antiques books. Some libraries will help you by phone, but a trip to the library is usually required. Doing your own research is always a good idea, as you can learn about other antiques in the process and perhaps gain some new interests.

There are many antiques publications, ranging from glossy color picture magazines devoted to expensive works of art to newspapers and newsletters on almost every subject. There are antiques shows in every area and often there are specialized shows for collectors of bottles or toys or paper antiques. The shows are listed in local newspapers as well as antiques publications. Browse through the shows and talk to some of the dealers and collectors; it is one of the best ways to learn. The antiques business is a friendly one. Most of the people involved are happy to give you information. Don't expect to get free appraisals. That is like asking your doctor or lawyer for free advice.

During the past ten years, collecting as well as collectors have changed. It is no longer a hobby for the rich or eccentric. Many well-known financial advisers are suggesting that "things," as well as stocks and bonds, should be considered as part of an estate. True collectors usually don't buy to resell. They buy for enjoyment, for the thrill of the chase, for a sense of history, or for furnishing a home. They rarely consider the eventual value of an antique.

Collections represent money. Various amounts of money are invested over a period of time until the antiques represent a large sum of money. The value of antiques has been rising faster than the inflation rate, so the value of your collection is constantly on the rise.

You may not consider your antiques as part of your assets, but insurance companies, the Internal Revenue Service, estate tax laws, and banks will treat your collection as cash. It is important to keep full records, so in case of loss, sale, or transfer, the problems of taxes and values can be well established.

Cataloging Your Collections

Buy a special inventory notebook or a card file as soon as you buy your first antique, even if the antique is something that cost only a few dollars. Record the name of the item, a description including size, color, markings, and condition, price paid, where purchased, and the date. The description is needed for proof of loss to an insurance company or for police reports in case of theft.

Be sure to keep all labels, stickers, auction catalogs, etc., with your records. Make a photocopy if necessary. The price paid is essential for your records should the antique be sold or placed into an estate. There are tax laws concerning the value of antiques and profit derived when the antiques are sold. This profit is based on the actual cost at the time of purchase; in some cases, the value at the time you received it.

The date and place of purchase is necessary because it is easiest to remember an antique if you can recall the day or circumstance when it was purchased. Sometimes information about an auction or sale can be a

clue to past history and will add to the value. A piece from an important collection has added prestige. It is also important to know if the antique was purchased at a retail shop, a show, or an auction. It puts the price in better perspective. For instance, auction prices are almost always lower than retail. If you got your antique as a gift or through a trade, list the approximate value at the time.

After an antique is listed in your files, record whatever information you feel may help the next owner. For example, if it is a piece of furniture, write on the bottom or in some inconspicuous area on the back the date you purchased it, your name, city, and any previous history of ownership.

Paintings or any type of framed antique should be identified in the same way. Also record how the piece was framed, if acid-free paper was used in the mounting, when it was restored, reframed, or opened, and whether the frame is old or new.

Silverware, porcelains, glassware, and toys cannot be marked this way because stickers or taped notes disintegrate or are destroyed in time through washing. You can mark these with special ink that is visible only under ultraviolet light.

Next, photograph the antiques. If it is possible, take a picture of each piece separately and attach the photo to the index card or notebook listing. This is important for identification purposes in case of theft or fire.

If individual photographs are impossible, have a friend who is a good photographer take a series of photographs of your home. Open the cupboard doors, drawers, etc., so all "hidden antiques" show. One picture of a breakfront filled with dishes is enough to establish a loss.

Be sure to file one set of pictures, your records, and any appraisals in a safe-deposit box, in the office, or in some place removed from the collection. It is of no help to have records that are destroyed in the same fire that destroyed the collection.

Of course, you don't have to do all of this at one time; but it is important to remember that the longer you wait, the bigger the job. We find it a great help to keep two kinds of listings. When an item is purchased, list it in a notebook with the date and brief description. Once a year, we go over these records and complete the entries with full measurements, photographs, etc. A chronological listing is helpful when it is time to review your insurance. (More about that later.) Be sure to delete any item you break, trade, or give away. These should be removed from your insurance lists as soon as possible.

Government Tax and Estate Records

One of the reasons for keeping good records is that sooner or later your antiques will be involved with the government, either when you sell them or when your heirs inherit them.

Tax laws keep changing and if you are concerned about a large collection to be sold, or about a future estate, it would be wise to consult the attorney or tax man who will be involved with your will.

Sometimes it can be to your advantage to give some of your antiques to charity or to a museum rather than sell them. There are times when you should give them to your children over a long time period to avoid a tax. If they are sold, you must pay taxes on the profit in the same manner as you would stocks.

Insurance

Antiques should be insured. You insure your house and its contents, and the antiques are part of this group. Most insurance policies give minimal protection for a fire or theft loss of antiques that are not specially listed—usually only $1,000 for any one loss of silver, $1,000 for loss of guns or books, $100 for one loss of coins or ingots, $500 for loss of jewelry.

Look around your house and imagine what your loss in antiques would be if there were a fire. The smoke and water damage could ruin many items—dishes craze and crack, furniture loses the finish, the upholstery is smoky and must be replaced, pictures must be cleaned, etc. None of them will be adequately covered if you do not carry fine arts insurance. Check with the insurance agent who carries your homeowner's policy. The added fine arts coverage is inexpensive but very important to all collectors.

Insure your items as follows: the furniture, silver, jewelry, books, country store pieces, and some other items should be covered for fire and theft; porcelains, glassware, oil paintings, and other pieces should be covered with the more expensive fire, theft, and breakage insurance.

Each year, go over the policy and add and delete antiques. Each year, reappraise the items, usually for higher values. A yearly reappraisal is necessary to keep prices up to date.

When you make a list for insurance coverage, divide the items into categories such as furniture, silver, porcelain, coins, jewelry, etc. List one kind to a page. *Number each entry.* Match these numbers to your inventory records.

If you should suffer a loss, you can remember that the Vienna art plate with the lady and the candle design was number 6 on both lists; the Vienna art plate with the lady in a red dress was number 7. It makes future listing and any claims much easier.

If it is possible to place a sticker with a number on the item, that is even better. This is often possible with furniture, paintings, or items that are not washed.

THE APPRAISAL

One of the biggest problems in applying for a fine arts insurance policy is the appraisal. Most insurance companies will take your word about the value of an antique if the individual piece is not too expensive (under $1,000) or if you are not insuring too many items.

If you have a special problem, such as an inherited collection of rare antiques, family heirloom furniture of a value unknown to you, a home so filled with antiques that your insurance listing runs into six figures, or just a stubborn company that won't believe the values you've given, you must have an appraisal.

Who to Have Do the Appraisal

In some cities, finding an appraiser can be difficult. Look in the Yellow Pages of the telephone book under "Appraiser." If none are listed, look in the Yellow Pages under "Antiques Dealer." The telephone display ads will often include the information that the dealer is also a qualified appraiser and will list the affiliation with an appraisal association.

If this information is not available, call an antiques dealer and ask him to direct you to an appraiser. Collectors and collectors' clubs often can suggest nearby appraisers.

There are a few national appraisers' associations that have directories. Some members will travel to your collection, but expect to pay a fee plus travel expenses and travel time. An out-of-town appraiser is not usually necessary unless you have a very specialized, large, or very expensive collection.

The appraisers' associations with national memberships are:

American Society of Appraisers
P.O. Box 17265
Washington, DC 20041

Antique Appraisal Association of
  America
11361 Garden Grove Boulevard
Garden Grove, CA 92643

Appraisers Association of America
60 East 42nd Street, Suite 2505
New York, NY 10165

International Society of
  Appraisers
P.O. Box 726
Hoffman Estates, IL 60195

International Society of Fine Arts
  Appraisers, Ltd.
P.O. Box 5280
River Forest, IL 60305

Mid-Am Antique Appraisers
  Association
P.O. Box 9681
Springfield, MO 65801

New England Appraisers
  Association
5 Gill Terrace
Ludlow, VT 05149

United States Appraisers
  Associaton, Inc.
886 Linden
Winnetka, IL 60093

One of the biggest problems with appraising is "conflict of interest." An appraiser should not offer to buy. A dealer who is buying cannot give you a fair appraisal. Separate appraising and selling completely.

Appraisal for Insurance

If your insurance company requires an outside appraisal, you must hire an appraiser with recognized credentials. You should have a written appraisal with pictures, if possible. Many antiques dealers can do the job, but it is best to find a qualified member of an appraisers' association.

The appraisal figure should be either retail or wholesale value. This is a matter of personal preference and only the person ordering the appraisal can make that decision. Remember, in the case of a death, the estate antiques will probably be valued at the prices listed for the insurance coverage.

If you are unable to find an appraiser who suits your insurance company, insist that they find an appraiser or permit you to do your own estimates of value. Sometimes it is very difficult to get an appraisal of a specialized collection, such as American pewter, music boxes, old radios, or dolls. Any specialized collection should be seen by an expert in that field of collecting. It will probably be a dealer specializing in that field or another collector with the same interest. The best way to find such people is through the collectors' clubs and publications devoted to the special field.

Appraisal for Charity

If you are donating some of your antiques to a museum or a charity, try to have the institution do the appraising. They tend to furnish high appraisals, which are to your advantage if the gift is tax deductible. You should receive a written appraisal and each item should be listed separately.

The institution should arrange for either professional or volunteer appraisers to furnish you with the needed records. If you give old clothes or furniture to the Goodwill or Salvation Army, the same rules apply. In some cases, you must do your own appraising for tax purposes. The Internal Revenue Service requires written appraisals. Without the proper papers you may be questioned about donations.

Appraisals for an Estate before Death

Should you do a complete appraisal of your collection in preparation for death? This causes many arguments among the experts. Unless the circumstances are unusual, we advise against it. When a complete appraisal of the antique contents of a home exists, the estate tax appraisal is often based on that list. If there is an appraisal of the estate by the average court appraiser, the antiques are usually undervalued. This is always to the advantage of those paying the estate tax.

Many times, an elderly collector wants to feel that the purchases of a lifetime have been wise; and the items are appraised at a high value. Unless there are plans for selling the collections soon after appraisal, there is no need for a formal written appraisal. Hire an appraiser to tell you the values, but don't get it in writing.

Appraisal for Division of an Estate

If you are part of a group of heirs and your attorney suggests you hire an appraiser for the antiques—don't. Ask for a regular court-appointed appraiser. An antiques expert will usually appraise at the high retail value of the collection. The court-appointed appraiser often considers many fine antiques as "old furniture."

It is illegal to hide any of the antiques in an estate, but you don't have to help the appraiser determine the value. Unless you are asked, don't offer any of the collector's records. You can always argue later that an appraisal is too high and use those records as proof.

If there is an insurance policy covering the collection, the appraiser will probably ask for a copy of the listing. That is just one of the reasons why it is not always advisable to insure antiques at the high retail price.

Sometimes the best way to divide antiques in an estate or divorce is with the help of an appraiser, who can set values. This is a special type of appraisal and you should be sure the appraiser knows what information you need. A formal written appraisal is usually not necessary.

Appraisal to Sell Your Collection

If you plan to sell a collection at auction, let the auction house give you an appraisal.

If you plan to sell the entire contents of your home at a house sale, ask the people running the sale to give you the approximate prices they expect to receive before you agree to allow them to sell. If the prices for the antiques are too low, remove them from the house sale and offer them to local dealers or an auction house.

If you wish to sell to a dealer, you should have exact asking prices in mind. A dealer cannot appraise your antiques and then buy them without having a conflict of interest.

Many appraisers are dealers who want to buy. Be very careful in this situation, as it is not always to your advantage. An appraisal is probably not needed if you are an active collector and know the market.

Appraisal Cost

An appraisal costs money and no dealer or appraiser can offer the services free of charge. Be sure to ask the fee, as it will vary from an hourly rate (usually including travel time) to a percentage of the appraised value. Many appraisal groups feel it is wrong to work on a percentage because it might influence the appraiser's judgment. Ask the appraiser for credentials, which should include membership in an appraisers' association, or local references. Ask for a written contract stating fees and type of appraisal to be furnished. There is a difference between a formal written appraisal and a quick listing for guidance purposes.

List your own items and have them in a convenient spot in your house. If the appraiser is working by the hour, it will help to reduce your costs. Some appraisers can do about sixty items an hour, but if you have rare paintings or special antiques that might require research, that number could change dramatically.

The cost of insurance and appraisals may be included in the basic cost of your collection when you sell and determine the taxes owed on the profit. The cost of storage, a safe deposit box, or other special equipment is also deductible. Ask your tax consultant about these specialized areas, but always be sure to keep exact records to help verify your claims.

SECURITY, BURGLAR ALARMS, AND OTHER PROBLEMS

Theft and fire are two of the biggest worries to antiques collectors. There are many ways to lessen these dangers—some inexpensive, some expensive. Consider the monetary value of your collection and the vulnerability of your home; then decide how to handle the problems.

Fire

The normal safety precautions against fire are of added importance if you are a collector. Be sure to remove all extra burnable trash, don't store inflammable materials in the house, and periodically check all appropriate safety features on furnaces, heaters, etc. If you refinish furniture, be very careful with the used rags. Rags soaked with linseed oil and turpentine mixtures can easily ignite by spontaneous combustion. If you have a collection of inflammable items like movie film, photographs, books, or paper items, try to keep them away from the furnace, fireplace, any open flame, or cigarette ashes.

A smoke detector is the one single investment that is probably most important to a collector. Buy several and place them at the top of stairs, near any library or collection of easily ignited articles, and, of course, near the bedrooms to warn you of fire at night. The alarms make a loud noise and wake you or, with some extra equipment, notify the fire department even if you are not at home.

Also, it is a good idea to keep small fire extinguishers in the house. Do not install a sprinkler system. The water can often do more damage than a small fire.

Theft Prevention

The least expensive form of protection is common sense. Don't talk about your collection in strange places. Check on the workmen you hire to repair your house. Be sure your household help is reliable. Don't give anyone a key to the house if it can be avoided. Don't tell the local paper, beauty parlor, gas station, or anyone else you meet casually that you will be away. Don't put your house key on the car key ring. Never let an unknown collector who calls to see your collection enter the house. Get some sort of reference first.

If you see a strange car near your home, write down the license number and a description of the car.

PROTECTION

Another inexpensive protection for your collection is the complete set of records and photographs you keep. It gives the police enough information to look for stolen items.

To add to this protection, write your social security number or driver's license number (check first to see if your state assigns a number on a permanent basis) on the antique with one of the new marking devices. There are two types of markers. One is an electric pencil, much like a dentist's drill, that etches the number into the piece. This is suitable for a limited number of antiques. Some cities have a program called Operation Identification. See if your town has one. The material needed to mark your collection can be borrowed from the program.

The other type of marker is a special pen filled with "invisible" ink that will fluoresce under a black (ultraviolet) light.

BETTER PROTECTION

After you have marked, photographed, and recorded your antiques, stop to consider how a thief would gain entry to your house. Every house has a weak spot.

Perhaps it is glass patio doors. You can't keep anyone from breaking the glass and entering, but you can make it difficult. Put dead bolt locks on the door, where they can't be easily reached through the broken glass. This way the burglar will have to make some noise to enter and won't be able to just push open an easily jimmied key lock. Use poles to "lock" sliding patio doors.

Lock all windows. Be sure the milk chute either locks from the inside or is too small for someone to enter. Put lights outside the house so the neighbors will notice intruders. Don't leave ladders outside the house.

Be sure the flat-roofed garage is not next to an open window. Be sure your garage door is closed and locked. Put bars over the basement windows or window wells. Don't put your name on your mailbox or doormat. A burglar often looks up the name in the phone book, calls to see if you are home, and then uses the empty house as an invitation. Keep lights on in the house when you are away.

An inexpensive timer is excellent, as you can arrange to turn on lights or a television set at a specified time. This makes the house seem occupied. There are special timers that can be set to turn lights on at a different time each night.

Tell the neighbors and police if you plan to be gone for a while. Be sure to do the obvious, such as stopping paper delivery, arranging for mail delivery, having the grass cut, or shoveling the snow, etc. Don't disconnect your phone, even temporarily. A phone answering machine can be a help, as it can give a message that says you are unable to come to the phone and will call back. The message should never say that you are away from home. If possible, have a neighbor put some trash in the trash cans each week. It is a good idea to leave a car in the driveway to block the way of a burglar with a truck.

BEST PROTECTION

Burglar alarm equipment is one of the best deterrents to robbery, but it must be the proper equipment for the job. Talk to people who own such systems, check with several suppliers, and then study the problems of your house and your collection before you decide on which alarm system to purchase.

The best protection for your family and your antiques is placed outside the house. No one ever wants to meet a burglar inside the house. He is nervous and so are you. Outside defenses should include lights in the yard, driveway, and garden; fences; bars on basement windows; good locks; and an automatic garage door opener or a locked garage door.

The next line of defense is at the door. There are several systems that set off bells, gongs, or silent alarms when a door is opened improperly or even when a window is broken. Many of these systems also notify police if a phone or power line is cut.

The next line of defense is up the stairs or across the halls. Detectors can be strategically placed in the home to warn you if anyone is moving in the house. This detector is useless if you have young children, dogs, cats, or sleepwalking family members.

The last hope for help is the "panic button." This is an alarm that can be pushed to silently call for help. It is either installed by a door or bed or is a portable unit.

Each type of installed alarm is designed for special conditions and special purposes. There are several brands of "tripalarms" that can be installed. These set off a loud noise when the window or door is opened. (Always be sure to buy the type that has to be turned off with a key. If the turnoff can be made with a switch, a burglar will have no trouble stopping the noise.) One of the major problems with this type of alarm is that each door and window must be wired with a separate unit. It is even possible for a clever burglar who knows the alarm system to go through a wall or remove the window in a special way that will not set off the alarm.

A more complex and expensive alarm is one with sensors attached to the windows and doors. This type sends a message to a control box that emits a noise, calls the police, turns on the lights, or whatever combination you choose.

Some of the expensive alarm systems have silent door and window alarms that alert the police or a listening station that your house is being entered. There is no noise and no visible sign because the theory is that the police will catch the burglar with the loot before he leaves the house.

If these fail, there are several types of alarms available that go off once a burglar is in the house.

Ultrasonic devices can be installed that will set off an alarm if anything is moving in the room. These alarms are usually placed in different zones throughout the house. For example, one may cover the living room, another the front stairs, and still another the basement stairs.

These alarms alert the police or a listening station and do not make any noise. This system cannot be used if you own dogs or cats. A good system will be activated if just a mouse runs across the floor.

Another type of alarm placed in specific zones is the electric eye. This is an almost invisible beam of infrared light that, when crossed, activates the silent alarm.

A similar type of alarm uses microwave installation and covers larger areas, such as an entire room.

A pressure-sensitive type of alarm installed under the rug is another device that detects people in the house. Many of these alarms can be purchased at retail stores and installed by an amateur.

One of the most popular alarms for private homes is a "bugging" system. This system is installed inside the walls or in inconspicuous spots throughout the house. Microphones will pick up any noise in the house. The system is usually installed with the addition of several of the door-opener alarms. If someone enters the home the noise is heard. The listening station can tell if the burglar is walking from room to room, packing antiques, or talking to a friend. The owners of a home with this system turn it off when they are in the house to maintain their privacy. Panic buttons are strategically placed throughout the house and can be activated instantly even if the system is off.

All of these alarms require a form of check-in and check-out with the alarm company. Some use keys; some have special combinations of buttons that must be activated in the proper sequence. Others require a phone call and a turnoff switch. All of the check-in procedures are a nuisance, but there is no way to have an alarm system without it.

The only way to decide which alarm you should use is by carefully considering how it will affect your daily lives. The consideration should include the size of the area to be covered, the number of people entering the house on a daily basis who must check in and out, the physical problems of installation, whether you have pets, and the type of police service available. Sometimes the best alarm is a large dog.

ADVANTAGES AND DISADVANTAGES OF ALARMS

Be sure to deal with a reliable burglar alarm company. There are cases on record where the alarm installation was done by the man who later robbed the house.

The "bugging" alarm has several good features. A smoke alarm can be installed that will give you full fire protection even when you are away. The alarm will pick up any signal of smoke or fire and transmit the sound to the main alarm center. The alarm service quickly calls the fire department. The installation is almost invisible.

You have personal contact with the alarm system company on a daily basis as you call in and out; so in case of exceptional problems, long trips, or other high-risk times, you can advise them.

Taped windows and zone coverage in the house are ideal for some homes. If your collection is displayed in a single area, this type of protection can be easily and inexpensively installed.

There are advantages to any system if you live alone. We know a collector who has told her alarm system company that if she does not check in each day by ten o'clock, they should send the police. She has no relatives nearby and this is a sort of insurance program for her in case of illness. Some services have their own security men who check out each alarm call. Most send the local police.

There are a few insurance companies that will lower fire and theft rates if you have an alarm. Many insurance companies will not insure a collection without proper protection.

Unsolved Questions

There are some questions about alarms that have never been answered satisfactorily. Should you put a sign in front of your house advising the world that you have an alarm? Should you tie in directly to the police station or is it best to use a listening service?

The sign in front alerts a burglar to the type of alarm and may give him the opportunity of working around it. Also, it suggests there are valuables inside. It could also suggest that the house next door without an alarm might be a better place to enter. If you have *no* alarm, the window decals saying you are protected by an alarm might help. If you are a known collector and the burglar is a professional, the sign probably will make little difference.

Some cities permit private homes to have a direct link to the police station. This means prompt service; but if you have a series of false alarms because you are checking in improperly (and this seems inevitable the first few months), the police may become very uncooperative. It is always a good idea to send a donation to the local police fund if you start having too many false alarms.

Some alarm owners prefer to use the listening station because the alarm people keep tabs on the progress of the police with continued follow-through until the attempted break-in is resolved.

Check with your local police department and ask about rules for alarms in your area. Call those alarm companies that offer the best protection.

One last note, all the alarm expense may be tax deductible in some way. Keep records because it could be a cost that can be added to the base price of your collection when it is sold. This will lower the taxes paid on any profit gained from the sale of the collection.

SELLING ANTIQUES

Selling an antique is almost as specialized a technique as buying an antique. It takes knowledge, time, and careful consideration. There is a best way to sell each type of antique.

Suppose you have just inherited the contents of a house from your ninety-year-old great-aunt. After a quick look, you decide there are only a few items you want to keep and you would like to sell the rest. Or, maybe you have collected antiques for years and now want to move to an apartment. How will you get the best sales results?

If it is an inheritance, lock the door of the house as soon as possible and be sure you are the only one with access. You may have to change the locks to be sure no one else has a key. There are several reasons for this.

Any inheritance is involved with the legalities of settling an estate, and the law does not permit you to move or sell property without the proper papers and permission. An inheritance usually involves other relatives and it is always amazing to see how many distant cousins will suddenly appear with requests for "mementos." It is equally strange that the memento is usually the antique with the greatest monetary value.

Tell all of the friends and relatives that you will be glad to consider their requests and will give them the first opportunity to have some of your aunt's things after the legal entanglements are settled.

Do not even let your attorney or his associates go into the house without you. Honest people often seem to think that the contents of an empty home are unwanted and therefore are free for the taking. Do not admit cleaning help, caretakers, apartment custodians, etc.

Do not clean the house. It is tempting to think that throwing out the piles of old magazines, papers, or bottles in the basement will make space and add to the desirability of what is left, but unknowing amateurs often throw out some of the most valuable items.

Don't invite any antiques dealers, friends, or other potential buyers into the house for them to pick and choose until you have finished getting all of your plans in order and have done the necessary research. An educated antiques collector can spot the best pieces and will probably try to buy them immediately. You might be tempted to take the first price offered, and that could be too low.

Ask your friends to suggest a collector who could help in determining what you have of value. (Still don't sell!) If you find an amateur with a fair knowledge of the general antiques market, you could have some good advice. Don't call in an antiques dealer either for advice or appraisal unless you plan to pay for the time. To ask a dealer over to look at the things is an invitation to buy and if you do not yet know the value of the antiques, you could be selling too low.

If you can't find a collector, go to the antiques shops, shows, flea markets, and auctions in your area. Go to house sales. Check the prices and types of items being sold. Make notes, ask questions.

This might be a good time to tell a few of the dealers that you may be calling them with some antiques for sale. Do not make definite appointments. Some dealers specialize in furniture, some in glass, etc. It is at this time that you should make your plans and get an idea of who would be interested in all or part of the collection.

Go to the library or your local bookstore. Buy or borrow some price guides. *The Kovels' Antiques Price List* by Ralph and Terry Kovel is an annual book listing forty-five thousand different antiques. Like all antiques price books, it assumes that you know enough about the antique to know its name. If you don't know pressed glass from cut glass, Queen Anne from Chippendale, pottery from porcelain, you need more help from an expert.

If you have done all of these things and still can't determine a fair market price, you will need help in selling the antiques. There are a limited number of ways to get rid of antiques. You can have an auction, assign the pieces to someone else's auction, have a house sale, put your items in someone else's house sale, sell to a dealer, take a table at a flea market and be a dealer, have a garage sale, place ads in the local papers or the national antiques publications and sell the pieces, or give the pieces to charity or a museum and take a tax deduction.

THE WAYS TO SELL AN ANTIQUE, AND THE ADVANTAGES AND DISADVANTAGES OF EACH

On-Premises Sale

If you have a house filled with an assortment of pieces ranging from kitchen pots and pans to golden oak furniture, you will probably get the most money by having an on-the-premises auction or a house sale. If your community allows an auction or a house sale, it is the easiest way to sell the items. Check your local papers and ask your friends. There is always a "best" auctioneer and a "best" house-sale manager. Contact these people and ask them to look over the collection. They can give you a rough estimate of the total value of the contents.

Be sure to get all pertinent information. Ask for references. These people will be handling *your money*. Be sure you are to be given copies of all bills of sale. Don't agree to a house sale unless each transaction is recorded. Request that your sale be the only one that the firm handles that particular day. You want their top people at your sale. Ask what rate is charged. It will probably be about 20 to 25 percent, although the commission is determined by the size and quality of the sale. Ask what advertising they will do. Be sure there is enough security to avoid thefts during the sale.

Once the sale is set, you have few worries. The auctioneer or house-sale person will know the approximate price to expect for an item, where to advertise the sale, how to handle the sales tax, keep the necessary records, and last, but far from least, furnish proper security.

If you wish, they will leave the house "broom clean." This means they will arrange either to sell out the last almost unsalable items at a very low price or to give them to a local charity. If the sale is for an estate, a gift to charity is sometimes better than the cash in hand. You should make this decision with your attorney or tax accountant before the sale.

Sometimes, there are special antiques that you might want to own that are of considerable value. It is proper for you to arrange for a minimum price before the sale. For example, there might be a table that is worth $300. You can arrange with the auctioneer or the house-sale manager to keep the table for you if it does not bring at least $250.

If there are only a few items like this, there is usually no problem. If there are many items with a "reserve" price, the auctioneer or sale person is justified in asking for a commission on the merchandise you keep.

The advantage in a sale of this type is that you have few worries, the pricing is near market value, and most of the junk is also sold. The almost new paperback books, the pots in the kitchen, the half-bag of grass seed, the lawn mower, and any other item brings cash. It is impossible to sell these items at other types of antiques sales.

Owner-Run House Sale

If you want to run your own house sale, it requires knowledge, elbow grease, and time. Check with your city to see if any sort of license is required. Learn whether your local laws allow you to post signs and have on-street parking. Find out if they require state sales tax and sale records. Learn what it is illegal to sell (in some states you cannot sell guns or liquor; some health departments forbid resale of mattresses; federal law forbids the sale of apparatus for making alcoholic beverages; etc.). It is considered poor taste to sell an American flag. Give it away.

Go to several local house sales and you will find it is easy to learn where items should be placed for best security. You can also learn how to guard the doors and how to tag merchandise. Pay particular attention to how the prices are reduced during the sale.

There is no easy way—running a sale is hard work. If you have a large, expensive collection of goods, it is probably better to hire a professional liquidator. What you save in commission by doing the sale yourself, you may lose in theft and poor pricing.

If it is a small sale and you have been going to house sales for years, you can probably handle it alone. There are a few books available giving guidelines, and many newspapers offer, as part of their services, a kit explaining how to have a house or garage sale.

Garage Sale

If you have less than a houseful and the antiques are varied, you might run a garage sale. The name itself indicates that the sale will contain bargains and low-priced pieces and that they are not all antiques. You should seek advice and help to run a garage sale.

Some of the larger newspapers that carry the ads for garage sales offer kits that give advice about selling and ads and even offer a sign for the front yard. If you are considering this type of sale, remember that each item must be priced. Have several friends or children help you sell, and be sure to have them watch to avoid theft.

Consignment to Auction

If you have a number of antiques but for some reason can't have the sale on the premises, you might send the pieces to auction. Top-quality antiques, rare art glass, early nineteenth-century American pewter, eighteenth-century furniture, rare toys, a choice doll collection, historic flasks, and the other antiques that sell in the hundreds and thousands of dollars usually can't be sold for top prices at an unadvertised local sale.

The consignment auction has the advantage of advertising that brings collectors and dealers from many parts of the United States and many foreign countries. Maybe you have only one or two expensive rarities. They will sell best at a sale with other items of the same type.

There are several disadvantages to the auction. There is no guarantee that the antique will sell for your price. You can usually sell it with a reserve (the lowest price it can be sold for), but if it does not sell above the reserve price, you pay the commission for an antique you still own.

The auction may be on a bad day. The weather or the mood of the crowd sometimes keeps the prices lower than usual. Most buyers go to an auction to buy a bargain.

If you plan to sell your items at auction, talk with the most reputable auctioneer in town. Ask about his auctions. There are some that are not as honest as they should be. Collecting your part of the money can be a problem with a disreputable auctioneer.

Most auctioneers are honest and fair. Some states require a license for the auctioneer and this helps to protect the buyer and seller.

Ask for an estimate of the value of your items. Check on the commission rate that you have to pay. Most firms charge 20 percent or a 10-percent buyer, 10-percent seller commission. This means you as seller pay 10 percent, the buyer pays an extra 10 percent added to the bid. If you have very valuable antiques (over $500 value for an item) or a collection of antiques with each piece worth over $200, consider an out-of-town auctioneer. Write a letter, describe the pieces, include pictures and history if possible. Some of these auction houses are listed here, others can be found at your library in the antiques publications. This list is for information only. It is not an endorsement.

AUCTION GALLERIES

Noel Barrett Antiques
& Auctions Ltd.
Carversville Rd.
Carversville, PA 18913
215-297-5109

Barridoff Galleries
87 Carroll St.
Portland, ME 04105
207-772-5011

Bill Bertoia
1217 Glenwood Dr.
Vineland, NJ 08360
609-692-4092

Frank H. Boos Gallery
420 Enterprise Ct.
Bloomfield Hills, MI 48032
313-332-1500;
fax 313-332-6370

Richard A. Bourne Co., Inc.
Corporation St.
P.O. Box 141
Hyannis Port, MA 02647
508-775-0797

Butterfield & Butterfield
220 San Bruno Ave. at 15th St.
San Francisco, CA 94103
415-861-7500

Christie's
502 Park Ave.
New York, NY 10022
general 212-546-1000
press office 212-546-1119
fax 212-752-3956

Cincinnati Art Galleries
635 Main St.
Cincinnati, OH 45202

Samuel Cottone Auctions
15 Genesee
Mt. Morris, NY 14510
716-658-3180

DeFina Auctions
1591 State Road 45
Austinburg, OH 44010
216-275-6674

Paul J. Dias
30 E. Washington St.
Route 58
Hanson, MA 02341
617-447-9057

Douglas Auctioneers
Rte. 5
South Deerfield, MA 01373
413-665-2877

Doyle Auctioneers & Appraisers
RD #3, Box 137, Osborne Hill Rd.
Fishkill, NY 12524
914-896-9492

William Doyle Galleries
175 East 87th St.
New York, NY 10128
212-427-2730

DuMouchelle's
409 E. Jefferson Ave.
Detroit, MI 48226
313-963-6255; 313-963-0248
fax 313-963-8199

Early Auction Co.
123 Main St.
Milford, OH 45150
513-831-4833

Robert C. Eldred Co., Inc.
Route 6A, P.O. Box 796
East Dennis, MA 02641-0796
508-385-3116; fax 508-385-7201

Garth's
2690 Stratford Rd.
P.O. Box 369
Delaware, OH 43015
614-362-4771

Morton M. Goldberg Auction
  Galleries
547 Baronne St.
New Orleans, LA 70113
504-592-2300; 800-882-7422
fax 504-897-0483

Guernsey's
108 E. 73rd St.
New York, NY 10021
212-794-2280

Hake's Americana & Collectibles
P.O. Box 1444
York, PA 17405
717-848-1333

Harmer Rooke Galleries
3 East 57th St.
New York, NY 10022
212-751-1900
fax 212-758-1713

Gene Harris Family Antique
  Auction Center
P.O. Box 476
Marshalltown, IA 50158
515-752-0600

Norman C. Heckler & Co.
Bradford Corner Rd.
Woodstock Valley, CT 06282
203-974-1634

Wills Henry Auctions
22 Main St.
Marshfield, MA 02050
617-834-7774
fax 617-826-3520

Leslie Hindman Auctioneers
215 West Ohio St.
Chicago, IL 60610
312-670-0010

James D. Julia
R.F.D. #1, Box 91
Skowhegan Road
Fairfield, ME 04937
207-453-7125; 207-453-9493

Lelands
151 W. 28th St., Suite 7E
New York, NY 10001
212-971-3111

Litchfield Auction Gallery
Susan Pico, PR
Rte. 202
Litchfield, CT 06759
203-567-3126

Joy Luke
300 E. Grove St.
Bloomington, IL 61701
309-828-5533

Lyons Ltd.
Charles R. Lyons
2700 Hyde
San Francisco, CA 94109

Neal Auction Company
4038 Magazine St.
New Orleans, LA 70115
504-899-5329
fax 504-897-3808

Northeast Auctions
Ron Bourgeault
P.O. Box 363
Hampton, NH 03842
603-926-9800;
  fax 603-926-3545

Oliver's (Auction Gallery)
P.O. Box 337
Kennebunk, ME 04043
207-985-3600

Richard Opfer
  Auctioneering Inc.
1919 Greenspring Dr.
Timonium, MD 21093
301-252-5035

Phillips
406 E. 79th St.
New York, NY 10021
212-570-4657
212-570-4830

David Rago
17 So. Main St.
Lambertville, NJ 08530
609-397-9374; 800-648-1431

Lloyd Ralston
173 Post Rd.
Fairfield, CT 06432
203-255-1233; 203-366-3399

Riba Auctions
P.O. Box 53, Main St.
South Glastonbury, CT 06073
203-633-3076

Roan Auctions
Box 118, R.D. #3
Cogan Station, PA 17728
717-494-0170

Skinner Inc.
Bolton Gallery, 357 Main St.
Bolton, MA 01740
508-779-6241

Sotheby's
1334 York Ave.
New York, NY 10021
212-606-7176;
fax 212-606-7027

Swann Galleries
104 East 25th St.
New York NY 10010
212-254-4710

Theriault's
P.O. Box 151; 2148 Renard Ct.
Annapolis, MD 21404
800-638-0422; 301-269-0680

Don Treadway
2128 Madison Rd.
Cincinnati, OH 45208
513-321-6742

Weschler's
905 E. St. N.W.
Washington, DC 20004
202-628-1281; 800-331-1430

Richard W. Withington, Inc.
Hillsboro, NH 03244
603-464-3232

Wolf's
1239 W. 6th St.
Cleveland, OH 44113
216-575-9653

Woody Auction
P.O. Box 618
Douglass, KS 67039
316-746-2694

House-Sale Consignment

If you do not want a sale in your home and you have a small number of items to sell, you might put them into someone else's house sale. Ideally, you can find a friend who is having a house or garage sale and put your items into the sale. The people who run house sales sometimes bring extra items into a house to enlarge the sale. The items are sold as part of the belongings of the house. If you consign some items to this type of house sale, the seller will keep separate bills to prove the price your items brought. Of course, you must pay a commission. In some cities, it is illegal to sell anything at a house sale that has been brought in for the occasion. Be sure to check the local laws.

Selling to a Dealer

If you have a few good pieces, it might be best to sell to a local antiques dealer. Once again, the more you know about your antique and the possible value, the better price you will receive. Look up the listed retail price in a book such as *The Kovels' Antiques Price List*.

A dealer should be able to pay you about half of the listed retail. Call some of the nearby dealers listed in the Yellow Pages of the telephone book. Tell them what you wish to sell and make an appointment, either to take the pieces to their shop or for the dealer to come to your home.

Please remember that the dealer is in business to make money. Sometimes, if you have a number of antiques, the dealer will offer you a very high price for one ordinary item and very low prices for others that you may not recognize as valuable. The dealer is in your home to buy and not to give you an appraisal. A dealer will usually ask you to set the price and many times your estimated value will be low.

If local dealers are not interested, you must do more homework. Take a picture of your antique or, if it is small, carry it to an antiques show. Each show will have dozens of dealers. Every antiques dealer who sells must buy, and it is usually harder to buy than to sell. Offer your pieces to dealers with similar items for sale.

Consignment

Some shops will sell on consignment. Many cities have resale shops or antiques shops that handle consignment merchandise. There are many dealers who will sell a few items this way. The antique is placed with a marked price in the shop. The shop is paid a commission after the sale is completed.

If you leave something for consignment sale, be sure to get a receipt listing the item, the price, and the condition of the antique. Set a time limit. If the item remains unsold for six months, take it back. If complete descriptions are given at the time of consignment, many arguments concerning damage and condition can be avoided.

Flea Market Table

If you have a few antiques and want to sell them yourself, the local flea market is an ideal spot. You can rent a table, check on the tax laws, price your antiques, and go into business. If you have priced the pieces too low, they will sell quickly; if your prices are too high, you will soon be told by the collectors who are shopping and not buying from you.

Friends

One of the best ways to dispose of antiques is by selling to friends. The problem of price is difficult, but otherwise the sale takes a minimum of effort. Look up the retail value and determine the price by your relationship with the friend. Friends are more important than high prices. If you have a liquidator run your house sale, explain to your friends that the liquidator determines the price and is paid a commission. There are circumstances when it is proper to invite relatives and friends in prior to the sale to see if they want to buy a cherished piece. Either ask them before you arrange for a dealer to sell your items or expect to pay the dealer the usual commission for the sale. Once the items have been priced for house sale or auction, you should not expect to avoid paying the commission.

Newspaper Sale

If you own some unusual or large antiques, such as a piano, wine press, or a popcorn wagon, you might place an ad in the local newspaper. Collectors, as well as dealers, read the ads. You will have many calls asking for a complete description and your asking price. Be sure to decide the value before placing the ad. Some dealers answer these ads in the hopes of buying other antiques once they are in your home.

If you advertise, make arrangements for someone to be home with you when a buyer appears. If possible, put the advertised item in the garage and do not allow strangers into your home. If the amount of money involved in your sale is large, ask for proper identification before accepting a check.

Giving Antiques to Charity

One of the best ways to dispose of unwanted antiques, especially part of an estate, is as a gift to a charity. The tax laws are such that in many cases it is better to take a $200 deduction for a gift than to sell the item for $100 cash. If there is high dollar value in the estate, the tax rate could be so high that the advantages of gifts are increased. Check with your attorney, the executors of the estate, or your accountant.

An antique can be given to a museum, a university, or for resale by a charity at either the present-day value or an adjusted value based on cost and present-day value. The laws are complicated, but the organization receiving the gift will be happy to give you an appraisal and the tax information.

Some things are almost unsalable, but have a good tax deduction value. We know of cases where an architect gave his original plans for fifty years of local work, an author gave original manuscripts, and a club group gave their early records and photographs. Designer-made clothes of any age could interest a local historical society.

Historical letters, photographs, and documents are in demand by specialized museums. Even unusual inventions, old tools, medical apparatus, old vacuum cleaners, typewriters, specialized books, etc., are wanted by some museums. Check on the gift value before you throw away the less decorative or less desirable antiques.

Specialized Collections

Some types of antiques require very special attention and the services of experts. Jewelry should always be taken to a reputable jeweler for appraisal. If the jewelry is antique, be sure the jeweler is knowledgeable in appraising old jewelry. Mine-cut diamonds or old jewelry might not look good to you. There are stories about a buyer at a house sale who purchased a real diamond ring for a dollar.

Autographs should be checked by an expert in the field, either a locally or nationally recognized expert.

Old books should be appraised by a local bookseller specializing in old books. First editions, special bindings, fore-edge painting, even historic interest in the original owner can add to the value of a book.

Old guns and musical instruments, coin and stamp collections, button collections, etc., should be examined by an expert in the field. The average antiques appraiser will not be good for this.

Oil paintings and marble sculpture, especially those signed by the artists, should be seen by an appraiser or a local museum.

If you have a very specialized collection, such as lithographed tobacco cans, telephone insulators, netsukes, barbed wire, or bitters bottles, you should contact an expert in that field. Ask about values and sales possibilities. Many of these pieces sell best through the major collector groups. A list of these organizations can be found in the back of the book *Kovels' Know Your Antiques* (Crown) or in the book *Encyclopedia of Associations.*

There are only a few sources you can use to check the price of an antique. Go to the local sales and shops and see how antiques sell in your neighborhood. Read the antiques publications with priced ads and see what is selling nationally. Check the price books that are available. Not surprisingly, we like *Kovels' Antiques Price List* the best.

Remember, prices change yearly and only current price books are accurate. All of the prices you see listed are retail prices, and unless you plan to open an antiques shop, you will get from one-half to one-third less.

Selling your antiques properly takes time and effort, but the extra money gained will pay you well.

2

Furniture, Victorian to Art Moderne

The ornate, carved, and usually uncomfortable furniture of the 1830–1900 period started to regain its popularity with collectors in the 1970s. Pieces of Belter furniture or Greco-Egyptian design can no longer be found in shops for just a few dollars. The swing back to Victorian was the result of the earlier furniture rising in price beyond the pocketbook of the average collector. This, combined with a major exhibition at the Metropolitan Museum of Art in 1970 where the finest pieces of the period were displayed, has caused the renewed interest.

The collector and dealer could finally differentiate between the good and the bad. They began to understand the various periods that are included under the heading "Victorian." Following are the major periods of Victorian usually referred to in books, sales, and auction catalogs.

10410—(b) "I'll Not Take Off Another Stitch If I Lose My Place"

Decorating a Victorian home meant filling all available space with pattern. This stereopticon slide shows a dining room of 1900. The slide is part of an old joke. Card one says, "Bridget, bring the salad without dressing." Card two says, "I'll not take off another stitch if I lose my place."

Gothic Revival: 1830–1850

Gothic Revival architecture was popular in England during the 1820s and 1830s and in the United States by the 1830s. Furniture to fill the pseudo-castles was a necessity. The furniture made for the period resembled small bits of Gothic architecture. Backs of chairs were made to look like church arches; headboards and footboards were made like the panels from a Gothic building; chairbacks were high, straight, and carved,

A rosewood Gothic center table made about 1845. Note the edging of the table, designed to resemble Gothic architectural trim.

These Gothic-style walnut side chairs were made about 1840 in the manner of John Jelliff of New Jersey.

resembling church chairs, or they were round with partitions to look like stained glass windows. Alexander Roux of New York and J. and J. W. Meeks of New York were the most important makers of this style.

Rococo Revival: 1845–1865

The French-influenced Victorian furniture of the Rococo Revival included highly ornamented curved pieces. Rococo lines, C & S scrolls, and a style called Louis XIV appeared. Cabriole legs, French scroll feet, carved flowers, grapes, leaves, oval-backed chairs, white marble tabletops, appeared. This was the period of the furniture made by John Henry Belter of

Many pieces of Rococo Revival furniture are unsigned. This set is in the Belter style but the maker is as yet unknown.

New York City. His laminated wood construction made some of the ornate designs possible. Other makers of note were Alexander Roux, Charles Baudouine, Joseph Meeks & Son, Charles Klein, Leon Marcotte of New York City, and Ignatius Lutz of Philadelphia.

Elizabethan Revival: 1840–1850

This was a very short-lived style that could be classified as part of the Rococo Revival. There was a group of furniture made that consisted mainly of chairs and sofas in what was called Elizabethan style. They featured spiral-turned legs and uprights plus needlework seats. A few pieces of this style remained in favor into the 1870s.

Louis XVI: 1860s

Some of the Rococo Revival pieces were based on the French eighteenth-century Louis XVI styles. Many of the cabinetmakers working in New York City were Frenchmen who had only recently come to America. Names like Marcotte, Roux, and Baudouine were common. This style of furniture often used ebonized maple or light fruitwood. The designs were neoclassical with narrow wooden trim and legs. It had restrained bits of ormolu, or gilded decoration, and perhaps a French porcelain plaque added for ornament. Some brass and mother-of-pearl was used as inlay.

Many chairs were mass produced by furniture makers in the 1850s. These two chairs are typical of the mass-produced chairs.

Many of the pieces were reasonably accurate copies of the eighteenth-century style with a nineteenth-century adaptation of color, upholstery methods, and even casters on the legs.

Louis XV: c. 1880–1900

Some Louis XV pieces were copied by American furniture makers with accuracy. They were mixed with pieces of Louis XVI furniture and this created a "French" look in a room. Louis XV pieces were more ornate and were often gilded or painted. Curves were found in the legs and chairbacks.

A rosewood library table by Alexander Roux.

Renaissance Revival: 1850–1875

The furniture of the Rococo period was heavy, ornate, and carved, but the furniture of the period that followed was even heavier, more ornate, and more deeply carved. Once again comfort was ignored by the designer as three-dimensional carvings protruded from every possible part of the chair or table. Massive pieces were made that were almost immovable. At first, the furniture was made by important East Coast manufacturers, but soon the mass-production furniture factories as far west as Michigan began manufacturing this style. The rectilinear look predominated. Sideboards and cabinets looked like massive architectural parts of a room.

Fifteenth- to eighteenth-century motifs such as columns, deep carvings, and cartouches were borrowed freely. The easy chair was made with thick upholstered back, seat, and arms. The headboards for beds were often over 8 feet high. Wooden carved drawer pulls appeared. As the style spread west the Cincinnati, Ohio, firm of Mitchell and Rammelsberg sold their wares in quantity. Christian Herter, Kimbel and Cabus, Alexander Roux, George Hunzinger, all of New York City; John Jelliff of New Jersey; and Grand Rapids, Michigan, firms such as Berkey and Gay, worked in this new style.

Renaissance Revival furniture took many forms. This pier table with étagères was probably made in New York. It has no use other than as a mirror and a shelf for three small pieces of sculpture. It is made of walnut and ebonized wood with porcelain plaques.

An American Renaissance Revival cabinet probably made in New York City.

John Jelliff also worked in the Revival styles. Sometimes this type of chair is called Italian Renaissance style. The fruit and tassel carving is characteristic of Jelliff pieces. This chair was made about 1860.

This is an astounding nineteenth-century American Egyptian Revival jewelry safe. The inside of the door has the inscription "Herring, Farrel & Sherman makers, 251 Broadway, New York."

Egyptian Revival pieces are hard to confuse with any other period. This chair, probably made in New York City, has appropriate Egyptian heads at the ends of the arms. The metal mounts for this chair and a matching sofa are marked "PS."

Greco-Egyptian: 1860–1870, 1890

An important collection of Egyptian artifacts arrived in America in 1852. The designers were delighted and perhaps too enthusiastic. The Victorian-Egyptian furniture of the 1860–1870 period was the result. Sphinx heads, animal paws, obelisks, and hieroglyphics were incorporated into designs on chairs and tables. The basic furniture had the curved lines of the Gothic Victorian but the embellishments were Egyptian. Some similar pieces made with hoof feet and with the classic shapes for chairs and stools were called "neo-Grec." There was a new flurry of interest in the Egyptian designs about 1889.

A Nebraska living room of the 1880s. Notice the chairs, and the desk that might be a Chautauqua desk.

Bentwood and Michael Thonet: 1840–present

Michael Thonet (pronounced "Tone-it") was a Viennese furniture maker of the nineteenth century. As early as 1830 Thonet was experimenting with different ways of making inexpensive furniture. In 1841, when he was forty-five years old, he received patents in England, Belgium, and France for new methods of using wood. The Austrian government asked him to move to Vienna where he could make furniture for the court. Thonet and his son established their own business in 1849 and it was in 1853 that they renamed it Thonet Brothers. They did special-order pieces. In 1851 they exhibited some chairs and won a first prize at the Crystal Palace Exposition in London, England. It was not until 1856 that the Thonets opened their first factory making mass-produced furniture, using Michael Thonet's methods and his specially designed machinery.

Bentwood furniture was made from prepared beechwood. Poles were boiled in water and bent to the proper shape and dried in ovens for several days. The finished chairs were shipped in parts and could be screwed together by the storekeeper. The most famous Bentwood chair, No. 14, was first made in 1859. Over 50 million were sold by 1910. The first Bentwood rocking chair was made in 1860.

A page from the Thonet catalog of 1904.

Michael Thonet died in 1871 but his sons continued to run the business. Bentwood furniture was so popular that by 1901 over fifty-two companies were making chairs using the Thonet patents, and hundreds of other furniture factories were making copies or pieces similar to Bentwood furniture.

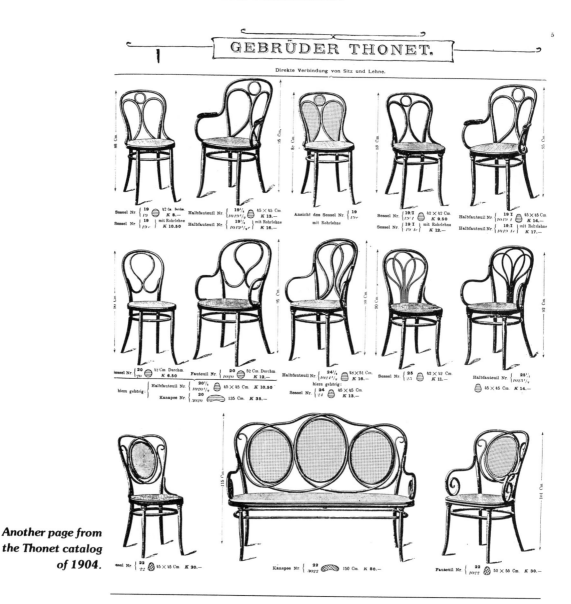

Another page from the Thonet catalog of 1904.

Bentwood chairs, tables, crib benches, hatracks, beds, and other useful objects were made.

The company headquarters moved to the United States in 1939. In 1962 Thonet in America was purchased by Simmons Company and the Thonet name is still in use.

A bentwood double bed made by Thonet in 1895.

Eastlake: 1870–1900

Charles Locke Eastlake was an architect and author in England. His book *Hints on Household Tastes in Furniture, Upholstery and Other Details* influenced design changes in England and the United States. He emphasized the importance of good taste and suggested that in simplicity there is beauty. The furniture designed in the United States under the style name Eastlake was very unlike the pieces recommended by Charles Eastlake. In general, the furniture was rectangular with several colors of contrasting woods, incised with lines that were often rubbed with gold. Sprigs of flowers or shallow carving were used. Turned spindles were popular. Sets of furniture for use in the parlor, bedroom, or dining room were in demand. The overall outline of the pieces was simple but the period was far from what a post–World War II eye would call "plain." Eastlake designs

An Eastlake-style walnut tambour front desk.

This Eastlake-style walnut dresser was made about 1875.

The term Eastlake refers to many different-looking pieces. This side cabinet made about 1890 is less Renaissance Revival than the walnut dresser and the walnut tambour front desk but is still part of the Eastlake style.

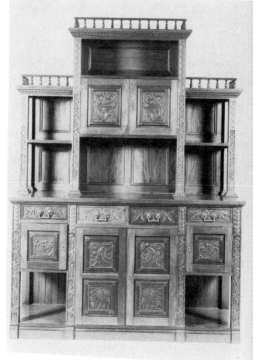

were made by many of the commercial furniture factories of the Midwest as well as some of the eastern manufacturers such as Herter Brothers, Kimbel and Cabus, and Charles Tisch.

Grand Rapids

The term *Grand Rapids furniture* that appears in books and casual conversation is sometimes meant as a comment on quality or as a description of design. The Grand Rapids, Michigan, furniture manufacturers as well as other furniture makers in the Midwest made mass-produced, machine-made furniture, primarily in the Renaissance Gothic and Eastlake styles. Grand Rapids pieces ranged from the top quality to the least expensive that it was possible to make. Elaborately carved custom-made Renaissance Gothic and Eastlake designs were reinterpreted for the machine-made product. The carving was flatter and the incised lines were often the main design element. Inlay was rarely used but large pieces of burled wood, especially walnut, were added for contrast. Furniture was made from solid walnut, oak, and other woods. The "look" of the geometric shape and flat surface areas created what we now refer to as "Grand Rapids style."

The West Coast made a similar style furniture but they made theirs with a painted veneer, not a burled wood trim. The western pieces date from the late nineteenth century and were probably made in California and other western states.

Japonisme: 1876–1885

The Centennial Exhibition of 1876 had a tremendous influence on design in America. One of the outstanding exhibits was a Japanese house that was built on the grounds. A craze for anything Japanese resulted. Japonisme, or the influence of Japanese design on European art, was prevalent in France from 1854, the year of Commodore Perry's visit to Japan, and soon spread to other countries. Famous artists such as Whistler placed Japanese decorative elements in their paintings. The Art Pottery movement in America was particularly affected by Japanese designs. Victorian furniture became a series of Japanese-inspired styles. Pseudo-bamboo was popular. Hardwoods like maple were turned to resemble bamboo (a style that could also be a reflection of the bamboo furniture that was popular in England during the 1790–1810 period). Actual bamboo pieces were imported. Light-colored woods like maple were also worked into more typical Victorian shapes with just a hint of Japanese influence. English or American tiles with Japanese scenes or flowers were incorporated into the design. Some pieces were even more Japanese in appearance and portrayed pagodalike forms with Oriental-type carved latticework.

Colonial Revival or Centennial Furniture: 1876–present

The idea of a "Colonial" kitchen or antique furniture is not new. Copies were being made of earlier pieces of furniture in the 1860s. By the time of

Another Colonial Revival rocking chair. It was made about 1900–1915 in mahogany.

This Colonial Revival chair has a shield back from the Federal period, knuckle armholds from the eighteenth century, and a late nineteenth-century look. It was one of many designs made under the name Colonial Revival that was not really a copy of any older period but rather a mixture of design elements from an earlier time.

the Centennial in 1876 the idea was accepted as part of good decorating. "Colonial" furniture included copies of any period of furniture from the 1500s to late Sheraton. Many Windsor chairs, Chippendale-style pieces, and William and Mary pieces were made. Reproductions of the Empire-style sofas of the 1840s were being made by the 1880s. The reproductions and adaptations of the earlier periods of furniture have now aged one hundred years and this is adding to the confusion of the collector. At first glance the appearance is often correct for the eighteenth century. It takes a careful study of the methods of construction, the woods used, and all of the fine points of a particular style to determine which are Revival pieces and which are originals. Collectors are not alone with this problem.

→

While all of these styles were being made another type of chair was being produced by chair factories. This is an ad for the Detroit Chair Factory in 1872.

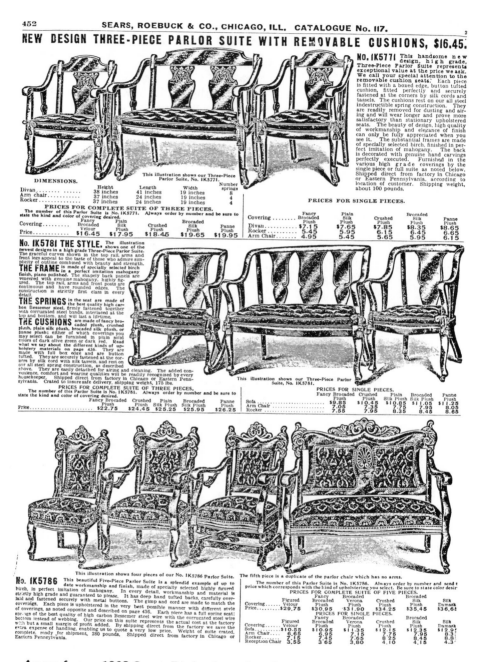

A page from a 1908 Sears, Roebuck catalog. By the 1900s Sears had furniture inspired by all of these styles, yet not exact copies.

Many museums and historical societies are just now finding out that the chair they thought was two hundred years old is one hundred years at the most.

At the same time that the accurate copies were made, many strange hybrid styles were produced and called Colonial. Even today these strange mixtures of style are offered for sale by furniture manufacturers. Included are pieces with wrought-iron hardware, knotty pine, spindles, and a pseudo-Windsor chair look.

Rustic Furniture: 1850–1900

The idea of making furniture from existing tree branches in a natural condition was an idea promoted for country houses during the 1850s. They were do-it-yourself projects. Branches, often with the bark still on, were joined together to make chairs or tables. It was the same type of furniture that was later made as Boy Scout projects in the twentieth century. The vacation homes of the wealthy in the Adirondack area of New York have some of this type of rustic furniture that was made during the 1875–1925 period. There were workmen in some areas who made pieces of furniture decorated with mosaics made from varicolored twigs.

Naturally shaped wood formed parts of this cedar wood "rustic" chair. It was used at a camp at Raquette Lake, New York.

View of a rustic interior at Camp Cedars, Forked Lake, in the Adirondacks. The photograph was taken about 1883.

SOME SPECIAL PIECES, ODDITIES, OR ORIGINAL DESIGNS

George Hunzinger

The Victorians were fascinated with machinery, power tools, and the possibilities of making something unlike anything ever previously made. A flurry of patented chairs appeared during the last quarter of the nineteenth century. Each chair suggests a very special use or special construction idea. One of the best-known makers of these special types of chairs was George Hunzinger of New York City, who worked in the 1860s and 1870s. He made chairs that looked like assembled plumbing pipes or other unique designs. He also made folding and reclining chairs. A myriad of folding, bouncing, reclining, or adjusting chairs were made. The barber's chair, the office chair, the platform rocker, tilt-back rocker, the adjustable child's chair that became a table, the invalid's chair, the reading chair, the swivel chair, and even the familar school desk and chair date from the 1875–1900 period.

George Hunzinger made chairs of unusual design. This platform rocker was made in 1885.

Perhaps the most unusual design made by John Belter, the set of furniture with the carved heads of the presidents. This is the sofa.

Belter slipper chair of laminated rosewood, pierce-carved with oak leaves, grapes, and flowers.

The Morris Chair

William Morris was an English designer who designed the Morris chair in England in 1860. It was immediately copied in America. A typical Morris chair had an adjustable cushioned back with a cushioned seat. It was made in many styles, from Renaissance Revival to Golden Oak and Mission.

Chautauqua Furniture

The Larkin Soap Company of Buffalo, New York, gave furniture premiums to customers who purchased enough soap. The Chautauqua line was their premium from the 1890 to 1905 era. Desks, chairs, and other furniture were offered. They were of the Golden Oak designs.

The English-designed Morris chair was quickly copied by many American furniture makers. This version, from a Larkin premium book of 1895, was offered free with a $10 case of Larkin soap. The chair came in oak or birch with mahogany finish. The cushions were covered in corduroy. The back was adjustable in four positions.

The famous "Chautauqua" desk offered free with a $10 case of Larkin soap. The 1895 catalog says this desk "has gladdened more than half a million hearts."

The strange look of the Westport chair made it seem odd when first patented in 1905, but it became a popular style in later years.

Westport Chair

Thomas Lee designed the Westport chair about 1900. He had it patented in 1905. The children's version was patented in 1922. The plain-line chair with flat wooden parts and an angled back was an oddity of style in its day, but thousands of similar chairs were made after Mr. Lee's original idea.

Pyro Mania

The mainstream carries most designers into the same general styles of architecture, furniture, or clothing. Occasionally, a startling new direction is taken by one designer. His styles may be accepted and may influence a new school, in the same manner as Frank Lloyd Wright or the Adams

Brothers. Then again, his styles may be ignored, and his designs might remain unique.

The George Stewart Company of Norwich, Ohio, seems to have had one of those offbeat design ideas that, while accepted by a few, was ignored in later years. About 1900, the firm put out a line of furniture for "the art-loving public." The pieces were "decorated in burnt work and stains and designed especially for those seeking something more artistic than the usual commercial styles."

The furniture was called art furniture and was entirely hand-decorated. The designs followed classic models. The firm also offered special-order pieces of furniture, leather wall hangings, pillows, and armor.

G. Stewart was working in Norwich for the C. W. Smith Company in 1890. The firm made hardwood and furniture specialties. Sometime before 1909, Stewart had founded his own company.

An undated catalog for the firm, which had offices in New York and Chicago, shows about forty pieces of the pyro-decorated furniture. The

This Turkish-style chair, pictured in an old catalog, decorated with burned lines, a deep blue background, green, red, and yellow designs, and a gold-leaf border, was really made in Norwich, Ohio. This type of furniture was made from 1900 to 1905.

introduction to the catalog mentions a home built in 1896. A catalog issued in 1909 shows much plainer furniture, so the pyro pieces must have been made for just a brief time, probably about 1900–1905.

The designs were inspired by Turkish, German, Scandinavian, Egyptian, and medieval sources. The prices were high—nine to sixteen dollars. Included in the line were leather screens, chests, bookshelves, writing tables, smokers, cradles, pedestals, umbrella stands, candlesticks, chests, music racks, chairs, fire screens, tables, tambourettes, and stools.

Today's collector might find one of these old pieces of furniture. The designs are so foreign-looking, it is doubtful that anyone would realize these are examples of high fashion of the early 1900s in the United States.

Wooton Desk

Indianapolis, Indiana, was the center of furniture manufacturers when William S. Wooton came to town in 1870. He had been in the furniture business with a partner in Richmond, Indiana. Mr. Wooton set up his own company in Indianapolis, making school, office, and church furniture. Mr. Wooton patented the "Wooton's Patent Cabinet Office Secretary" on October 6, 1874. This was the first of the famous desks. The Wooton desk was made in sections with innumerable cubbyholes and drawers. The desk was made to be closed or even locked at night. It furnished security with a minimal use of space while the office was cleaned. The desks were very heavy but were made on bracket feet with rollers, and they could easily be moved.

Four grades of desks were made: Ordinary, Standard, Extra, and Superior. There were three sizes of each grade, ranging from 4 feet 7½ inches to 5 feet 1½ inches high. They originally retailed from $90 to $750. The desks were made in the Eastlake style, using black walnut with pine, maple, poplar, holly, ebony, Spanish cedar, or satinwood. The hardware was bronze or gold-enameled bronze. The carvings were elaborate.

The company catalogs offered a Ladies' Secretary that was smaller than the others, and there was a "Lawyer's own desk," two cases with pivoting sections holding the top. Wooton also made rotary desks with cylinder tops. Other companies made similar types of desks.

The Wooton company went out of business in America about 1884. The desk was made and sold by both Canadian and English firms after that time.

A Wooton desk patented 1880.

Another model of the Wooton desk, opened to show the advantages of such a piece of furniture.

Rolltop Desk

The Victorian rolltop desk made its comeback during the 1970s. It had been a relatively unwanted piece of furniture that sold for under fifty dollars until collectors began to appreciate the amount of space and convenience that was offered by this furniture form. The standard rolltop desk had a flat top with a tambour front that rolled back into the desk. The earliest examples were made of black walnut. The later ones were of cherry, mahogany, and finally oak. Many manufacturers used a combination of woods. They were factory-made from about 1875 to the early 1920s. The desks were made for use in offices and stores but not in homes.

A typical rolltop desk offered by a Cincinnati office furniture company in the early 1900s. (Levy & White, Store, Office & Bar Fixtures catalog)

The rolltop desk with Eastlake decoration and a solid rollback top dates from the 1875 to 1890 period. It was usually made of walnut or mahogany.

Hoosier Kitchen Cabinet

The Hoosier cabinet was at the height of popularity about 1913. A complete line of cabinets was made under the Hoosier name in the early 1900s. The cabinets, made for kitchen storage, had special places for flour, sugar, spices. They also contained a breadboard, cupboards, and many other working sections. The cupboards became so popular that today the brand name "Hoosier" has taken on a generic meaning and all of the multisectioned kitchen pieces are referred to as Hoosier cabinets. The style lasted until the built-in kitchen cabinet became popular in the 1920s, but was still offered in an early-1940s Montgomery Ward catalog.

The Brooks Manufacturing Company of Saginaw, Michigan, offered this version of a Hoosier-style cabinet in the 1915 catalog. Notice the flour sifter, the aluminum top, and bins for storage of sugar, salt, and spices.

Golden Oak

Collectors have named the period of the light-colored heavy oak furniture of 1880–1920 the "Golden Oak" period. Included in this general category is not only the honey-colored oak but also the darker-finished pieces of oak. This was one of the first mass-produced furniture types in America. Golden Oak was made for use in the office, factory, and home. All types of furniture were made, ranging from dining room sets to baby furniture. The earliest of the Golden Oak was made in simplified Victorian styles. Tables had carved pedestals and the chairs had turnings and carving with backs curved. The 1890s brought a new form of china cabinet– mirror desk that resembled no other period of design. The asymmetrical piece has a glassed-in china cabinet on one side with a fall-front desk over drawers on the other side. There were a few bits of applied carving added. Variations of this asymmetrical design appeared in other dining or bedroom cabinet pieces. By the end of the nineteenth century Golden Oak was designed in the Mission style. Straight sides, squared chests of drawers, plain legs, and undecorated surfaces were favored. The furniture was still heavy in weight as well as appearance. With the approach of the 1920s the appearance of weight diminished until the last of the Golden Oak pieces were made with an Art Deco appearance.

The furniture was made not only of oak but also of combinations of woods like ash, beech, maple, and hickory.

Sideboard. Solid Oak, Golden Finish. Top, 21x42. Mirror, 14x24.
No. 110-76-11½. Each $29.90

Sideboard. Solid Oak, Golden Finish. Full swell, quartered oak top drawer.
Top, 22x42. Mirror, 14x24.
No. 105-76-13½. Each $33.50

Sideboard. Solid Oak, Golden Finish. Full swell, quartered oak top drawer.
Top, 22x46. Mirror, 18x36.
No. 109-76-17½. Each $44.00

Sideboard. Solid Oak, Golden Finish. Full swell, quartered oak drawer.
Top, 22x42. Mirror, 16x28.
No. 114-76-11. Each $35.00

Line No. 100. Shipped F. O. B. New York City.

Golden Oak sideboards and tables offered in the fall 1916 catalog of Peck & Hills Furniture Company of New York City.

755   SEARS, ROEBUCK & CO., Cheapest Supply House on Earth, Chicago. CATALOGUE No. III.

Golden Oak furniture was a perennial best-seller for Sears, Roebuck. These desks were offered in the 1902 catalog.

Still more Sears, Roebuck Golden Oak: a page of bookcases from 1908.

$7⁹⁵ COMBINATION $27⁴⁵ BOOKCASES

BIG REDUCTION IN PRICES.

AT $7.95 TO $27.45 WE SHOW THE FOLLOWING HANDSOME HIGH GRADE, NEW STYLE COMBINATION BOOKCASES; THESE VALUES CANNOT BE EQUALED. OUR LOW PRICES ARE NOT MADE AT THE EXPENSE OF QUALITY. WE GUARANTEE EVERY BOOKCASE LOWER IN PRICE THAN THE SAME QUALITY OF GOODS CAN BE BOUGHT ELSEWHERE.

OUR COMBINATION BOOKCASES this season, for beauty of design, high quality of construction and finish, and convenience in arrangement and for extraordinary value, are positively unequaled. They embody all the new ideas in bookcase construction, the designs are greatly improved over any previous season and every one represents the product of the most up to date and modern machinery, the best material to be obtained and put together by the best skilled workmanship that money can buy.

THE WOOD used in the construction of our combination bookcases is specially selected, highly figured oak. It is thoroughly air seasoned and kiln dried before being put through the factory. Great care is taken to get the highest quality and the choicest flaky grained lumber.

THE CONSTRUCTION of our combination bookcases is strictly high grade, the best that modern machinery and skilled workmanship can produce. The framework is carefully joined and mortised evenly together and grooves carefully fitted. The drawers are dovetailed on the sides and grooved on the backs and bottoms. The panels are made of transverse layers of highly figured, flaky grained oak, which prevents warping or shrinkage. Every part and piece is carefully and perfectly fitted. The drawers all work smoothly without friction, and the doors close without binding. The hand carving is finely executed and new and original in design.

THE MIRRORS used in our combination cases are the very best quality of genuine heavy thick French bevel plate, with a perfect beveled edge and a perfect reflection. We do not use any cheap, domestic plate mirrors.

$10.85 FOR THIS MAGNIFICENT NEW DESIGN high grade combination bookcase. Is made of specially selected, thoroughly air seasoned and kiln dried oak, high gloss golden finish, exceptionally attractive in design, high grade in construction and beautiful in finish; without question the most wonderful value ever offered. The equal of combination bookcases generally sold at $16.00 to $18.00. It stands 75 inches high and 38 inches wide. New design pattern shaped mirror is best quality French bevel plate, size 12x12 inches. Writing desk has drawer and pigeonholes for stationery, etc. Below desk is a roomy drawer and spacious cupboard; book compartment has four swell bent glass door and adjustable shelves to fit any size book. Note especially the ornamental hand made carvings on the top and the bric-a-brac shelf below mirror. Fitted with locks, keys and best quality cast brass handles and casters. The workmanship is strictly first class throughout, doors and drawers carefully fitted and entire frame extra well constructed, perfectly rigid and strong. Our price $10.85 at which we offer our customers this beautiful combination bookcase and writing desk, a price that is possible only by reason of our advantageous and extremely large contract direct with the manufacturer and because we add but the narrowest kind of a profit to the actual cost of material and labor. Shipping weight, 140 pounds.

HOW WE ARE ABLE TO MAKE QUICK DELIVERY

of this bookcase and save time and freight charges to our customers. Our sales on this magnificent high grade combination bookcase have grown so large from every section of the country that, in order that we may be able to get one of these splendid and deservedly popular combination bookcases to our customers in the WEST and NORTHWEST in a day or two from the date we receive your order, to insure its reaching you in perfect condition, to remove the liability of breakage or damage and reduce the freight charges to the smallest possible amount, we have arranged warehouse facilities at St. Paul, Minn., and Kansas City, Mo. We ship this combination bookcase in solid car lots receiving from the railroad company the very lowest carload freight rates, so that when we receive your order here in Chicago for this combination bookcase, No. 1K1113, we immediately send your order by special mail delivery to the warehouse nearest you and order the combination bookcase shipped to your railroad station on your order at once. It will leave the warehouse in perfect condition and will reach you in a few hours to a day or two at the farthest from the time it leaves the warehouse, and when you get it you will need to pay the small freight charges for the short distance from the warehouse to your railroad station. The total cost of this combination bookcase to our customers in the WEST and NORTHWEST will amount to considerably less than if shipped to you singly as one shipment from the factory in Illinois to your nearest railroad station. Shipping weight, 140 pounds.

No. 1K1113   Price at factory in Northern Illinois..$10.85
Price at warehouse in Kansas City, Mo... 11.78
Price at warehouse in St. Paul, Minn.. 11.75

No. 1K1113

No. 1K1101 This Combination Bookcase is made of thoroughly seasoned oak, high gloss golden finish. Height, 72 inches; width, 34 inches. Mirror is best quality French bevel plate, size, 10x12 inches. Writing desk has drawer, pigeonholes and pen rack. Below desk is a spacious cupboard and imitation drawer. Roomy book compartment has four adjustable shelves and double strength glass door. Best quality cast brass knobs and casters. Sells in retail stores at $11.00 to $12.00. Exceptional value at the price we ask. Shipped direct from factory in Northern Illinois. Shipping weight, 125 pounds.
Price **$7.95**

No. 1K1103 This New Design Combination Bookcase and Writing Desk is made of solid oak, high gloss golden finish. Height, 72 inches; width, 36 inches. Pattern shaped mirror, size, 12x12 inches; is best quality thick French bevel plate. Note the bracket shelf below mirror and convenient arrangement of interior of writing desk. Below writing desk is a spacious compartment with imitation drawer. Book section has adjustable shelves to fit any size book and will hold 100 to 125 ordinary size books. Sells in stores at $15.00 to $16.00. Shipped direct from factory in Northern Illinois. Shipping weight, 130 pounds.
Price...... **$9.45**

No. 1K1110 This Handsome Combination Bookcase and Writing Desk is made of quarter sawed oak with a high gloss golden finish. Height, 72 inches; width, 39 inches. Fitted with pattern shaped French bevel mirror, size, 12x12 inches. Inside of desk is provided with drawer and pigeonholes for envelopes, writing paper, etc. Below desk is a convenient drawer and roomy cupboard for books, magazines, newspapers, etc. Ornamented with smooth cut handsomely designed hand carvings. Adjustable shelves, to fit any size book, thoroughly seasoned. Fitted with locks, keys and best quality cast brass handles and casters. Shipped direct from factory in Northern Illinois. Shipping weight, 130 pounds.
Price **$10.65**

No. 1K1105 This Combination Bookcase and Writing Desk is made of selected oak with a high gloss golden finish. Height, 72 inches; width, 36 inches. Interior of desk is fitted with drawer and pigeonholes. Below desk is a imitation drawer and spacious cupboard. Book section has double thick glass door. Shelves adjustable to any size book. Fitted with best quality of French plate mirror, size, 12x12 inches. Note the ornamental, deep smooth cut, hand carved decorations and French shaped front legs. Fitted with the best quality cast brass handles, locks and casters. Sells in retail stores at $12.00 to $14.00. Securely crated and shipped direct from factory in Northern Illinois. Shipping wt., 135 lbs.
Price **$8.95**

No. 1K1106 Full Swell Bent Glass Door Combination Bookcase at $9.85, the equal of those offered in retail stores at $15.00 to $16.00. Made of thoroughly seasoned quarter sawed oak, except the ends, which are made of plain oak. High gloss golden finish; height, 72 inches; width, 37 inches. Writing desk has drawer, pigeonholes and pen rack. Book compartment fitted with four adjustable shelves and will hold 125 average size books. Mirror is best quality French bevel plate, size, 12x12 inches. Material, construction and finish first class. Fitted with locks, keys, cast brass handles and casters. Shipped direct from factory in Northern Illinois. Shipping weight, 130 pounds.
Price..... **$9.85**

No. 1K1116 This Combination Bookcase and Writing Desk is made of quarter sawed oak in a high gloss golden finish. Height, 72 inches; width, 39 inches. Interior of desk is arranged for stationery, below which are three spacious drawers. Pattern shaped French bevel plate mirror, size, 12x14 inches. Shelves adjustable to any size book. Note the convenient shelf above mirror. Decorated with ornamental smooth cut hand carvings. High grade in construction, beautiful in wood and finish. Fitted with best quality of cast brass handles, locks and casters. Exceptional value at our price. Shipped direct from factory in Northern Illinois. Shipping weights, 135 pounds.
Price **$12.45**

Pressed-back chairs with backs that are made by actually pressing the wood to resemble carving.

Oak and maple chairs from a catalog of the Evansville Furniture Company of Evansville, Indiana. Some of these appear to have carved backs, others pressed backs. Many of the catalogs of the day call all of these chairs "carved."

Pressed-Back Chairs

For some inexplicable reason the name pressed-back chair today not only refers to the chairs made with—what else?—a pressed back, but also to the carved solid wood chairs that have the same type of designs as the pressed-back chair.

Furniture manufacturers made these chairs from 1890 to 1910. They were inexpensive utilitarian wooden chairs that were made to sell in quantity. Thousands of these chairs in hundreds of varieties were mass-produced in Grand Rapids, Michigan, and other cities. The 1897 Sears, Roebuck catalog pictures pressed-back chairs ranging in price from $2.25 to $12.00. Rockers, children's rockers, children's chairs, dining sets, armchairs, desk chairs, and side chairs were made. The expensive models were made of solid wood with carved decoration. Most of them were made by pressing the wood to create the design. Oak, walnut, birch, elm, and other hardwoods were used. Seats were upholstered in fabric or were made of wood, cane, or leather.

Pressed-back rocker made in Michigan in the early nineteenth century.

The ubiquitous photographer's prop of the late nineteenth century, a fancy wicker chair.

Wicker Furniture

Wicker furniture can be traced back to the ancient Egyptians and through many centuries. Most collectors are interested only in the nineteenth- and twentieth-century pieces.

Some cargoes sent to the United States from China in the nineteenth century were tied in place with rattan. Cyrus Wakefield, a Boston grocer, realized that the rattan was being discarded and removed from the docks as a fire hazard. He experimented with the material and soon found that it was suitable for many types of furniture and especially for chair seats. He corresponded with his brother-in-law in Canton, China, and eventually hired ships to import cane and rattan for furniture makers. By the 1850s Mr. Wakefield moved to South Reading, Massachusetts, where he started a rattan factory. Before long he was employing large numbers of workers making rattan, cane, or willow furniture. The literature of the eighteenth and early nineteenth century does not differentiate between the various types of materials used in what they referred to as "wicker" chairs. It was not until the late nineteenth century that the makers explained the difference in their advertisements.*

Wicker furniture became popular in America about 1850. The curved lines of the Victorian French Rococo style were easily interpreted with the pliable wicker. Some of the early furniture was made of bent wood that was covered with rattan. In England the 1850 chairs were much less curved, and a basket chair was popular.

Rattan was temporarily in short supply in 1856 because of the war in China. Cyrus Wakefield kept experimenting until he developed a method of using the reed, or inside section, of the rattan. Before this, only the outer "skin" of the vine was used. The new processed reed was found to be more pliable, and easier to stain and paint.

There was great interest in the various types of wicker furniture during the years just after the Civil War. A combination of materials was used. All types of styles were made, including Rococo, Classical, Gothic, and many variations of designs. Wicker was ideally suited for porch and garden furniture. It was lightweight and very durable. Many wicker pieces were left natural or lightly stained. Some of the wicker pieces were used indoors but most of those pieces were painted.

The 1876 Centennial exhibition influenced the design of wicker furni-

---

* Makers are now using different materials for "wicker" furniture and the difference is often described on the label. *Rattan* is a vine in the palm family. It is bent to shape. Some rattan is peeled and the peel is used for weaving or tying. *Reed* is a grassy plant similar to straw. This was the material used on the early American wicker chairs. The term *reed* is sometimes used for the core of the rattan vine. *Bamboo* is the tropical Asian grass with jointed, hollow stems, used for many types of furniture. *Willow* is a tree shrub. The willow is woven. It can be easily identified because the diameter of each strand becomes smaller near one end.

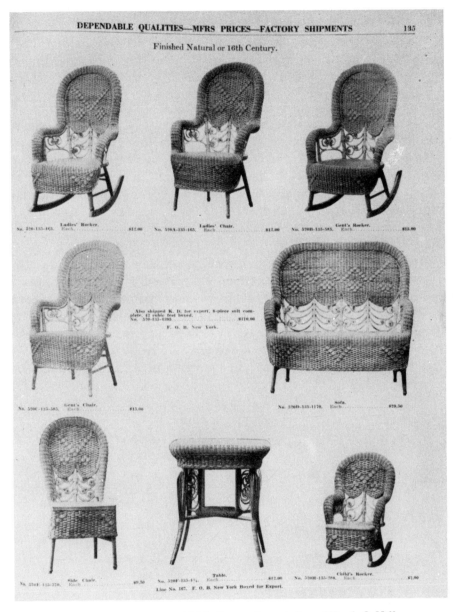

Wicker of the style popular in 1916. From the catalog of Peck & Hills.

ture. Chinese wicker furniture was shown and the hourglass chair was copied in America for several years. Painted wicker furniture made from reeds was seen in many Victorian rooms. There were wicker plant stands, easels, shelves, and wicker tables. The wicker could be shellacked, stained, enameled, or gold-leafed. Chairs were often painted in several colors and draped with fabric. Wicker baby carriages, invalid chairs, wheelchairs, and baby furniture were made. Less expensive wicker was made and sold by the Sears, Roebuck Company and Montgomery Ward.

Oriental designs were clearly seen as an influence in later Victorian wicker pieces. The idea of the mysterious Far East and wicker were intertwined by the 1880s. The slightly wicked erotic connotations of the Orient were suggested. Many photographers began using an ornate, asymmetric wicker chair as a prop for a picture of an attractive woman. Many brothels were elegantly furnished with wicker furniture.

The turn of the twentieth century brought a change in decorating tastes. The Eastlake ideas of less decoration were considered. Sanitation, health, and country living became part of a fad. Central heating was in use. Many porches were enclosed as sun parlors, with the outdoor porches left for those who desired fresh air. Wicker was the ideal furniture that could be used in both rooms. More sedate designs were made with fewer curves. The hourglass chair design that was so popular in 1876 returned and

An American wicker table of the 1920s.

Pseudo-bamboo furniture was part of the Victorian style influenced by Japanese design. The pseudo-bamboo chair was made about 1885. The lady's secretary desk was made in the same style. These pieces are either American or English.

complete sets of furniture, including chairs and tables, were made in that shape. Many were imported from China. Most wicker was the straight-line Mission-type furniture. "Cape Cod" weave was the tight weave, and the "Bar Harbor" weave was the loose weave.

A new type of "wicker" furniture was made from fiber in 1904. It was a type of fiber reed made from twisted paper that was stiffened with glue. It did not break easily and was very inexpensive. The fiber reed pieces were usually made in a closely woven style. This type of paper-wrapped reed was not popular until 1920. It can be recognized by the braided legs on chairs or tables. The paper material could not be rolled like wicker.

Marshall B. Lloyd invented a machine in 1927 that made a woven fiber fabric that could be attached to the frame of the furniture by hand. The

This American maple and bird's-eye maple bed was made to resemble bamboo about 1880.

fiber is a twisted paper woven into a cloth. It is reinforced with steel wire, making it durable. Today this woven wicker fabric is often used for bathroom hampers and porch furniture.

Art Deco designs were introduced in 1920 and the wicker makers immediately adapted the designs to their wares. Removable seats and upholstered wicker pieces were popular. A small diamond design of a contrasting color was the feature of many Art Deco pieces. Table and floor lamps, tea carts, and almost all types of chairs, tables, dressers, and shelves were made.

The day of wicker almost ended in the 1930s. The public no longer considered wicker stylish and furniture dealers or secondhand stores couldn't give it away. It was not until the 1960s that wicker again became a popular mass-produced furniture. Copies of many of the older styles were made in the Orient and shipped to the United States. Wicker pieces were also being manufactured in American factories. Collectors began their search for the antique wicker pieces and it was once more in demand.

A history of wicker furniture in America is impossible without the inclusion of the history of the most famous maker, the Heywood Wakefield Company.

Heywood Wakefield

Cyrus Wakefield was the clever Boston grocer who realized that the discarded rattan of Boston was suitable for furniture. He started buying and importing cane by 1845 and by the 1850s moved to South Reading, Massachusetts, to build a factory to make wicker furniture. He developed a way to use the inside of the rattan for some of the pieces. It was not long before his reed furniture gained popularity in the market. Wakefield had ten acres of floor space devoted to the furniture business in the early 1870s but during a financial crash he died and the company went bankrupt. Just prior to his death he incorporated as the Wakefield Rattan Company. His wife paid the bills from money inherited from her father, and Cyrus Wakefield II, a nephew, became manager.

Levi Heywood founded Heywood Brothers in 1861 and the company began buying rattan seats for his factory from Wakefield in the 1870s. Mr. Heywood made wooden furniture, and invented several machines that could bend wood or otherwise improve the manufacture of chairs. One machine made a groove that allowed sheet caning to be used for chair seats. His firm was the largest chair manufacturer in the United States by 1870. They sold mainly Windsor and Bentwood chairs, but by 1875 the firm began making wicker furniture. By the 1880s they were making so many wicker baby carriages that they printed a special catalog.

The competition between the two firms continued with both companies making similar products. The main building of the Wakefield Rattan Company burned in 1881, and was rebuilt. But in 1888 Cyrus Wakefield II died, leaving inexperienced management. Levi Heywood died in 1882 and his nephew Henry Heywood became the new head. He expanded the lines, opened warehouses overseas, and the company prospered. The firms of Heywood and Wakefield merged in 1897.

They purchased the Lloyd Manufacturing Company in 1921. The acquisition gave them ownership of the firm that had developed the loom that could produce the very popular closely woven wicker. The firm is still working and makes wicker and other types of furniture.

Care and Restoration of Wicker

Wicker is more pliable when it is damp. Like a basket, it should be washed or wetted from time to time. A wicker chair that makes small popping noises is too dry and should be soaked or dampened.

The most valuable wicker pieces are those that are still in their natural or unpainted condition. Clean the piece and if necessary coat it with a colorless lacquer. Touch up all repairs with the proper stain. Painted wicker can be stripped, but it is very difficult and not always successful. Wicker can be repainted but must be completely clean and sanded where necessary. Fill all of the cracks with plastic wood. It is best to use spray paint. Use several light coats instead of one heavy one. Let each coat dry completely outdoors in warm, dry weather before painting again. To do it right is not an easy job.

Some paints may not be compatible with the original finish. Try a little of the paint over the varnish, paint, or lacquer in an area that is not visible. Wait a few days to see whether it blisters, peels, or stays tacky. If any of these troubles appear, try using a different type of paint.

Brass Beds

The brass bed was an English fashion that started about 1835. The bed was designed for use on the farm or in a village home. Mahogany was still the only suitable material for an in-town home. The wooden bed of the day had a carved wooden headboard, sides, and a canopy that was draped with side curtains. The curtains were drawn to keep out the night air. The metal bed offered more air circulation, avoided woodworms, bedbugs, ticks, and was more hygienic.

The first patented design of an English metal bed was issued in 1849. The brass bed was shown at the Great London Exhibition in 1851 and the English middle class immediately began ordering copies. The idea quickly spread to the United States and the Continent and the English brass bed manufacturers made and exported thousands of beds. The brass bed of the 1850s was of the Renaissance style and was often made with a canopy, hangings, and even cupids that held up the corners. The design of the bed gradually changed, the canopy disappeared, and the decorations became more symmetrical and open.

Birmingham, England, became the headquarters of the brass bed industry. American manufacturers produced beds but they could not make them fast enough, so imports remained high. There were few design changes until the 1920s and the Art Deco period when the typically rectilinear Art Deco designs were made. The demand for brass beds ended in 1930 and it was not until the 1960s that they again gained favor. Reproductions and new versions of brass beds are being manufactured as the supply of old beds dwindles.

Several types of brass were used in the beds. The most common was iron tubing that was wrapped with brass sheet metal. There was a seam on the rod where the end of the brass was crimped. A magnet will stick to this type of bed but the brass sheeting is usually so thick that it will probably never be polished away.

Some of the best beds were made of all brass. They had no supporting iron core and for structural reasons were made only with straight lines. They are plain in appearance and no seam can be seen.

The least desirable type of brass bed was made using brass-plated

Typical Victorian brass beds.

metal. It is not unusual to find one with the plating wearing off. A limited number of beds were made of cylindrical hollow brass tubing for the main crosspieces and seamed brass tubing for the smaller decorative parts.

Brass beds were expensive, so manufacturers made similar beds of iron at the same time. These were usually painted. The iron bed was usually much lighter in weight because the iron rods were smaller than the brass tubing. They were often less than one-quarter inch in diameter. Some of the iron beds had brass ornaments, especially at the corners.

Condition of Brass Beds   Always test a brass bed with a magnet. A magnet will stick to brass-plated steel or to brass-covered iron but not to solid brass. The painted bed should be tested in an inconspicuous place with a knife. Scrape away some of the paint and examine whether it is the typical yellow color of brass or the dull gray of iron.

Beds that have rusted are usually of the plate brass variety. Tarnished beds with a green color may be fine after a good polishing. A painted brass bed is also satisfactory after removing the paint. Be sure that it is really brass and not an iron bed.

To remove paint or lacquer the bed must be dismantled. Use paint remover to strip the covering. Then polish with a good brass polish or even a combination of vinegar and salt. It is not an easy job and a professional furniture stripper can usually do it easier and faster. The polished bed should be lacquered with a spray lacquer. If you are handy this could be a do-it-yourself job.

MISSION

The ornate Victorian furniture began to lose its popularity by the twentieth century. Gustav Stickley founded a company in Eastwood, New York, in 1898. He made furniture in a style that was popular with William Morris of England. He and many others began making functional, simple furniture, usually of oak. Their pieces had very straight lines with little if any decoration. Only the prominent mortise-and-tenon joints relieved the smooth oak surface.

Why was this furniture called Mission? Some sources, including catalogs of the day that offered the furniture, claimed the pieces were inspired by the Franciscan missions of California. Some say the name came about because the makers felt the furniture had a mission and was to be used and appreciated by the public. It was simple, and of a dignified style without elaboration or ornament. The chairs were made to be comfortable and the tables were made to fit the space provided. The Mission style of

Stickley became so popular that many others made pieces of similar design. The ideas spread to the Sears, Roebuck catalog and finally to the do-it-yourself manual for school woodworking shops.

Gustav Stickley

Gustav Stickley (1857–1942) was the originator of Mission furniture and he called his line Craftsman. Stickley began working as the Gustav Stickley Company in Eastwood, New York, in 1898. His first public exhibition was at a furniture show in Grand Rapids, Michigan, in 1900.

His furniture was made of native American or fumed oak. Fumed wood was exposed to ammonia fumes, which created an immediate aged look. He used leather, canvas, or simple fabrics for chair seats. The hardware was iron or copper. He decided to promote the name Craftsman and marked his pieces with a joiner's compass and the words "Als ik Kan," meaning "As I Can." He added his written signature. In 1901 he added a semicooperative group to his firm called United Crafts. They were dropped by 1904.

A Gustav Stickley reclining oak chair, stamped with the name.

Stickley bought a building in 1902, which became the Craftsman Building. It was there that he published a magazine extolling the virtues of Ruskin, Morris, and the Mission furniture ideas. He had furniture and metalworking shops plus a library and lecture hall. He tried to organize his workers in the style of the medieval craft guilds to prove that he believed in the philosophy of the Arts and Crafts movement of England. It was an idealized view of the single workman creating a total piece of furniture in an honest and sincere manner.

A Gustav Stickley round oak dining table with six leaves. It is 53¾ inches in diameter.

This Gustav Stickley library table has the hardware favored by the firm. The oak table is 5 feet 6 inches long.

Harvey Ellis designed for Gustav Stickley's United Crafts. This chair, from an early catalog, has the inlaid metal patterns on the back.

A sideboard from the Gustav Stickley catalog of 1910. Notice the copper tray on the sideboard.

601 Desk
Height, 34½ in.
Top, 20 x 34 in.

602 Desk
Height, 36½ in.
Top, 22 x 40 in.

604 Desk
Height, 36½ in.
Top, 22 x 40 in.

601

602

913 Desk Chair
Height, 37½ in.
Width, 16 in.
Wood seat

610 Desk
Height, 39 in.
Top, 22 x 40 in.

**1313
Desk Chair**
Height, 37½ in.
Width, 16 in.
Leather uphol-
stered seat

609 Desk
Height, 36½ in.
Top, 22 x 44 in.

913

604

1313

610

609

33

A page from the L. and J.G. Stickley catalog showing typical oak pieces.

Stickley drew house designs, made textiles, rugs, lighting fixtures, and copper and brass objects. They were all made to go with the Mission-style furniture.

In 1905, after changing his name from Gustave Stickley to Gustav, he moved his offices to New York City, but the workshops remained in Eastwood. He continued his many projects, including a model farm, until he went bankrupt in 1915. There were too many others imitating his styles and making Mission furniture at lower prices. This did not stop his creative talents and he tried some very different styles of furniture, which included one type with a painted finish called Chromewald.

Another type of furniture was made in the Chinese Chippendale style. In less than two years he stopped manufacturing all types of furniture and took a job in Kenosha, Wisconsin, which lasted less than a year. He died in 1942.

Stickley Brothers Company (George and Albert)

Gustav Stickley had been in business in 1886 with several brothers. George and Albert moved to Grand Rapids, Michigan, in 1891 to make furniture. They made furniture at a firm called Stickley Brothers Company. It resembled the oak furniture made by Gustav, but their pieces were mass-produced and were not as well made or well designed. The pieces were marked "Quaint Furniture," one of the line names, or "Arts and Crafts" with the name "Stickley Bros. Co." The firm stopped working sometime after 1907.

L. & J.G. Stickley Company

Two brothers, Leopold and George Stickley, opened a furniture factory in Fayetteville, New York, in 1900 with the name L. and J.G. Stickley Company. They made furniture that also followed the designs of Gustav Stickley. At times they used veneers and laminated woods. Their pieces were marked in red with the name "L. and J.G. Stickley." The firm also made furniture that was designed by Frank Lloyd Wright, plus the Morris chair and reproduction furniture. They purchased the Gustav Stickley factory in 1916 and continued operating it as the Stickley Manufacturing Company. The firm is still working and making many types of reproductions.

The Stickley-Brandt Furniture Company

There were other Stickley relatives. Some married into the Brandt family. In 1884 in Binghamton, New York, The Stickley-Brandt Furniture Company was formed and run by Charles Stickley, a brother of Gustav, and some members of the Brandt family. The company did not work in the Mission style but made late-Victorian-style furniture of the Golden Oak type. The firm went bankrupt in 1919.

Elbert Hubbard–Roycroft

Elbert Hubbard (1856–1915) was born in Bloomington, Illinois. He sold soap for many years until he joined with John Larkin to found the Larkin Soap Company in 1875. The company was one of the classic success stories in American industry. Their advertising genius, use of premiums in exchange for soap labels, and the family sales plan of Elbert Hubbard turned the Buffalo, New York, company into a major concern.

After ten years Hubbard decided that money was not the most important part of life, and he sold his interests in the soap company in 1893. He was living in East Aurora, New York, and decided to become a book publisher. He wrote, edited, and published a magazine called *The Philistine* and that too became a financial success. Hubbard had been influenced by the thought of William Morris of England and he created a community dedicated to superior craftsmanship, edifying thoughts, and with the motto "Not How Cheap, But How Good." He started the Roycroft Print Shop in 1897 and produced books having high-relief molded leather or limp chamois covers, and elaborately decorated pages. The print shop grew into the community where workshops made leather place mats, boxes, purses, copper, silver, and brass pieces, rugs, baskets, wood carvings, and furniture.

Mission-style furniture was first mentioned in the 1901 catalog. Heavy oak or mahogany chairs and tables were made with a Roycroft mark. The Roycroft community made many types of furniture, chairs of all sorts, slant-top desks, lamps, library tables, picture frames, chests of drawers, serving tables, and bedroom sets. The hardware was often copper or brass that was handcrafted in the shops. An adaptation of the trademark has been used since 1977 on pieces made by Roycrofters-at-Large Association, a group interested in promoting the Roycroft community.

The men and women employed at Roycroft worked in an apprentice system. Mr. Hubbard lectured, wrote, and inspired many. He printed the famous pamphlet *A Message to Garcia* in 1899. This was only one of the

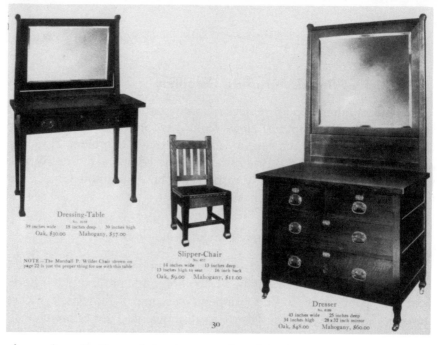

Dressing-Table
No. 0
39 inches wide   18 inches deep   30 inches high
Oak, $30.00   Mahogany, $57.00

NOTE—The Marshall P. Wilder Chair shown on page 22 is just the proper thing for use with this table

Slipper-Chair
No. 0
14 inches wide   13 inches deep
13 inches high to seat   16 inch back
Oak, $9.00   Mahogany, $11.00

Dresser
No. 0100
43 inches wide   25 inches deep
34 inches high   28 x 32 inch mirror
Oak, $48.00   Mahogany, $60.00

A page from the Roycroft furniture catalog of 1912.

many words of wisdom produced in the community. His mottoes were printed, framed, and offered for sale.

Elbert Hubbard and his wife, Alice, died on the *Lusitania* when it was sunk in 1915. The Roycroft shops were managed by Elbert Hubbard II until they were sold at auction in 1938.

Other Important Mission Makers

William H. Bradley

Will Bradley (1868–1962) was a designer and not a manufacturer. Any study of Mission-period furniture must include knowledge of the Bradley room designs that were made for the *Ladies' Home Journal,* November 1901 to August 1902. The designs incorporated the best of the English and American ideas of Mission plus the additional skills of Bradley.

Harvey Ellis

Harvey Ellis (1852–1904) was a designer for Gustav Stickley's United

Crafts. He did pieces for the *Craftsman* magazine from July 1903 until his death in 1904. The furniture that he designed had inlaid patterns of copper, pewter, or other details that were unlike the usual Stickley oak furniture. His designs were made for only a short time after his death.

Charles and Henry Greene

The Greene Brothers, Charles (1868–1957) and Henry (1870–1954) were practicing architects in Pasadena, California, in 1892. They designed a house, its grounds and furniture. Their furniture was made from walnut or fruitwood and trimmed with ebony or semiprecious stones.

Limbert Guild

Charles P. Limbert Company of Grand Rapids, and Holland, Michigan, made several lines of Mission furniture from 1902 to 1944. It was called Holland Dutch Arts and Crafts, and was marked with a branded label. Pieces were made of fumed oak with leather or tapestry seats, and copper hardware. A few pieces were inlaid with ebony designs.

Charles Rohlfs

Charles Rohlfs (1853–1936) was a New York City furniture maker who worked in many styles, including Mission. By the 1890s, he was making plain oak pieces that were similar to those popularized by Stickley. He often lectured as a guest of Elbert Hubbard. Some of Rohlfs' pieces were marked with the brand "R" and the date.

Rose Valley Association

The Rose Valley Community was founded in 1901 by Philadelphia architect William Price. They made furniture in the Mission manner and marked their pieces "Rose Valley Shops." The pieces were medieval in design and more ornate than the Stickley Mission designs. The community went bankrupt in 1909.

Frank Lloyd Wright

The famous modern architect Frank Lloyd Wright (1867–1959) designed some Mission-style furniture for use in his studio and for several of the homes that he designed. The early pieces were made by hand under his direction. Later, he became interested in the possibilities of machine-made designs.

Other Styles

Tobey Furniture Company

The Tobey Furniture Company of Chicago, Illinois, was started in 1875 by Charles and Frank Tobey. The company produced expensive furniture, often made to order. Art Nouveau pieces were made, also Mission or Arts and Crafts style. The company closed in 1974.

Another company working in Chicago at the turn of the century making top-quality Art Nouveau pieces was S. Karpen and Brothers.

Wallace Nutting

Wallace Nutting was a clergyman who became famous as a photographer, manufacturer, antiquarian, and author of books. He wrote several books about furniture, *Furniture Treasury, Furniture of the Pilgrim Century, Windsor Handbook,* a book about clocks, the "States Beautiful" series, and several others. The Nutting prints were hand-colored photographs of landscapes, flowers, Colonial interiors, architectural exteriors, and other attractive scenes.

His furniture was made to copy original pieces that he had acquired to furnish the rooms pictured in his photographs. It was not until 1917 that he started a workshop in Framingham, Massachusetts, to make furniture. All Nutting pieces were made by hand by craftsmen in the old manner, but they did use some motor-driven machinery. The name "Wallace Nutting" was burned on each piece and some also had paper labels. Script letters were used from 1917 to about 1921.

Nutting furniture was primarily made from oak and maple in the style of the seventeenth century. He also made eighteenth-century pine, walnut, and maple cupboards, tables, and Windsor chairs. His catalogs stated, "Those who are looking for 'Mahoganized imitations will waste their time. . . .'" He did make mahogany furniture and by the late 1920s the most popular pieces were those of the late eighteenth-century styles and not the seventeenth-century oak. Over two hundred fifty different designs were used.

Some of the Nutting furniture was resold as authentic antiques and Mr.

Nutting warned buyers of this problem. He sold his business and later bought it back because the quality and controls were not to his liking.

The furniture business was never a monetary success. He sold many pieces but it was the print sales that made the money.

The furniture workshop was sold by 1941 when Mr. Nutting died, and his designs were purchased by the Drexel Furniture Company. They decided that most of the pieces were too expensive to manufacture and apparently never made any of the Nutting line.

Art Deco

The European designs used about 1910 brought the development of a new style named Art Deco. The twining tendrils and the sensuous mood of the Art Nouveau design disturbed many designers and they began making furniture in straight lines and geometric shapes. Symmetry and simplicity returned to the furniture. Low, wide geometric patterns in fabric or inlay came into vogue. Some designers used expensive and rare materials such as ebony, amboyna, sharkskin, and fruitwoods. Other designers just made simple furniture, using new materials such as plastics.

An Art Deco-style bedroom set shown in the 1935 issue of Home Furnishing Arts. *The furniture is finished in brown and cream, the draperies and bedspreads in tones of green.*

An Art Deco-style dining room shown in an advertisement for rugs in 1935.

A burled elm and walnut desk designed by Gilbert Rohde about 1937, a fine example of American Art Deco furniture.

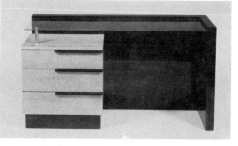

The Art Deco designs were not important in the United States until the 1920s, when many buildings were made in the style. The Rockefeller Center Radio City Music Hall is a prime example. Mass-produced furniture was made in the Art Deco style until 1940. Many American designers worked in the Art Deco style but most of the famous pieces made by American manufacturers were designed by Europeans, such as Emile-Jacques Ruhlmann, Marcel Breuer, and Mies Van Der Rohe.

And All the Others after 1920

It is not too soon to be collecting the furniture made after 1920. Many reproductions were made of earlier styles of furniture. The 1920s version of Jacobean was made in large dining room sets with table, chairs, cup-

A page from the **House Beautiful Furnishing Annual** *of 1925, showing Grand Rapids furniture in a variety of earlier styles.*

boards, and other pieces. The carved solid oak furniture of this type was difficult to sell until the late 1970s, when those who were buying older homes with large rooms discovered that very little modern furniture was scaled for the older rooms. "Flemish" high-backed chairs with caned seats, carved oak library tables, and even bedroom sets were made.

Reproductions have been made of all the periods from 1700 to the present. A well-made Sheraton-style table made in 1910 is of interest to buyers today because of its solid construction and attractive price when compared to the quality of new reproductions.

Top-quality modern designers such as Breuer, Charles Eames, and Mies Van Der Rohe have made furniture that is already collected by those interested in art and design.

Copies of earlier styles have been popular in America in the twentieth century. This chair is in the style of Charles II.

The everyday modern furniture of the 1940s, the Art Moderne designs, are just beginning to interest some collectors. Those Hollywood-inspired sets with round mirrors and blond wood are available in all qualities from poor to custom-made. Usually they are found in secondhand shops, not antiques shops.

A piece from the Quaint Furniture catalog of Stickley Brothers Company, the Old House, Grand Rapids, Michigan. The catalog is No. 50, undated, but evidently from about 1915 to 1925.

BIBLIOGRAPHY

General

Agius, Pauline. *British Furniture, 1880–1915.* Suffolk, England: Antique Collectors' Club, 1978.

The American Heritage History of Antiques from the Civil War to World War I. New York: American Heritage, 1969.

Andrews, John. *Price Guide to Victorian, Edwardian & 1920s Furniture.* Suffolk, England: Antique Collectors' Club, 1980.

Bishop, Robert. *Centuries and Styles of the American Chair, 1640–1970.* New York: Dutton, 1972.

Denker, Ellen and Bert, *The Rocking Chair Book.* New York: Mayflower Books, 1979.

Eastlake-Influenced American Furniture, 1870–1890. Yonkers, New York: Hudson River Museum, 1974.

Hanks, David A. *Innovative Furniture in America from 1800 to the Present.* New York: Cooper-Hewitt Museum, 1981.

Kane, Patricia E. *300 Years of American Seating Furniture.* Boston: New York Graphic Society, 1976.

Kovel, Ralph and Terry. *American Country Furniture, 1780–1875.* New York: Crown, 1965.

Morningstar, Connie. *American Furniture Classics.* Des Moines: Wallace-Homestead, 1976.

Ormsbee, Thomas H. *Field Guide to American Victorian Furniture.* Boston: Little, Brown, 1952.

Renaissance Revival Victorian Furniture. Grand Rapids, Michigan: Grand Rapids Art Museum, 1976.

A Selection of 19th Century American Chairs. Hartford: Stowe-Day Foundation, 1973.

Swedberg, Robert and Harriet. *Victorian Furniture.* Book 2. Des Moines: Wallace-Homestead, 1981.

Terry, Berry. *Nineteenth-Century America: Furniture and Other Decorative Arts.* New York: Metropolitan Museum of Art, 1973.

Mission

Cathers, David M. *Stickley Craftsman Furniture Catalogs.* New York: Dover, 1979.

Clark, Robert Judson. *The Arts and Crafts Movement in America, 1876–1916.* Princeton: Princeton University Press, 1972.

Makinson, Randell L. *Greene & Greene Furniture and Related Designs.* Santa Barbara: Peregrine Smith, Inc., 1979.

Rubin, Jerome and Cynthia. *Mission Furniture.* San Francisco: Chronicle Books, 1980.

1920s

Battersby, Martin. *The Decorative Twenties.* New York: Walker, 1969.
———. *The Decorative Thirties.* New York: Macmillan, 1971.

McClinton, Katharine Morrison. *Art Deco: A Guide for Collectors*. New York: Clarkson N. Potter, 1972.

Morningstar, Connie. *Flapper Furniture and Interiors of the 1920s*. Des Moines: Wallace-Homestead, 1971.

Wallace Nutting

Freeman, John. *Wallace Nutting Checklist of Early American Reproductions*. Watkins Glen, New York: American Life Foundation, 1969.

Oak

Blundell, Peter S. *Market Place Guide to Oak Furniture*. Paducah, Kentucky: Collector Books, 1980.

Collector's Illustrated Price Guide: Oak Furniture. Paducah, Kentucky: Collector Books, 1977.

Hill, Conover. *Value Guide to Antique Oak Furniture*. Paducah, Kentucky: Collector Books, 1972.

Oak Furniture Styles and Prices. Des Moines: Wallace-Homestead, 1980.

Rickabaugh, Phil. *The Rainbow Identity Guide to Pressed-Back Chairs for Antique Dealers & Collectors*. Portland, Oregon: Rainbow Identity Guides, 1971.

Rustic

Stephenson, Sue Honaker. *Rustic Furniture*. New York: Van Nostrand Reinhold, 1979.

Thonet

Thonet Bentwood & Other Furniture, The 1904 Illustrated Catalog. New York: Dover, 1980.

Wilk, Christopher. *Thonet: 150 Years of Furniture*. Woodsbury, New York: Barron's Education Series, 1980.

Wicker

Corbin, Patricia. *All About Wicker*. New York: Dutton, 1978.

Saunders, Richard. *Collecting & Restoring Wicker Furniture*. New York: Crown, 1976.

Shirley, G. E. *Great Grandmother's Wicker Furniture, 1880–1920s*. Burlington, Indiana: Privately printed, 1978.

Thompson, Frances. *The Complete Wicker Book*. Des Moines: Wallace-Homestead, 1978.

Wooton

Walters, Betty Lawson. *The King of Desks, Wooton's Patent Secretary*. Washington, D.C.: Smithsonian Institution Press, 1969.

3

American Art Pottery, 1876 to 1930

The term *art pottery* has several meanings, but this is true of many of the words used by antiques collectors. To the scholar and researcher, art pottery is a type of ware that was made in America from about 1870 to 1920. It was made in the spirit of the Arts and Crafts movement. Art pottery was handmade or primarily handmade and produced with a major concern for the art and not just for its commercial value. Consequently, a pottery may have made art pottery and industrial or florist wares at the same time.

The collector is more pragmatic. In general usage today, the term *art pottery* refers to any of the works of the myriad companies included in the list of potteries working during the 1870–1920 era. The term has even been extended by some to include factories that were working later, up to and including the 1940s.

Abraham Lincoln was shown on this blue tile by the Mosaic Tile Company. It is made of jasperware.

This Buffalo Pottery emerald Deldare plate was made in 1911.

The Art Deco designs were favored by the Cowan Pottery, as can be seen in this blue, gold, and maroon figure of a man. It is 9 inches high.

The typical crackle glaze found on Dedham ware makes it easy to identify. This plate is in the moth pattern.

The art pottery movement in America started in Cincinnati, Ohio. In 1872 Maria Longworth Nichols started a class in china painting for a group of well-to-do women. One of her students, Mary Louise McLaughlin, saw some French Haviland pottery at the Centennial Exhibition and after experimenting began to make pottery with similar decorations. Others soon discovered the new style of pottery. Mrs. Nichols founded the Rookwood Pottery in 1880, which became a successful commercial enterprise. Other Cincinnati area potters included the Cincinnati Art Pottery Company, the Matt Morgan Art Pottery, and the Avon Pottery. Some of the potters trained at Rookwood left to found other companies such as the Van Briggle Pottery of Colorado Springs, Colorado. Some firms took advantage of the natural assets and potters available in Ohio and opened competing firms, including the Roseville Pottery, Weller Pottery, and Lonhuda Pottery. At the same time potteries were working in other parts

The matte green glaze used by Grueby was so popular it was copied by others for lower prices until Grueby finally was forced out of business. These vases were made between 1893 and 1903.

of the country. New England potters had discovered the same French pieces at the Centennial and soon art potteries like Chelsea Keramic Art (later Dedham), Volkmar, and Low Art Tile Works were founded.

Eventually the art pottery movement spread to all parts of the United States. George Ohr of Biloxi, Mississippi, made his own style of crumpled vases while the Newcomb Pottery in New Orleans, Louisiana, perfected a matte glazed ware with stylized floral decoration. Grueby Pottery, made in Boston, Massachusetts, was decorated with a matte green glaze that became so popular and so widely copied in less expensive wares that it eventually forced the company to close. Other potteries opened in Michigan, Illinois, and California.

The companies either found the problems of making a high quality artistic ware too difficult and closed, or they kept making more and better designs while enlarging the plants. By the 1920s many of the firms, especially in Ohio, were making both art pottery and commercial quality wares to sell for lower prices. Gradually the quality of the work suffered as the pricing became more important and by the 1920s most of the art potteries had closed or discontinued the art lines. Those who wanted to make special pottery worked alone in small shops and became known as "studio potters."

The history of the art pottery movement is well documented in several easily available books. Listings of all of the marks, the artists, and the designs used by the factories can be found. The following is a quick reference to the potters, dates, and marks.

The Fulper Pottery did a variety of glazes on their vases. This same shape vase can be found glazed in crystalline glaze, blue of several shades, or matte green.

The Low Art Tile Works made many types of decorative tiles for use in fireplaces, or on walls. Some were framed and sold as pictures. This brown-glazed tile was sold originally in this frame but the frame was covered with velvet.

AMERICAN ART POTTERY

Pottery and Location	Dates of Manufacture	Pottery and Location	Dates of Manufacture
Alberhill Pottery Alberhill, California	1912–1920 **ALBERHILL**	American Terra Cotta & Ceramic Company Terra Cotta, Illinois	1881–1929
American Art Ceramic Company Corona, New York	c. 1901	Arc-en-ceil Pottery Zanesville, Ohio	1903–1905
American Edgerton Art Clay Works Edgerton, Wisconsin	1892–1899	Arequipa Pottery Fairfax, California	1911–1918

Pottery and Location	Dates of Manufacture	Pottery and Location	Dates of Manufacture
Avon Pottery Cincinnati, Ohio	1886–1888	Chelsea Keramic Art Works Chelsea, Massachusetts	1872–1899
Avon Works (Avon Faience Company) Wheeling, West Virginia	c. 1905	Chelsea Pottery U.S. Chelsea, Massachusetts	1891–1896
Bennett, Edwin Baltimore, Maryland	1895–1897	Chicago Terra Cotta Works Chicago, Illinois	1866–1879
Biloxi Art Pottery. See Ohr, George.		Cincinnati Art Pottery Company Cincinnati, Ohio	1879–1891
Brouwer Pottery. See Middle Lane.			
Brush McCoy Pottery Roseville, Ohio Zanesville, Ohio	1911–1925	Clewell Canton, Ohio	1902–1955
Brush Pottery Roseville, Ohio	1925–present	Clifton Art Pottery Newark, New Jersey	1905–1911
		Corona Pottery. See Volkmar.	
Buffalo Pottery Buffalo, New York	1901–1956	Cowan Pottery Studio, Inc. Rocky River, Ohio	1912–1931
Byrdcliffe Pottery Woodstock, New York	c. 1902	Craven Art Pottery. See Jervis.	
		Dayton Porcelain Co. Dayton, Ohio	1882–1884
California Pottery & Terra Cotta Works Oakland, California	1875–1887	Dedham Pottery Co. East Dedham, Massachusetts	1896–1943
Cambridge Art Pottery Cambridge, Ohio	1898–1909	Dell, Wm. Pottery Cincinnati, Ohio	1891–1892

Pottery and Location	Dates of Manufacture	Pottery and Location	Dates of Manufacture
Denver Art Pottery. See White Pottery.		Gay Head Pottery Cottage City, Massachusetts	c. 1879
Denver China & Pottery Co. Denver, Colorado	1900–1905	Geijsbeek Pottery Golden, Colorado	c. 1899
Desert Sands Pottery Boulder City, Nevada Barsfor, California	1962	Charles Graham Chemical Pottery Works Brooklyn, New York	1880– c. 1903
Dorchester Pottery Dorchester, Massachusetts	1895– present		
Durant Kilns Bedford Village, New York	1910–1920	Grand Feu Art Pottery Los Angeles, California	1912– c. 1916
Edgerton Pottery Edgerton, Wisconsin	1894–1901	Grueby Faience Co. Boston, Massachusetts	1894–1910
Enfield Pottery Laverock, Pennsylvania	1906–1928	Halcyon Art Pottery Halcyon, California	1910–1913 1931–1940s
Faience Manufacturing Co. Greenpoint, New York	1880–1892	Hampshire Pottery Keene, New Hampshire	1871–1927
Florentine Pottery Cambridge, Ohio Chillicothe, Ohio	1900–	Hull Pottery Co. Crooksville, Ohio	1905– present
		Jervis Pottery Oyster Bay, New York	1908–1912
Frackleton Pottery Milwaukee, Wisconsin	1883– c. 1930		
Fulper Pottery Flemington, New Jersey Trenton, New Jersey	1814–1955	Jugtown Pottery Jugtown, North Carolina	1921– present

Pottery and Location	Dates of Manufacture	Pottery and Location	Dates of Manufacture
Kenton Hills Pottery Erlanger, Kentucky	1937–1945	Mosaic Tile Co. Zanesville, Ohio	1894–1967
Lonhuda Pottery Steubenville, Ohio	1892–1900	Mueller Mosaic Tile Co. Trenton, New Jersey	1909–1938
Low Art Tile Works Chelsea, Massachusetts	1877–1907 J.&J.G.LOW	Muncie Pottery Muncie, Indiana	1922–1926 MUNCIE
Marblehead Pottery Marblehead, Massachusetts	1905–1936	Nashville Art Pottery Nashville, Tennessee	1884–1899
Markham Pottery Ann Arbor, Michigan National City, California	1883–1921	Nelson McCoy Pottery Roseville, Ohio	1910– present
Matt Morgan Pottery Cincinnati, Ohio	1883–1884	Newcomb Pottery New Orleans, Louisiana	1895–1945
McCoy, J. W. Pottery Co. Roseville, Ohio	1899–1911 LOY–NEL–ART McCOY	New Milford Pottery Co. New Milford, New Jersey	1888–1890
Menlo Park Ceramic Co. See Volkmar.		New Orleans Art Pottery New Orleans, Louisiana	1888–1890
Merrimac Pottery Co. Newburyport, Massachusetts	1897–1908	Niloak Pottery Benton, Arkansas	1909–1946
Middle Lane Pottery East Hampton, New York	1894–1902	Nonconnah Pottery Shelby County, Tennessee Skyland, North Carolina	1901–1916
Moravian Pottery & Tile Bucks County, Pennsylvania	1897–1956 MORAVIAN	Norse Pottery Co. Rockford, Illinois	1904–1913

Pottery and Location	Dates of Manufacture	Pottery and Location	Dates of Manufacture
North Dakota School of Mines Grand Forks, North Dakota	1892–1960s	Pewabic Pottery Detroit, Michigan	1903–1961
Northwestern Terra Cotta Chicago, Illinois	1886–1950s	Pisgah Forest Pottery Arden, North Carolina	1920–present
George Ohr Biloxi, Mississippi	1883–1906	Poillon Pottery Woodbridge, New Jersey	1904–1928
Ouachita Hot Springs, Arkansas	1879–1890	Radford Pottery Co. Tiffin, Ohio Clarksburg, West Virginia Zanesville, Ohio	1890–1912
Overbeck Pottery Cambridge City, Indiana	1911–1955		
Owens Pottery Co. Zanesville, Ohio	1896–1928	Red Wing Potteries, Inc. Red Wing, Minnesota	1936–1967
Pauline Pottery Chicago, Illinois Edgerton, Wisconsin	1883–1893 1902–1909	Rhead Pottery Santa Barbara, California	1913–1917
Paul Revere Pottery Boston, Massachusetts Brighton, Massachusetts	1906–1942	Robertson Art Tile Co. (Robertson Manufacturing Company) Morrisville, Pennsylvania	1890–present
Pennsylvania Museum & School of Industrial Art, School of Pottery Philadelphia, Pennsylvania	c. 1903	Robertson Pottery Los Angeles, California Hollywood, California	1934–1952
Peters & Reed Pottery Co. Zanesville, Ohio	1897–1920	Roblin Pottery San Francisco, California	1899–1906

Pottery and Location	Dates of Manufacture	Pottery and Location	Dates of Manufacture
Rookwood Pottery Cincinnati, Ohio	1880–1967	University City Pottery University City, Missouri	1910–1915
Rosemeade Wahpeton Pottery Wahpeton, North Dakota	1940–1961	Upjohn, C. B. Zanesville, Ohio	1904–1905
Rose Valley Pottery Rose Valley, Pennsylvania	1901–1905	Valentien Pottery San Diego, California	1911–1914
Roseville Pottery Roseville, Ohio Zanesville, Ohio	1890–1954	Van Briggle Pottery Colorado Springs, Colorado	1901– present
		Vance-Avon. See Avon Works.	
Rumrill Pottery Red Wing, Minnesota	1930–1939	Volkmar Pottery (Volkmar Kilns; Volkmar Keramic Company; Charles Volkmar & Son) Greenpoint, New York Corona, New York Brooklyn, New York Metuchen, New Jersey	1879–1911
Shawnee Pottery Zanesville, Ohio	1935–1961		
Shawsheen Pottery Billerica, Massachusetts Mason City, Iowa	1906–1911		
Stockton Terra Cotta Company Stockton, California	1891–1902	Walley Pottery West Sterling, Massachusetts	1898–1919
Teco. See American Terra Cotta & Ceramic Company.		Walrich Pottery Berkeley, California	1922–1930
Tiffany Pottery Corona, New York	1898–1920	Wannopee Pottery Co. New Milford, Louisiana	1892–1903

Pottery and Location	Dates of Manufacture	Pottery and Location	Dates of Manufacture
Weller Pottery Zanesville, Ohio	1895–1948 WELLER	White Pottery Denver, Colorado	1893– c. 1955 White Denver
Wheatley Pottery Co. Cincinnati, Ohio	1903– c. 1910 WP		
		Zane Pottery Zanesville, Ohio	1920–1941
T. J. Wheatley & Co. Cincinnati, Ohio	1879– c. 1882 TJWheatley	Zanesville Art Pottery Zanesville, Ohio	1900–1920 LA MORO

This Rozane ware mug of the Roseville Pottery has the typical brown-colored glaze of the time.

This Matt Morgan vase was made about 1880. The decorations are brown and green.

The American Terra Cotta and Ceramic Company used the mark "Teco" on vases. This semimatte-glazed vase has the impressed mark.

A 9-inch vase with semimatte seagreen glaze impressed with the mark "Teco," by the American Terra Cotta and Ceramic Company.

The yellow daffodil pictured against a brown-glazed background was drawn by Delores Harvey on this Owens Utopian vase.

The Japanese style of design was copied on this Weller vase of the "blue and decorated" line. It has a cream-colored crackle glaze and pink and gray trailing blossoms.

"Despondency" is the name of this vase design by Van Briggle Pottery. It was first made in 1903. The turquoise-glazed vase depicts a brooding nude man at the top.

George Ohr made folded and twisted clay "pots" that are unique. His ability to mold clay enabled him to produce vases and mugs of unusual design. The glazes used by Ohr are often flawed.

Full figures of men were rarely found as the decoration on Rookwood pieces. Sometimes heads were used, often Indians. This samurai warrior was produced by Matt A. Daly, a Rookwood artist, in 1889. When sold in 1979 this piece set a world record for a piece of Rookwood.

The swirled design seen on this Niloak vase was made by the various colored clays used, not by a glaze. The vase is 8 inches high.

After American Art Pottery, or the Studio Potter

The art pottery movement gradually disappeared during the 1930s in the United States, although there were a few "studio potters" working and making very limited productions of handmade pottery during these years. The studio potter was usually a single person or at most a group of under five. Some were artists who had worked for the larger art potteries in their waning days. There has been little research on the smaller potteries, and collectors who study about their local potters should be able to find bargains in the works of "undiscovered artists." A few studio potters working before 1946 whose names have appeared in the records are listed here. There are still studio potters working in all parts of the country.

Note: These dates are taken from published records and exhibits; the potter may have worked before or after the dates given.

Laura Anderson Los Angeles, California	c. 1945	Clara Maud Cobb Hilton Marion, North Carolina	c. 1930
Alexander Archipenko New York, New York	c. 1935	Edgar Littlefield Columbus, Ohio	c. 1940
Arthur E. Baggs Columbus, Ohio	c. 1930	Glen Lukens Los Angeles, California	c. 1945
Carlton and Kathryn Ball Oakland, California	c. 1940	Marie Martinez New Mexico	c. 1940
Charles Fergus Binns New York, New York	c. 1930	Reuben Nakian New York, New York	c. 1930
Paul Bogatay Columbus, Ohio	c. 1935	Gertrud and Otto Natzler Los Angeles, California	1939–1972
Cornelius Brauckman Los Angeles, California	c. 1910	Dorothea Warren O'Hara Darien, Connecticut	c. 1940
Paul E. Cox New Orleans, Louisiana	c. 1935	Henry Varnum Poor New York, New York	c. 1930
Hunt Diederich New York, New York	c. 1925	Antonio Prieto Oakland, California	c. 1945
Edris Eckhardt Cleveland, Ohio	c. 1935	Ruth Randall Syracuse, New York	c. 1935
Marion Lawrence Fosdick New York, New York	c. 1940	Louis Benjamin Raynor Alfred, New York	c. 1945
Bernard Frazier Lawrence, Kansas	c. 1945	Harold E. Riegger New York, New York	c. 1945
Waylande Gregory Bound Brook and Metuchen, New Jersey	c. 1940	A. Robineau Syracuse, New York	c. 1930
		Edwin & Mary Scheier New Hampshire	c. 1945
Maija Grotell New York, New York	c. 1935–1950	Viktor Schreckengost Cleveland, Ohio	c. 1940
Sam Haile Ann Arbor, Michigan	c. 1940	Susi Singer Pasadena, California	c. 1945

Albert Valentien c. 1915 San Diego, California	Marguerite Wildenhain c. 1945 Guerneville, California
Carl Walters c. 1930 Woodstock, New York	Thelma Frazier Winter c. 1940 Cleveland, Ohio
Valerie Wieseltheir c. 1930 New York, New York	

BIBLIOGRAPHY

General

Barber, Edwin A. *Marks of American Potters.* Southampton, New York: Cracker Barrel Press, 1904.

Boger, Louise Ade. *The Dictionary of World Pottery and Porcelain.* New York: Scribner's, 1971.

Clark, Garth and Hughto, Margie. *A Century of Ceramics in the United States, 1878–1978.* New York: Dutton, 1979.

Darling, Sharon S. *Chicago Ceramics and Glass: An Illustrated History from 1871–1933.* Chicago: Chicago Historical Society, 1979.

Donhauser, Paul S. *History of American Ceramics: The Studio Potter.* Dubuque: Kendall/Hunt, 1978.

Evans, Paul. *Art Pottery of the United States.* New York: Scribner's, 1974.

Kovel, Ralph and Terry. *The Kovels' Collector's Guide to American Art Pottery.* New York: Crown, 1974.

Club: American Art Pottery Association, P.O. Box 2374, Grand Rapids, Michigan 49501. (Issues a newsletter)

Publication: Pottery Collectors Newsletter, P.O. Box 446, Asheville, North Carolina 28802

Buffalo Pottery

Altman, Vi and Si. *Price Guide to Buffalo Pottery.* 4th ed. Clarence, New York: Privately printed, 1981.

Natzler Ceramics

Herman, Lloyd E. *Form and Fire: Natzler Ceramics, 1939–1972.* Washington, D.C.: Smithsonian Institution Press, 1973.

Newcomb

Ormond, Suzanne and Irvine, Mary E. *Louisiana's Art Nouveau.* Gretna, Louisiana: Pelican, 1976.

North Dakota School of Mines

Barr, Margaret Libby; Miller, Donald; and Barr, Robert. *University of North Dakota Pottery: The Cable Years.* Grand Forks, North Dakota: Privately printed, 1977.

Overbeck

Postle, Kathleen R. *The Chronicle of the Overbeck Pottery.* Indianapolis: Indiana Historical Society, 1978.

Pewabic

Pear, Lillian Myers. *The Pewabic Pottery.* Des Moines: Wallace-Homestead, 1976.

Redwing

Simon, Dolores. *Red Wing Pottery with Rumrill.* Paducah, Kentucky: Collector Books, 1980.

Rookwood

Kircher, Edwin J. and Agranoff, Barbara and Joseph. *Rookwood, Its Golden Era of Art Pottery, 1880–1929.* Cincinnati: Privately printed, 1971.

Peck, Herbert. *The Book of Rookwood Pottery.* New York: Crown, 1968.

Roseville

Buxton, Virginia Hillway. *Roseville Pottery for Love or Money.* Nashville: Tymbre Hill, 1977.

Huxford, Bob and Sharon. *The Collector's Encyclopedia of Roseville Pottery.* Paducah, Kentucky: Collector Books, 1976.

Van Briggle

Arnest, Barbara M. *Van Briggle Pottery: The Early Years.* Colorado Springs: Colorado Springs Fine Arts Center, 1975.

Bogue, Dorothy McGraw. *The Van Briggle Story.* Colorado Springs: Dentan-Berkeland, 1968.

Weller

Huxford, Bob and Sharon. *The Collector's Encyclopedia of Weller Pottery.* Paducah, Kentucky: Collector Books, 1979.

Purviance, Louise and Evan and Schneider, Norris F. *Weller Art Pottery in Color.* Des Moines: Wallace-Homestead, 1971.

4

American Dinnerware, 1930 to 1970

In the period between 1930 and 1940 some of the commercial potteries made many collectible pieces. During the 1970s many people who had never thought about collecting became interested in the wares from some of the commercial potteries.

The prices were low and the items were readily available at flea markets and garage or house sales. The dream of a full set of attractive dishes was not only a possibility but a reality for many. Fiesta ware, Hull pottery, McCoy, Roseville, Shawnee, and others were eagerly collected and studied. These and other minor potteries became firmly entrenched in the inventories of many antiques shops, and collectors continued to try to find the ideal items.

A Blue Ridge plate.

Blue Ridge (Southern Potteries, Inc.)

Southern Potteries Incorporated was founded in 1920, in Erwin, Tennessee. The company used a hand-painted decoration under glaze. The wares marked "Blue Ridge Hand Painted Under The Glaze" were made after 1938. The company closed in 1957.

Catalina Pottery

William Wrigley, Jr., started a pottery on Catalina Island, California, about 1927. The company first made bricks, roof tiles, floor tiles, and garden pots from native clays. By 1930 the Catalina pieces were decorated and glazed. From 1927 to 1932 their wares were usually brown clay. From 1932 to 1937 their wares were made mainly with white clay bodies, and from 1937 to 1941 they were of white clay exclusively. The Gladding McBean Company of Glendale, California, makers of Franciscan pottery, bought the Catalina molds and designs in 1937. They produced a line in their plant with the trademark "Catalina." This remained in use until 1947. There was an attempt in 1963 to start making Catalina pottery on Catalina Island, but it failed.

A Fiesta plate.

Fiesta creamer with
full circle handle

Fiesta Ware and Similar Potteries

Bauer ware was the first in the brightly colored pottery dinnerware line. It was made in Los Angeles, California, by the J. A. Bauer Company between 1932 and 1962.

John Andrew Bauer made pottery in Paducah County, Kentucky, and in Atlanta, Georgia, but it was his work in California after 1915 that interests today's collector. He started a plant in Los Angeles, making redware pots and flower containers. The firm made the famous ring pattern dinnerware in 1932. They also made pots, jars, dinnerwares, and other useful pieces. The company marked pieces "Bockman's Quality" pottery for a short time in the 1940s and they even purchased some pieces from the Red Wing Pottery of Minnesota. During the 1950s the firm made some pottery lines marked "Brusché." The company closed in 1962.

The first and most famous Bauer pattern was the "ring" pattern, sometimes known as "Beehive" because the cups look like little beehives when turned upside down. Concentric rings covered the entire surface of pieces such as pitchers, sugar bowls, and salt and pepper shakers, but only the edges of the plates.

The original colors of the Ring pattern were shades of orange, burnt orange, dark blue, yellow, green, ivory, maroon, and black. Pastel colors were made during World War II when ingredients for the bright glazes were scarce.

Other Bauer patterns included Modern Pattern, Smooth Line, Monterey Moderne, and the Brusché Line. Most Bauer pieces were marked in the mold with the incised name "Bauer Pottery," "J. A. Bauer," or with the name "Brusché" for a 1952 line.

A Harlequin plate.

Fiesta ware was introduced in 1936 by the Homer Laughlin China Company, redesigned in 1969, and withdrawn in 1973. The design was characterized by a band of concentric circles, beginning at the rim.

Cups had full-circle handles until 1969, when partial-circle handles were made. The original Fiesta colors were bright green, blue, yellow, and red; later ivory, turquoise, gray, rose, forest green, light green, and chartreuse were added. The redesigned New Fiesta Ironstone, made from 1969 to 1973, was made only in mango red, antique gold, and turf green.

Harlequin jug with triangular handle

Most Fiesta ware was marked with the incised word "Fiesta." Some pieces were hand stamped before glazing.

Harlequin and Riviera were related, less expensive wares produced by Homer Laughlin. Harlequin was made from 1938 to 1964, and sold without trademark by the F. W. Woolworth Company stores. Like Fiesta, it had a concentric ring design, but the rings were separated from the rim by a plain margin. Cup handles were angular, almost triangular in shape.

Harlequin was made in all the Fiesta colors except ivory and green. It was also made in the non-Fiesta colors of maroon, mauve blue, and spruce green. In February of 1979 a reissue was offered by Homer Laughlin through the Woolworth stores. Turquoise, green, yellow, and a new deep coral color are being used.

A Riviera plate.

Riviera ware was made from 1938 to about 1950. It was unmarked, and sold exclusively by the Murphy Company. Plates were square, and cup handles were squared. Colors were mauve blue, red, yellow, light green, ivory, and, rarely, dark blue.

Riviera creamer with squared handle

Russel Wright (1905–1976)

American modern designs came into fashion in the 1930s. The Hall pottery teapot called Airflow, the dinnerware called Raymor by the Roseville Pottery, and the American Modern pattern by Russel Wright are the most memorable.

Russel Wright was an industrial designer. He made home furnishings of wood, glass, chrome, and pottery. In the early 1930s, he made spun aluminum stove-to-table dishes. His blond maple furniture made in 1935 set the style of the time. In 1938, his American Modern dinnerware was introduced. It was made in colors that were unfamiliar for dinner sets—muted tones called seafoam blue, spruce green, and chutney. The dinnerware shapes were different from those used by others. The dish had no rim, the celery dish was a curved free form, the cups turned in at the rim. Eventually, dishes marked with the Russel Wright name were made by the Iroquois China Company, Syracuse, New York; the Harker China Company of Chester, West Virginia; the Steubenville Pottery Company of Steubenville, Ohio; and the Paden City Pottery of Paden City, West Virginia, distributed by Justin Tharaud and Sons. Later in his career, Russel Wright designed plastic dinnerwares. His personal notes show sketches or mention of work for Edwin Knowles China, Ravenware, Rustic Dinnerware, and Sterling China.

Russel Wright
MFG BY
STEUBENVILLE

Steubenville Pottery Co.

Russel Wright designed his American Modern dishes in radically different sizes and shapes. His coupe shaped plates eventually became as well known as the standard rim shapes that had been used since the eighteenth century.

Hall China

Robert T. Hall started the Hall China Company in East Liverpool, Ohio, in 1903. He first made a glazed low-grade yellowware and soon after developed several other clays and glazes. He eventually produced a white body with colored glazes that was fireproof and strong. The firm also made decorated wares such as Autumn Leaf, 1933–1977; restaurant wares, 1914; teapots, 1920; kitchenwares, 1932; dinnerwares, 1936; and refrigerator wares, 1938. Most of these products are still being made by the firm.

Hall Teapots

(colors listed are most commonly found
  for that pattern)

Airflow, canary; 1940
Aladdin, camellia; 1939
Albany, emerald; 1930s
Automobile, Chinese red; 1938
Baltimore, emerald; 1930s
Basket, canary with silver; 1938
Basketball, Chinese red; 1938
Birdcage, maroon; 1939
Boston, warm yellow; c. 1920
Cleveland, emerald; 1930s
Doughnut, Chinese red; 1938
Football, delphinium; 1938
French, decorated; c. 1920
Globe; 1940s
Hollywood, maroon; late 1920s

Hook Cover, cadet; 1940
Illinois, cobalt; late 1920s, early 1930s
Los Angeles, stock brown; 1926
Manhattan, stock brown; 1930s
Melody, canary; 1939
Moderne, ivory; 1930s
Nautilus, canary; 1939
New York, blue turquoise; 1930s
Parade, canary; 1942
Philadelphia, cadet; 1923
Rhythm, Chinese red; 1939
Saf-Handle, canary; 1938
Sani-grid, cadet; 1941
Star, turquoise; 1940
Streamline, canary; 1940
Surfside, emerald; 1939
Windshield, camellia; 1941

Other Teapot Lines by Hall

T-Ball designed for Bacharach, Inc., in
  1948; maroon, daffodil, delphinium;
  round and square McCormick, 1907;
  maroon, turquoise, green, and silver.

Lipton, same shape as French, label on
  bottom; black luster, warm yellow,
  daffodil cozy

Twin-Tee, flat top, decorated in gold or
  decal, 1926; stock brown, cobalt, light
  russet, pansy

Tea for Two, angled top, undecorated,
  1930s; sandust, old rose

Cube (made by other companies); red,
  green cobalt

Twinspout (round), made for the
  Teamaster Co., late 1940s; maroon

Teataster (oval), made for the
  Teamaster Co., late 1940s; still in
  production; cobalt, lettuce, daffodil

Victoria & Albert, 1940s; celadon/gold

Gladstone; pink/gold

Disraeli; pink

Miss Terry

Hall China

Hall Coffeepots

Deca-flip; red and hi-white

Big Boy; maroon/silver

Step-round; ivory

Step-down; red, black, and green (some
  decals)

Armory; warm yellow

Blaine; cadet

Carraway; Chinese red

Coffee Queen; Chinese red

Drip-o-lator

This is a line of pots made for the Enterprise Aluminum Company from the 1930s to the present. Enterprise Aluminum ordered the pots from Hall, added an aluminum drip section, and marketed them under the name Drip-o-lator.

Sash
Sweep
Bullseye
Bell
Petal
Crest
Bricks'n'ivy
Trellis

Basketweave
Step-round (only one that had been
   previously designed)
Monarch
Arch
Panel

Hall Cookie Jars

Little Red Riding Hood
Zeisel; Monterey/medallion and pink/
   basket

Hall Autumn Leaf

In 1975 a group of collectors began publicizing their search for Autumn Leaf dishes. These apparently were Depression Glass and Fiesta ware collectors looking for other wares from the 1930s.

Autumn Leaf was first made for the Jewel Tea Company, a grocery firm, by the Hall China Company of East Liverpool, Ohio. The first of these dishes was made in 1933 and was called by several names. It was named Autumn Leaf in the 1940s. The Autumn Leaf dishes by Hall were sold only through the Jewel Tea outlets. Several other companies made Autumn Leaf, including the Crooksville China Company of Crooksville, Ohio; Columbia Chinaware, Harker Potteries of Chester, West Virginia;

Taverne by Hall China Company is one of several dinnerware sets to be decorated with simple black silhouettes. The rim is platinum.

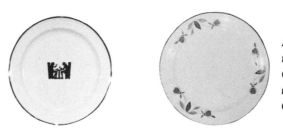

Autumn Leaf is probably the most famous Hall China Company pattern. It was made for the Jewel Tea Company.

and the Paden City Pottery of Paden City, West Virginia. Their wares were not necessarily made for Jewel Tea. Fabrics, glassware, cooking utensils, tinware, and flat silver were also made in a similar design. The design is still being made.

Hull Pottery

The A. E. Hull Pottery Company was established in 1905 in Crooksville, Ohio, by Addis E. Hull, W. A. Watts, and J. D. Young. Their first product was stoneware. The firm made pottery and also purchased European pottery to be resold. Tiles were made after 1927. Art wares were made from 1930 to 1950. Matte glazes were discontinued after 1950. A flood and fire in June 1950 burned the factory but it was reorganized as the Hull Pottery Company and reopened in 1952.

McCoy Pottery

The McCoy name on pottery has caused confusion for years because several firms have the name McCoy. The J. W. McCoy Pottery was founded in Roseville, Ohio, in 1899 by James McCoy. The pottery made commercial wares and artwares. It was destroyed in 1903, rebuilt and enlarged. George S. Brush managed the firm after his own pottery was destroyed in 1909. The McCoy pottery became the Brush McCoy Pottery Company about 1911. This firm became the Brush Pottery Company in 1925. It closed in 1982.

James McCoy of the J. W. McCoy Pottery helped his son Nelson form the Nelson McCoy Sanitary and Stoneware Company in Roseville, Ohio, in 1910. They made kitchenwares, but by 1926 they too were producing artwares. The name became the Nelson McCoy pottery in 1933. After several corporate changes, the company became a subsidiary of Designer Accents in 1986. It closed in 1990.

Shawnee Pottery

The Shawnee Pottery Company started in Zanesville, Ohio, in 1937. Addis E. Hull, Jr., of the Hull Pottery Company headed the firm. Most of the early production was decorated pottery that was sold to dimestores and Sears, Roebuck and Company. Each customer ordered special patterns.

The firm made pottery for Rumrill Pottery in 1938. Addis Hull, Jr., left the firm in 1950 to run the Western Stoneware Company of Monmouth,

Illinois. The most popular collector's item made by Shawnee is the pattern called Corn-King or, later, Corn-Queen. Full sets of dishes, vases, ashtrays, and kitchenwares were made. The yellow and green pieces were made to resemble an ear of corn, with molded grains of corn and leaves. The pottery closed in 1961.

Stangl Pottery

There has been a pottery plant in Flemington, New Jersey, since the early 1800s. In 1860 the pottery was purchased and run by Abraham Fulper. After his death his three sons continued the company. In 1919 the company began to make art pottery. Johann Martin Stangl had been hired at the company in 1910 as a ceramic chemist and plant superintendent; he became president in 1926. Some pieces made at this time were marked with his name. The main pottery in Flemington burned in 1929. Mr. Stangl acquired the company in 1930. Work continued at a second plant in Trenton, New Jersey. The company made artwares and dinnerwares through the 1940s. Animal and bird figurines were popular in the 1940s and giftware items were also made. In 1965 another fire destroyed the plant. The firm continued until 1973, when it was bought by the Wheaton Glass Company. The assets were sold in 1978 and the plant closed.

Stangl dinnerwares featured hand-decorated pieces in bright colors. This yellow-bordered plate is called Blueberry.

Vernon Kilns

The history of Vernon Kilns begins with George Poxon, an Englishman who settled in California about 1912. He made ceramic wares in Vernon, California, in 1914 under the company name "Poxon China." He sold his company in 1931 but he continued making and selling his pottery.

Faye G. Bennison bought the Poxon pottery and called it Vernon Potteries Ltd. He later changed the name to Vernon Kilns. The company made dinnerwares and figurines, many designed by some of the famous artists of the day: Rockwell Kent, Don Blanding, Walt Disney, and others. Plaid patterns and solid-colored dinnerwares were also made.

Vernon Kilns went out of business in 1958. Some of its assets, including the name "Vernon Ware," were purchased by Metlox Potteries of Manhattan, California. Metlox Vernon Ware is still being made.

OTHER POTTERIES

Pottery and Location	Dates of Manufacture	Pottery and Location	Dates of Manufacture
American Art Clay Co. Indianapolis, Indiana	1919– present	Guernsey Earthenware Co. Zanesville, Ohio	1909–1925
Atlas Globe China Co. Cambridge, Ohio	1926–1933	Haeger Potteries, Inc. Dundee, Illinois	1914–
Cahoy Pottery Colome, South Dakota	1973– present	Harker Pottery East Liverpool, Ohio Chester, West Virginia	1840–1931
Chesapeake Pottery Co. Baltimore, Maryland	1880–1924	Herold China and Pottery Co. Zanesville, Ohio	1910–1920
Crescent Pottery Trenton, New Jersey	1881–1892	H. F. Coors Co. Golden, Colorado	1925–c. 1940
Crowley's Ridge Pottery Bloomfield, Missouri	c. 1920	Homer Laughlin Co. Newell, West Virginia	1877– present
Dickota Pottery Grand Forks, North Dakota	1934–1938	Ironton Pottery Ironton, Ohio	c. 1880
Dryden Pottery Ellsworth, Kansas Hot Springs, Arkansas	1946–1956 1956– present	Iroquois Syracuse, New York	1905–1969
Ecanada Hamilton, Ontario Canada	1926–1952	Knowles, Taylor and Knowles East Liverpool, Ohio	1870–1934
Elgee Pottery Zanesville, Ohio	1946–1952	Muncie Clay Products Co. Muncie, Indiana	1926–1939
Fairhope Fairhope, Alabama	c. 1918	Nelson McCoy Sanitary & Stoneware Co. Hartford, Connecticut	1910–1933
Frankoma Pottery Sapulpa, Oklahoma	1936–1983	Ohio Pottery Zanesville, Ohio	1905–1923
Fraunfelter China Co. Zanesville, Ohio	1923–1939	J. B. Owen Floor & Wall Tile Co. Roseville, Ohio Zanesville, Ohio	1885–1891 1891–1928
Globe China Co. Zanesville, Ohio	1925–1926		
Gonder Ceramic Arts, Inc. Zanesville, Ohio	1941–1957		

Pottery and Location	Dates of Manufacture	Pottery and Location	Dates of Manufacture
Pennsbury Pottery Morrisville, Pennsylvania	1950–1971	Stangl Pottery Co. Flemington, New Jersey	1929–1972
Pfaltzgraff Pottery York, Pennsylvania	1811– present	Sterling China Co. Sebring, Ohio	1917– present
Plymouth Pottery Plymouth, Massachusetts	1836– present	Steubenville Pottery Co. Steubenville, Ohio	1879–1959
Pope-Gosser China Coshocton, Ohio	1902–1929 1934–1958	Swastika Keramos Minerva, Ohio	1903–1932
Rowantrees Blue Hill, Maine	1934– present	Trenton Potteries Trenton, New Jersey	1892–1960
Rozart Pottery Kansas City, Missouri	1970– present	Triangle Novelty Co. Carrollton, Ohio	1933–1949
Shearwater Pottery Ocean Springs, Mississippi	1928– present	Walker China Bedford, Ohio	1923–1980
Silver Springs Silver Springs, Florida	c. 1938	Wheeling Potteries Co. Wheeling, West Virginia	1879– c. 1933

Special Objects

Some pottery and porcelain is collected by shape, not by the maker. The bone dish, beer stein, mustache cup, toothpick holder, shaving mug, potlid, fairing, and butter pat have been in demand for quite some time. More recent shapes and varieties of ceramics are now part of the collecting scene.

Cookie Jars

The 1930s and after saw manufacturers producing modeled, colorful cookie jars. McCoy Pottery made the best-known jars, including covered wagons, log cabins, antique autos, locomotives, clowns, and animals. Two-faced cookie jars were made by the Leeds China Company of Chicago, Illinois, many picturing Disney characters. Shawnee Pottery made many cookie jars, including a sitting elephant, a Dutch boy, Puss-in-Boots, Mr. and Mrs. Pig, and a sailor boy. Roseville Pottery made a water lily and a magnolia pattern. Hull Pottery made several styles, including a bean pot, baby duck, and an apple. Red Wing made the Dutch girl, and a French chef, as well as many jars to match their dishwares.

The Robinson-Ransbottom pottery of Roseville, Ohio, made many styles of cookie jars until 1959. Cookie jars are still being made by many firms in a variety of shapes.

Sewer Pipe Collectibles

One collector of sewer pipes was so enthusiastic about his collection that he opened a private museum in Cleveland, Ohio. His collection, however, does not include sewer pipe figures, which have been of great interest to collectors in the Midwest. Some of the workers in the sewer pipe factories often had extra time and imagination at the end of the day and used the dark sewer pipe clay in unique ways. Many small figurines such as lions, dogs, rabbits, frogs, and turtles were made. Banks, flowerpots, and

It seems strange that sewer pipe clay should inspire workmen to a special form of folk art. This "sewer pipe" lion, 28½ inches long, was made in an Ohio factory.

even tombstones were modeled from the clay and glazed in the characteristic dark brown or other colors. Sewer pipe figures were complicated to make, as the workman had to make a wooden pattern, then a plaster of Paris casting, and finally the clay figure was fired. The molded clay figure was often completed with detail lines pressed in with a sharp stylus.

Some of the sewer tile figures were signed with the workman's initials, dates, or even stamped with his name. Most of them were made in Ohio, although sewer pipe firms in other parts of the country also had workmen who made sewer pipe figures.

Sewer pipe pieces are now considered folk art. The best is very good, while the worst looks, and probably was, the work of a person with no talent: the children of some workmen would come to the factory after school and model figures from the unused clay.

The bricks made in America are related to the sewer pipe work. Collectors of bricks not only want the normal red clay bricks but also unusual types, including glazed sewer pipe bricks made in fancy designs.

Old Sleepy Eye

Sleepy Eye is the name of an Indian chief, a town in Minnesota, and a brand of flour. The Sleepy Eye pottery was created to advertise the flour, made in the town of Sleepy Eye, and it pictures an Indian. Heavy stoneware pieces were given away or sold by the flour company from sometime between 1899 and 1905 and until 1937. The design was revived in 1952 and special pieces were made for the town of Sleepy Eye's one hundredth anniversary in 1972.

Old Sleepy Eye pottery was made by several potteries. The earliest piece was probably a mug made by the Minnesota Stoneware Company. It was created with the design of the Indian printed in blue, and a verse. The Weir Pottery Company of Monmouth, Illinois, made a variety of Old Sleepy Eye pieces in blue and gray stoneware from about 1899 until 1906. The Western Stoneware Company of Monmouth, Illinois, made the Old Sleepy Eye premiums after that time. Cobalt blue and white pitchers and steins were made as late as 1937. Other pieces in the same pattern were made but not used as premiums.

A group of twenty-two- and forty-ounce steins were made at the Western Stoneware Company in 1952. In these the Indian has a larger nose than on the earlier pieces. A few were made as late as 1968. They were marked with a maple leaf under the glaze.

While most of the Old Sleepy Eye pieces were stoneware with blue decoration, other types were produced—green, brown on yellow, blue on white, or brown on white.

BIBLIOGRAPHY

General

Kovel, Ralph and Terry. *The Kovels' Illustrated Price Guide to Depression Glass and American Dinnerware.* New York: Crown, 1980.

Lehner, Lois. *Complete Book of American Kitchen and Dinner Wares.* Des Moines: Wallace-Homestead, 1980.
———. *Ohio Pottery and Glass Marks and Manufacturers.* Des Moines: Wallace-Homestead, 1978.
Publications: The Glaze, P.O. Box 4929, Springfield, Missouri 65804; *The National Journal,* P.O. Box 3121A, Wescosville, Pennsylvania 18106

Autumn Leaf

Cunningham, Jo. *The Autumn Leaf Story.* Springfield, Missouri: Privately printed, 1976.
———. *1979/1980 Update: The Autumn Leaf Story Price Guide.* Springfield, Missouri: Privately printed, 1979.
Club: National Autumn Leaf Collectors, 4002 35th St., Rock Island, Illinois 61201

Blue Ridge

Newbound, Betty and Bill. *Blue Ridge Dinnerware.* Paducah, Kentucky: Collector Books, 1980.
Publication: National Blue Ridge Newsletter, Highland Dr., Rt. 5, P.O. Box 198, Bountville, Tennessee 37617

Catalina

Fridley, A. W. *Catalina Pottery: The Early Years, 1927–1937.* Costa Mesa, California: Rainbow, 1977.

Fiesta

Hayes, Barbara Jean. *Bauer, The California Pottery Rainbow.* Venice, California: Privately published, 1975.
Huxford, Bob and Sharon. *The Collector's Encyclopedia of Fiesta.* Paducah, Kentucky: Collector Books, 1981.
Riederer, Lahoma and Bettinger, Charles. *Fiesta III.* Monroe, Louisiana: Privately printed, 1980.
Clubs: Fiesta Collectors and Dealers Association, P.O. Box 100582, Nashville, Tennessee 37210; Fiesta Collectors Club, P.O. Box 106, Buttzville, New Jersey 07829
Publication: Fiesta Dishpatch, P.O. Box 106, Buttzville, New Jersey 07829

Frankoma

Cox, Susan N. *Collector's Guide to Frankoma Pottery.* El Cajon, California: Privately printed, 1979.

Hall

Duke, Harvey. *Superior Quality Hall China: A Guide for Collectors.* Otisville, Michigan: Depression Glass Daze, 1977.

Hull

Coates, Pamela. *Hull.* Indianapolis: Privately printed, 1974.

Felker, Sharon Loraine. *Lovely Hull Pottery.* Book 2. Des Moines: Wallace-Homestead, 1977.

McCoy

Coates, Pamela. *The Real McCoy.* Cherry Hill, New Jersey: Reynolds Publishers, 1971.

Huxford, Bob and Sharon. *The Collector's Catalog of Brush McCoy Pottery.* Paducah, Kentucky: Collector Books, 1978.

————. *The Collector's Encyclopedia of McCoy Pottery.* Paducah, Kentucky: Collector Books, 1978.

————. *The Collector's Encyclopedia of Brush McCoy Pottery.* Paducah, Kentucky: Collector Books, 1978.

Old Sleepy Eye

Meugniot, Elinor. *Old Sleepy Eye.* Tulsa: Privately published, 1973.

Club: Old Sleepy Eye Collectors' Club of America, Inc., P.O. Box 12, Monmouth, Illinois 61462

Red Wing

Bougie, Stanley J. and Newkirk, David A. *Red Wing Dinnerware.* Monticello, Minnesota: Privately printed, 1980.

Club: Redwing Collectors Society, Inc., Rt. 3, P.O. Box 146, Monticello, Minnesota 55362

Shawnee

Simon, Dolores. *Shawnee Pottery.* Paducah, Kentucky: Collector Books, 1977.

Stangl

Rehl, Norma. *The Collector's Handbook of Stangl Pottery.* Milford, New Jersey: Privately published, 1979.

Vernon Kilns

Nelson, Maxine Feek. *Versatile Vernon Kilns.* Costa Mesa, California: Rainbow Publications, 1978.

Russel Wright

Eaklor, Thomas W. *A Collector's Guide to Russel Wright.* Washington, D.C.: Privately printed, 1978.

Kerr, Ann. *The Steubenville Saga.* Sidney, Ohio: Privately printed, 1979.

5

American Porcelain, Eighteenth Century to Today

Porcelain in America has a history dating back to the eighteenth century. There are records of an attempt by Andrew Duche to make porcelain in Georgia as early as 1739. The next porcelain manufactory in America that appeared to be successful was in Philadelphia in 1769. Bonnin and Morris of Philadelphia, Pennsylvania, made a few pieces that have survived. Other attempts were made by Dr. Henry Mead of New York City in 1816: Abraham Miller of Philadelphia, Pennsylvania, in 1824; and the Jersey Porcelain and Earthenware Company of Jersey City, New Jersey, in 1825. Reports of porcelains made by these firms can be found in the records but there is still some question about the product, which may have been pottery and not porcelain.

The first famous American porcelain was manufactured by William Ellis Tucker in 1826. He worked alone until 1828, then with a partner, Thomas Hulme, for several years under the firm name of Tucker and Hulme (1828–1832). It later became Tucker and Hemphill, a partnership of Judge Joseph Hemphill and William Tucker, then the judge and Thomas Tucker from 1832 to 1838.

This small cream pitcher, marked "T & H" for Tucker and Hemphill, was found at a house sale in the 1960s and given to the White House collection. It is part of a set of dishes, but the other pieces are still missing.

Other firms, including Smith, Fife and Company (c. 1830) and Kurlbaum and Schwartz (1853–1855), also made porcelain in the Philadelphia area. William Boch and Brother of Greenpoint, New York (1844–1862), made porcelain under several names, including "Empire Porcelain."

Charles Cartlidge of Greenpoint, New York, started a porcelain factory in 1848. His firm closed in 1856. William Boch reopened the firm between 1857 and 1861. Thomas C. Smith bought it in 1861 and renamed it the Union Porcelain Works. The firm continued operation until 1890.

This pitcher has been attributed to the factory of William Ellis Tucker.

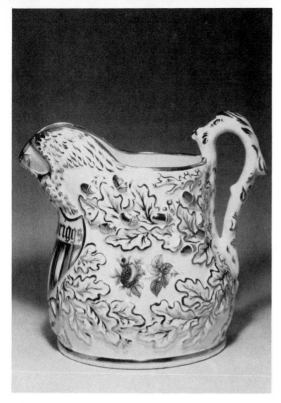

This large pitcher is marked "Cartlidge and Company."

There are several versions of this Union Porcelain Wor[k]s century vase made at the time of the Centennial. Som[e] are this size, 22¼ inches high; others are larger and ha[ve] very elaborate decorations covering the center of th[e] vase.

Edward Marshall Boehm, Inc. (Early)

Edward Marshall Boehm, Inc. (1957)

Edward Marshall Boehm, Inc.

The animal and bird figures made by Edward Marshall Boehm, Inc., are known throughout the world.

Edward Marshall Boehm was born in Baltimore, Maryland, in 1913. He attended a school for boys until he was sixteen, then went to Maryland University and studied animal husbandry. He managed a farm from 1934 to 1942. He joined the army, married, and in 1945 returned to Great Neck, Long Island, where he worked for a veterinarian. Edward Boehm made models of animals and birds as a hobby and worked with several experts to create a suitable hard-paste porcelain. In 1949 he succeeded. He rented a studio in Trenton, New Jersey, and started making models. The firm was named the Osso China Company in 1950. His wife, Helen, joined the company and their models received immediate acceptance. Several of their pieces were purchased for the Metropolitan Museum of Art in 1951. Although it was an artistic success the firm had financial problems. The company was reorganized in 1953 and named Edward

Marshall Boehm, Inc. Helen Boehm was the saleswoman, and Edward Boehm made the porcelains. The company prospered under this arrangement. Edward Marshall Boehm died in 1969. The Malvern Boehm studio of England was established soon after Mr. Boehm died and produced wares based on his old designs. Bone china figures were made there. Hard-paste porcelains are still made in New Jersey and also in England. Some of his designs can be found on limited edition plates by Lenox China.

Cybis

Cybis Porcelains was founded by Boleslaw Cybis, a Polish artist who served in the Ukrainian army in 1917. He was born in 1895 in Lithuania, lived in Poland, and moved to the United States in 1939. Cybis Art Pro-

"Catbird with Hyacinths" is a limited edition porcelain made by Edward Marshall Boehm in 1965.

These Cybis figurines depict "The Enchanted Princess Aurora" and "The Enamoured Prince Florimund." Each was issued in a limited edition of five hundred.

Cybis Porcelains 1976

ductions was started on Long Island, New York, in 1940. In 1942 Mr. Cybis moved to Trenton, New Jersey, and worked for Cordey, a company founded in the 1930s. Cybis Porcelains was started by 1950. Mr. Cybis died in 1957 but the company is still working. The company in Trenton makes numerous models of figurines in limited and unlimited editions.

Pickard China

The earliest known mark used by the Pickard China Company was found on this 10-inch jardiniere. It was made in 1893–1894.

W. A. Pickard was a salesman for the Pauline Pottery Company of Edgerton, Wisconsin, in 1889. He decided to start a pottery business with his wife in Chicago, Illinois, in 1893. They decorated and fired white china and sold it to stores in all parts of the country.

| 1893-1894 | 1895-1898 | 1930-1938 | 1938 to Present |

The firm moved to another Chicago location in 1905 and continued to prosper. It was renamed the Pickard Studios in 1925, and it was making its own china by 1935. It became Pickard, Inc., in 1938 and is still working.

Pope-Gosser

This Pope-Gosser vase was mentioned in Pottery and Glass magazine, June 1909.

Pope-Gosser China Company was founded in Coshocton, Ohio, in 1902 by I. Bentley Pope and Charles Gosser. Their early wares were elaborately decorated. Some were marked "Clarus Ware" but by 1908 "Pope-Gosser" became part of the trademark.

The company made a variety of wares for home use. They merged with other companies and in 1929 became the American China Corporation, located in Canton, Ohio. The company closed in 1931. Pope-Gosser reopened in 1933, but then closed again in 1958.

Pope-Gosser

Syracuse China

W. H. Farrar built a pottery in Syracuse, New York, in 1841. After a few years the company was reorganized as the Empire Pottery. It was refinanced in 1871 and became the Onondaga Pottery Company. It made white graniteware and in 1888 started manufacturing with the trade name "Imperial Geddo." One type of ware was marked "Syracuse China" in 1891. The company did not officially become the Syracuse China Corporation until 1966, although it had been known as Syracuse China since 1891. The firm is still in business.

O. P. CO.
CHINA
SEMI-VITREOUS

Syracuse China
Early

Syracuse China
After 1966

The strange decorations on this plate are examples of the special designs that could be made to order from Syracuse China. Each of the designs on this sample plate was meant as a center design on a finished plate for a restaurant or club.

Warwick

Warwick china was probably first made in 1884 even though the firm was not incorporated until 1887. The Wheeling, West Virginia, firm was founded by C. E. Jackson and a group of four other men. They decided to make only vitrified chinaware, which was an unusual product for an American company. Their most desirable nineteenth-century pieces were decorated with portraits of monks or Indians. Some of their other pieces had floral decorations, birds, animals, and fraternal emblems. Most of the early pieces were finished with a brown tone that was made to resemble the art pottery popular at the time. They retained this style until about 1914. The firm made many types of useful wares, including tablewares, and vases in all colors. Most of their decorations were applied decals. The factory closed in 1951. Warwick china was marked with the name "Warwick" and a picture of the head from a suit of armor. One mark included the word *IOGA*.

IOGA

AMERICAN PORCELAIN

Some other firms making porcelain in the nineteenth and early twentieth century are listed here. Examples from most of these companies are rare.

American China Co.

B & M
CHINA

Burroughs &
Mountford Co.

Porcelain Firms and Location	Dates of Manufacture	Porcelain Firms and Location	Dates of Manufacture
American China Co. Toronto, Ohio	1894–1910	Burroughs & Mountford Co. Trenton, New Jersey	1879–1882

The Wheeling Pottery made many types of useful wares. This humidor is in honor of Admiral Dewey and is dated 1898. It is decorated in appropriate red, white, and blue.

Pottery and Location	Dates of Manufacture	Pottery and Location	Dates of Manufacture
French China Co. Sebring, Ohio	c. 1907–1916	Sevres China Co. East Liverpool, Ohio	1900–1908?
Homer Laughlin China Co. East Liverpool, Ohio	1874– present		
		Trenton Potteries Co. Trenton, New Jersey	1892–1923
New Jersey Pottery Co. Trenton, New Jersey	1869–1883		
		University City Pottery University City, Missouri	1909–1918
Ohio Valley China Co. Wheeling, West Virginia	1889–1900		
		Wheeling Potteries Co. Wheeling, West Virginia	1879–1909
Prospect Hill Pottery Trenton, New Jersey	1880–1926		

American Belleek

O & B

Ott & Brewer Circa 1876

The word *belleek* has changed in meaning through the years. Irish Belleek has been made in County Fermanagh, Ireland, since 1857. The thin porcelain with the pearllike glaze and the ivory color inspired similar porcelains in the United States. Several firms were making wares they called Belleek in the 1880s. In 1929, a court case established the sole right to the name "Belleek" as part of a mark or an advertisement to the Belleek Pottery Limited of Ireland. There is confusion among collectors because the term is still used in a general way.

The First American firm making a ware it called Belleek was probably Ott and Brewer of Trenton, New Jersey. The company of Bloor, Ott and Booth was founded in 1863 and in 1873 its name was changed to Ott and Brewer. It started experimenting with Belleek porcelain. About 1876 the firm made "ivory porcelain," similar to Irish Belleek, and in 1882 was producing true Belleek.

Ott & Brewer
After 1883

Ott and Brewer made many other types of porcelains and nonporcelains. Walter Lenox, Jonathan Coxon, and other workmen from their firm later established other manufacturing firms in the Trenton area. Isaac Broome, who joined Ott and Brewer in 1875, developed the line of Parian ware busts. The company of Ott and Brewer closed in 1893.

Ott & Brewer
After 1883

Knowles, Taylor and Knowles

Isaac W. Knowles founded a pottery in East Liverpool, Ohio, in 1853. He made Rockingham-type pottery and yellowware. In 1870, Isaac Knowles's son, Homer S. Knowles, and John N. Taylor joined the company and it was renamed Knowles, Taylor and Knowles. "Company" was added to the name in 1891 when the firm was incorporated.

They made ironstone, whiteware, semi-porcelain, and dinnerware. From 1891 to 1896 Knowles, Taylor and Knowles made a Belleek-like ware called Lotus. It has been rumored that the company made a true Belleek in 1889 but that a fire destroyed the pottery and the ware was discontinued. Lotus ware was being made during the same period. The thin, fragile ware was sold either plain or decorated at the factory. Amateur china painters often purchased plain pieces. After decorating the ware at home, those who lived nearby brought their newly decorated pieces back to the kiln to be baked.

Knowles, Taylor and Knowles

Most items that are marked "Lotus" are the white bone china that resembles Belleek. A limited number of pottery pieces were made with a dark green glazed body and white china decorations. They too are marked "Lotus." The firm went out of business in 1934.

Lenox, Inc.

Jonathan Coxon, Sr., and Walter Scott Lenox met while working at the Ott and Brewer pottery. In 1889 they decided to form their own company and named it the Ceramic Art Company. Walter Lenox bought out his partner in about 1896 and the company continued operating as the Ceramic Art Company until he changed the name to Lenox, Inc. The company made dinnerwares and many decorated and undecorated pieces.

Lenox, Inc.

They made the china for the White House in 1918. Walter Lenox died in 1920.

The designs used by the company changed with the prevailing styles. The early pieces were similar to Irish Belleek. They were often thin with a nacreous glaze and the creamy color that is still being used by the firm. Art Nouveau patterns were introduced during the 1900 to 1910 period. Many of the pieces were made with a sterling silver overlay. Elaborately painted

c. 1896

BELLEEK

1894–1906

LENOX

Lenox
c. 1896

BELLEEK

Lenox
1906–1924

This pitcher, originally made by Walter Scott Lenox in 1887, has recently been reissued by the company. Inscribed on the base of this piece of Belleek porcelain is the mark "W.S.L./1887." The pitcher is 8½ inches high.

fish and game sets were made. The Art Deco look was in style by the 1920s and Lenox made many figurines and dishes in the new manner. The firm started making pastel-colored wares in light pink, blue, green, gray, or yellow about 1940. The company continues to make both old and new designs for the giftware market.

Willets Manufacturing Company

Three brothers, Joseph, Daniel, and Edmund R. Willets, founded the Willets Manufacturing Company in Trenton, New Jersey, in 1879. The company made plumber's specialties, white and decorated pottery, and

LENOX

Lenox, Inc.
1906–1930

Cherub candlesticks made about 1895–1905 by the Willets Manufacturing Company of Trenton, New Jersey.

LENOX

MADE IN USA

Lenox, Inc.
after 1950

WILLETS

Willets Manufacturing Co.

*Willets made a
paper-thin Belleek
ware. This tea
service has gold
and brown
decorations.*

the famous Belleek ware. According to the accepted reports, the company stopped making Belleek about 1909. They seem to have closed in 1912.

OTHER AMERICAN PORCELAIN FIRMS PRODUCING BELLEEK-LIKE WARES

Porcelain Firm and Location	Dates of Manufacture	Porcelain Firm and Location	Dates of Manufacture

American Art China Works
    Trenton, New Jersey
	1891–1900?	Cook Pottery Co.
		    Trenton, New Jersey
			1894–1929

Edwin Bennett Co.
    Baltimore, Maryland
	1886
	(Belleek)
		Delaware Pottery
		(Mr. Oliphant, Thomas Connelly)
		    Trenton, New Jersey
			1884–1892

Columbian Art Pottery
(Morris & Willmore)
    Trenton, New Jersey
	1893–1902	Greenwood Pottery Co.
		(Originally Stephen Tams & Co.; est. 1861)
		    Trenton, New Jersey
			1893–1886
			(Belleek)

BIBLIOGRAPHY

Boehm

Cosentino, Frank J. *Edward Marshall Boehm, 1913–1969*. Trenton: Edward Marshall Boehm, Inc., 1970.

Palley, Reese. *The Porcelain Art of Edward Marshall Boehm*. New York: Abrams, 1976.

Cybis

Collier, Mary Elizabeth. *Cordey: Past—Present—Future*. San Jose: Privately printed, 1981.

Cybis in Retrospect. Trenton: New Jersey State Museum, 1970.

Lenox, Inc.

Robinson, Dorothy and Feeny, Bill. *The Official Price Guide to American Pottery and Porcelain.* Orlando: House of Collectibles, 1980.

Pickard

Platt, Dorothy Pickard. *The Story of Pickard China.* Hanover, Pennsylvania: Everybody's Press, 1970.

Warwick

Hoffmann, Donald C., Sr. *Warwick China Collector's Guide.* Aurora, Illinois: Privately printed, 1979.

———. *Why Not Warwick.* Aurora, Illinois: Privately printed, 1975.

6

British Art Pottery, 1865 to 1930

Art pottery was first made in Great Britain about 1865. The mood of the philosophers of the time was against industrial production and its lack of "art." It was now time for a craftsman to create an individual piece rather than become part of the mechanized, ugly world of the machine. John Ruskin, William Morris, and others encouraged the artist-craftsman to produce pottery in the manner of the Arts and Crafts movement.

Most of the British art potteries had small shops with just a few workmen. The style created by them influenced the larger potteries, and some, like the Doulton company, began making similar wares in a special art department.

The style and products of the art potteries fell from favor after World War I. They were considered Victorian and old-fashioned.

The collector can often find examples of this pottery. Most books on the subject did not appear until 1975. They are easily available in England but are difficult to find in the average public library in the United States.

The smiling cat is wearing a medallion of a dog, probably the reason she is smiling. This 13-inch earthenware figure was made by Emile Gallé.

BRITISH ART POTTERY

Dragons climb on this faience vase by Burmantofts Pottery. The vase, made about 1885, is 24¼ inches high.

Pottery and Location	Dates of Manufacture	Pottery and Location	Dates of Manufacture
Adams & Co. Scotswood-on-Tyne, Northumberland	1904–1914	Bishops Waltham Hampshire	1866–1867 BISHOPS WALTHAM
Allander Pottery Milngavie, Dunbartonshire, Scotland	1904–1908 ALLANDER	Bramfield ware. See Pearson, James, Ltd.	
		Brannam, C. H. Barnstaple	1895–1938 *C H Brannam Barum*
Aller Vale Pottery Newton, Abbot, Devon	1865–1901 ALLER VALE DEVON ENGLAND	Bretby Art Pottery Woodville, Derbyshire	1883–1887 BRETBY
Ashby Potters Guild Woodville, Derbyshire	1909–1922 ASHBY GUILD	Burmantofts Pottery Leeds	1880–1904 BURMANTOFTS FAIENCE
Ault & Tunnicliffe Woodville, Derbyshire	1923–1937 Aultcliff MADE IN ENGLAND	Carter, Stabler & Adams (Poole) Dorset	1921–c. 1930 POOLE ENGLAND / CARTER STABLER ADAMS LT POOLE ENGLAND
Ault, William Swadlincote	1887–1923 AULT	Cliff, Clarice Staffordshire	1928–d. 1972 *Clarice Cliff*
Bailey, C.J.C. & Co. Fulham, London	1864–1889 BAILEY FULHAM		
Barons Pottery Rolle Quay, Barnstaple	1895–1939 BARON N.DEVON	Coldrum Pottery See also Wells, R. F. West Malling, Kent, Chelsea	1908–1924 COLDRVM
Barum. See Brannam, C. H.			
Bellevue Pottery Rye	1869–1969 R S W RYE	Commondale Pottery Stokesley, Yorkshire	1872–1884 COMMONDALE POTTERY
Bingham, Edward (Hedingham Art Pottery) Castle Hedingham	1864–1901 E. BINGHAM	Compton Pottery Guildford	1896–1956 COMPTON POTTERY

Moorcraft designed for James Macintyre from 1897 to 1913. This earthenware jardiniere, decorated with yellow, green, white on a blue ground, is marked with the double mark and the name "Florian Ware."

The lion is on a 8¼-inch-high Pilkington Tile and Pottery Company earthenware vase decorated in orange and olive. The other Pilkington vase, also orange and olive, is impressed "Royal Lancastrian."

Sunflowers were a popular design in the 1890s when this earthenware vase was made by Edmund Elton. It is 7½ inches high.

Pottery and Location	Dates of Manufacture	Pottery and Location	Dates of Manufacture
Cooper, Susie Staffordshire *Susie Cooper* [Susie Cooper Production, Crown Works, Burslem, England mark]	1922–1966	Grovelands Potteries (Silchester ware) Reading	1850s–1910
		Hedingham Art Pottery. See Bingham, Edward.	
Crane, Walter London [monogram mark]	1867–1915	Kensington Fine Art Pottery Hanley [crown K.F.A. mark]	1892–1899
Dalton, William London [WB mark]	c. 1899– c. 1940	Lauder & Smith Barnstaple, Devon, Pottington *Lauder Barum*	1876–1914
Della Robbia Pottery Birkenhead, Cheshire [ship mark]	1894–1906	Leach, Bernard St. Ives [BL mark]	1920–
De Morgan, William Chelsea, Merton Abbey, Fulham [rose mark]	1860s–1907	Linthorpe Pottery Middlesbrough, Yorkshire **LINTHORPE**	1879–1890
		Longpark Pottery Torquay LONGPARK TORQUAY	1905–1940
Devonmoor Art Pottery Liverton, Newton Abbey DEVONMOOR	1913–1914 1922–	MacIntyre & Co. Burslem [mark]	1890s–1913
Doulton & Co. (Doulton & Watts) ("Royal Doulton" mark used) (see also Chapter 7) Burslem Lambeth [marks]	1858–1956 1815–1858 After 1901– present	Mansfield Bros. Ltd. Woodville, Church Gresley **M.B.**	1890–
		Martin Brothers London, Southall, Fulham *R W Martin 85 London*	1873–1920
Dresser, Christopher Yorkshire, Swadlincote, London (others) *Chr. Dresser*	c. 1870– 1890s	Maw & Co. Shropshire MAW & CO. BROSELEY	1851–
Eltons Sunflower Pottery (Sir Edmund Elton) Clevedon, Somerset *Elton*	1879–1922	Minton's Art Pottery Staffordshire, Gore, Kensington, London [marks]	1869–1875

Bernard Leach made low-temperature faience called Raku, as well as some English slipware and stoneware. He had studied in Japan. This is a 7½-inch stoneware jug by Bernard Leach.

The Martin Brothers are best remembered for the grotesque bird figures they made. This is a tobacco jar made about 1895.

Pottery and Location	Dates of Manufacture	Pottery and Location	Dates of Manufacture
Moorcroft, William Burslem, Staffordshire	1897–1945	Ruskin Pottery Smethwick, Worcestershire	1898–1935
Moore, Bernard Stoke-on-Trent, Staffordshire	1905–1915	Rye Pottery (Cadborough Pottery, Bellevue Pottery) Sussex, Bellview, Rye	1840–1871 1869–1947
Murray, William Staite	1919–1940	St. Ives Pottery Cornwall	1920–
Newport Pottery Co. Ltd. Burslem	1920–	Salopian Art Pottery Co. Shropshire	1882–1912
		Silchester ware. See Grovelands Potteries. See also Wells, R. F.	
Norton, Wilfred & Lilly London	1920–1956	Spode (Copeland & Garrett) (W. T. Copeland) (W. T. Copeland & Sons) (see also Chapter 7) Stoke-on-Trent	1762–1833 1833–1847 1847–1867
Orange Tree Pottery Durham	1952–		
Pearson, James, Ltd. (Bramfield ware) London	c. 1890–1939	Stiff, James & Son Lambeth	1840–1913
		Tooth, Henry. See Bretby Art Pottery.	
Pilkington Tile & Pottery Co. (Pilkington Royal Lancastrian) Manchester	1893–1938 1948–1957	Torquay Terra-cotta Co. Hele Cross	1875–1909
		Upchurch Pottery Rainham, Kent	1913–1961
Poole Pottery (Formerly Carter, Stabler and Adams) Dorset	1873–1921	Vyse, Charles London	c. 1919
Royal Essex Art Pottery Castle Hedingham	c. 1901	Wardle Art Pottery Art Co. Ltd. Hanley	1871–1935

Pottery and Location	Dates of Manufacture	Pottery and Location	Dates of Manufacture
Watcombe Pottery Co. Staffordshire, Torquay, Devon	1867–1962	Wells, Reginald Fairfax See also Coldrum Pottery. Kent, Chelsea	1909–1951
		Winchombe Pottery Gloucestershire	1926–1939
Wedgwood, Josiah & Sons Ltd. Burslem Etruria Barlaston	1759– 1769– 1940–	Wren, Denise K. Surrey	1907–

The Watcombe Pottery Company made this earthenware vase about 1880. It is 13½ inches high.

BIBLIOGRAPHY

General

Battie, David and Turner, Michael. *The Price Guide to 19th and 20th Century British Pottery.* Woodbridge, England: Baron Publishing, 1979.

Coysh, W. A. *British Art Pottery.* Rutland, Vermont: Charles E. Tuttle, 1976.

Godden, Geoffrey A. *British Pottery: An Illustrated Guide.* New York: Clarkson N. Potter, 1975.

———. *Encyclopedia of British Pottery and Porcelain Marks.* New York: Crown, 1970.

Haslam, Malcolm. *English Art Pottery, 1865–1915.* Suffolk, England: Baron Publishing, 1975.

Hughes, G. Bernard. *Victorian Pottery and Porcelain.* London: Spring Books, 1959.

Reynolds, Ernest. *Collecting Victorian Porcelain.* New York: Praeger, 1968.

Thomas, Lloyd, E. *Victorian Art Pottery.* London: Guildart, 1974.

Wakefield, Hugh. *Victorian Pottery.* New York: Thomas Nelson, 1962.

Goss

Andrews, Sandy. *Crested China: The History of Heraldic Souvenir Ware.* London: Springwood Books, 1980.

Pine, Nicholas. *Price Guide to Crested China.* Horndean, Portsmouth, Hants: Milestone Publications, 1981.

———. *Price Guide to Goss China.* Horndean, Portsmouth, Hants: Milestone Publications, 1981.

Ward, Roland. *The Price Guide to the Models of W. H. Goss.* Suffolk, England: Antique Collectors' Club, 1975.

Leach

The Art of Bernard Leach. London: Victoria and Albert Museum, 1977.

Martin Ware

Hillier, Bevis. *The Martin Brothers Potters.* London: Richard Dennis, 1978.

Moorcroft

William Moorcroft and Walter Moorcroft, 1897–1973. (Exhibition catalog). London: Richard Dennis, 1973.

Poole

Hawkins, Jennifer. *Poole Potteries.* London: Barrie & Jenkins, 1980.

Rowland & Marcellus

Arman, David and Linda. *Historical Staffordshire: An Illustrated Checklist.* Danville, Virginia: Arman Enterprises, 1975.

Royal Doulton

Eyles, Desmond. *The Doulton Burslem Wares.* London: Barrie & Jenkins, 1980.
———. *Royal Doulton Character & Toby Jugs.* Stoke-On-Trent, England: Royal Doulton Tableware Ltd., 1979.
Eyles, Desmond and Dennis, Richard. *Royal Doulton Figures Produced at Burslem c. 1890–1978.* Stoke-On-Trent, England: Royal Doulton Tableware Ltd., 1978.
Irvine, Louise. *Royal Doulton Series Ware.* London: Richard Dennis, 1980.
Kovel, Ralph and Terry. *The Kovels' Illustrated Price Guide to Royal Doulton.* New York: Crown, 1980.
Club: Royal Doulton International Collectors Club, P.O. Box 1815, Somerset, New Jersey 08873

Royal Worcester

Sandon, Henry. *Royal Worcester Porcelain from 1862 to the Present Day.* New York: Clarkson N. Potter, 1975.

Royal Worcester Spode

Whiter, Leonard. *Spode.* New York: Praeger, 1970.

Ruskin

Ruston, H. James. *Ruskin Pottery.* England: Metropolitan Borough of Sandwell, 1975.

Shelley

Watkins, Chris; Harvey, William; and Senft, Robert. *Shelley Potteries.* London: Barrie & Jenkins, 1980.

Tile

Barnard, Julian. *Victorian Ceramic Tiles.* Greenwich, Connecticut: New York Graphic Society, 1972.

————. *Victorian Tiles.* Wolverhampton, England: Wolverhampton Art Gallery, 1978.

Lockett, A. Terence. *Collecting Victorian Tiles.* Suffolk, England: Baron Publishing, 1979.

Wedgwood

Buten, David. *Wedgwood: Guide to Marks and Dating.* Merion, Pennsylvania: Buten Museum of Wedgwood, 1976.

Keilly, Robin and Savage, George. *Dictionary of Wedgwood.* Suffolk, England: Antique Collectors' Club, 1980.

Klamkin, Marian. *The Collector's Book of Wedgwood.* New York: Dodd, Mead, 1971.

Mankowitz, Wolf. *Wedgwood.* New York: Dutton, 1953.

Museum: Buten Museum of Wedgwood, 246 N. Bowman Ave., Merion, Pennsylvania 19066

7

European Pottery and Porcelain, Collector's Choice

Collectors have chosen several late-nineteenth- and twentieth-century porcelain companies as favorites. The quality of the work, ranging from good to excellent, is no different from that of many other firms, but the fact is the proper mark on a piece can mean greater interest and higher prices. Other factories will probably be added to this list in the future as collectors continue to discover the charms of special types of wares.

When you buy pottery and porcelain from these factories, remember that good taste, humor, historic interest, and decorative value are the price-determining factors. What may appear to be attractive to one person is considered poor quality to another. In recent years the desire for a collection that is a series has grown. Buyers like wares from Royal Doulton or Goebel Hummel because there are a few thousand known patterns and it might be possible to buy one of each. The supply is large enough to make the search interesting. Slight differences in the pattern or decoration can mean big differences in price, so be sure to do the necessary research into marks and patterns.

Austria—Teplitz

"Teplitz" refers to a town in Central Europe in what is now called Austria. Several companies in the Turn-Teplitz area manufactured art pottery during the late nineteenth and early twentieth centuries. The Amphora Porzellanfabrick (Amphora Porcelain Works) was run by Reissner, Stellmacher, and Kessel. The firm used a variety of marks with the word "Amphora" or the initials "RS&K." Another firm making pottery was the Alexandra Porcelain Works, founded by Ernst Wahliss. Wahliss sold RS&K wares until 1894, when he bought his own factory.

Amphora Porcelain Works

Amphora Porcelain Works   *Amphora Porcelain Works*   *Alexandra Porcelain Works (c.1899–c.1918)*   *Alexandra Porcelain Works (c.1900–c.1921)*

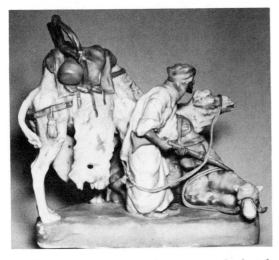

This camel and driver figure is marked with the Amphora, Austria, crown mark. It is 24 inches long, decorated in pale earth tones.

The Art Nouveau-inspired Teplitz pieces are eagerly sought by collectors. This vase has raised gold decorations. It is marked with the Amphora mark.

Austria—MZ Austria

MZ Austria is the firm of Moritz Zdekauer, working in Alt-Rohlau, Austria, from about 1900.

Moritz Zdekauer c. 1900	**Moritz Zdekauer** c. 1920–1938	**Moritz Zdekauer** c. 1938–1945

Czechoslovakia—Royal Dux

The Duxer Porzellanmanufaktur (Dux Porcelain Manufactory) was founded in Dux, Bohemia, in 1860 by E. Eichler. By the turn of the century the firm specialized in porcelain statuary and busts of Art Nouveau–style maidens, large porcelain figures, and ornate vases with three-dimensional figures climbing on the sides.

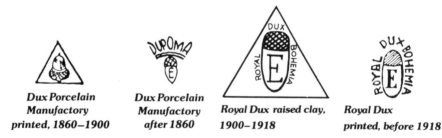

Dux Porcelain Manufactory printed, 1860–1900	**Dux Porcelain Manufactory** after 1860	**Royal Dux raised clay,** 1900–1918	**Royal Dux** printed, before 1918

An early mark of Eichler's firm used an acorn, because *Eichel* in German means "acorn." The mark used later (1900–1918) was a raised triangle of clay with a stylized acorn and initials. After 1918 "Bohemia" was no longer part of the mark because World War I changed Dux, Bohemia, into Duchcov, Czechoslovakia. The firm is still in business.

Denmark—Bing & Grondahl

Bing & Grondahl was established in Copenhagen, Denmark, in 1853 by Frederick Vilhelm Grondahl, who had worked at the Royal Copenhagen Porcelain Manufactory, and M. H. and J. H. Bing, owners of a stationery department store. Mr. Grondahl died a year later and other artists were hired to work at the factory. At first overglaze and biscuit porcelains were

The leering man and posturing lady are posed in a Royal Dux figurine. The clothing is decorated with royal blue and gold; the figures are lifelike in coloring.

made. Underglaze blue decoration was started in 1886. The annual Christmas plate series was introduced in 1895. Dinnerwares, stoneware, and figurines are still made today.

B & G

Bing & Grondahl
1853

Danish China Works
COPENHAGEN
B. & G.

Bing & Grondahl
1895

B&G
COPENHAGEN
DANISH CHINA WORKS
B & G

Bing & Grondahl
1898

B&G
KJØBENHAVN
DANISH CHINA WORKS
B & G

Bing & Grondahl
1899

B & G
KJØBENHAVN
MADE IN DENMARK
B & G

Bing & Grondahl
1902

B & G
KJØBENHAVN
COPENHAGEN
B & G

Bing & Grondahl
1914

B & G
KJØBENHAVN
DANMARK
B & G

Bing & Grondahl
1915

B&G
KJØBENHAVN
DANMARK
B & G

Bing & Grondahl
1948

B&G
KJØBENHAVN
MADE IN
DENMARK

Bing & Grondahl
1952

B&G
KJØBENHAVN
MADE IN DENMARK

Bing & Grondahl
1958

B&G
KJØBENHAVN
DENMARK

Bing & Grondahl
1962

COPENHAGEN PORCELAIN
B&G
MADE IN DENMARK

Bing & Grondahl
1970

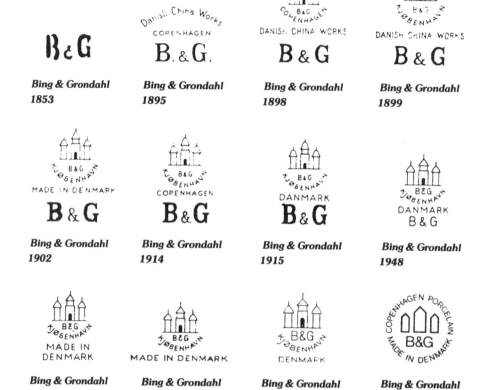

A smoking mountain is modeled on the face of this plate by Arnold Krog for the Royal Copenhagen Porcelain Manufactory about 1893. It has a grand feu colored glaze.

The annual Christmas plate by Bing & Grondahl has been made since 1895. This is the 1919 plate, decorated in the typical blue colors.

Denmark—Royal Copenhagen

A factory to produce hard-paste porcelains was founded in Copenhagen, Denmark, in 1775. The firm had been supported by the Royal Family and in 1779 ownership was taken over by the king. The firm was named the Royal Copenhagen Porcelain Manufactory. Although the firm was put into private ownership in 1868, the name remained.

Early wares included low-cost blue decorated porcelain and more elaborate types, including the famous Flora Danica service started in 1790. Tablewares such as the Blue Fluted dinner service, made since 1775, Blue Flowers, Julian Marie, and Saxon Flower, of about 1800, are still in production.

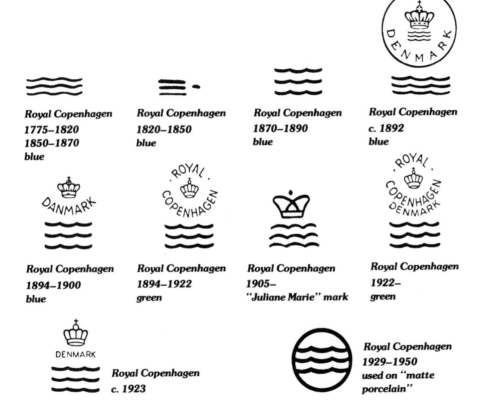

Royal Copenhagen
1775–1820
1850–1870
blue

Royal Copenhagen
1820–1850
blue

Royal Copenhagen
1870–1890
blue

Royal Copenhagen
c. 1892
blue

Royal Copenhagen
1894–1900
blue

Royal Copenhagen
1894–1922
green

Royal Copenhagen
1905–
"Juliane Marie" mark

Royal Copenhagen
1922–
green

Royal Copenhagen
c. 1923

Royal Copenhagen
1929–1950
used on "matte porcelain"

The underglaze-blue-decorated wares developed by Arnold Krog about 1884 have remained popular. Christmas plates were first made in 1908. Figurines with underglaze blue decoration and colored decorations have been in production since the nineteenth century.

Denmark—Dahl-Jensen

The Dahl-Jensen Porcelaensfabrik was founded in Copenhagen, Denmark, in 1925 by J. P. Dahl-Jensen, a sculptor, and his son Georg Dahl-Jensen. The same family is still running the firm.

Dahl-Jensen
mark used 1925–
1928

Dahl-Jensen
1928–present

England—Carlton Ware

Carlton ware was made from about 1890 to 1957 at the Carlton Works of Stoke-on-Trent by a firm named Wiltshaw and Robinson. The firm was renamed Carlton Ware Ltd. in 1958. The Oriental-designed luster wares are the wares most popular with collectors.

Carlton Ware

Carlton Ware

England—Clarice Cliff

Clarice Cliff was a Staffordshire pottery decorator and designer. She worked for A. Wilkinson Ltd. subsidiaries, including the Royal Staffordshire Pottery, Newport Pottery, and an association of Wilkinson and Foley Pottery. She did Art Deco designs in the 1930s. She died in 1972.

Clarice Cliff

Goss China souvenir pieces were often shaped like houses. This is a small Tudor-style house less than 3 inches long.

England—Goss China

William Henry Goss founded his factory at Stoke-on-Trent in 1858. He specialized in ornamental Parian ware, figures, terra-cotta, and jeweled porcelain. In 1883 he began making china souvenir items. Goss became a part of Cauldon potteries in 1934 and ceased production in 1940.

Goss china souvenir items were designed to represent specific tourist attractions. They were sold only in the town that was represented by the souvenir.

W. H. GOSS
COPYRIGHT

Goss China
c. 1858–1865
impressed or printed

Goss China
1862–1930

Goss China
1930–c. 1940

England—Minton

Thomas Minton, after working for other potters, started his own firm at Stoke-on-Trent in 1793. The family business made a wide variety of tablewares and decorative pieces. By 1846 it was making Parian ware, later made majolica, tiles, bone china, and art pottery. The firm became part of the Royal Doulton Tableware Group in 1968 but the wares continue to be marked "Minton." From 1873 to about 1912 the name on the mark was usually "MINTONS," then it again became "MINTON." A special code of symbols was stamped or impressed on wares from 1842. Each year was represented by a different picture. Any good book on English porcelain marks will list these symbols.

Minton
1860s
printed

Minton
1863–1872
printed

Minton
c. 1873–
printed "England"
added 1891; "Made in
England" added
c. 1902–1911

Minton
c. 1912–1950
printed

Minton
c. 1951–present
printed

This 9-inch-tall Minton earthenware vase was made about 1900. It is decorated with red and avocado green glaze.

This Minton pâte-sur-pâte vase is fancifully decorated with a child spinning a spiderweb. It dates about 1870.

England—Moorcroft; James Macintyre and Company

William Moorcroft worked from 1897 as a designer for James Macintyre and Company of Burslem, England. In 1913 he set up his own firm, making many of the wares he had developed in the other factory. His designs often featured stylized flowers and distinctive glaze colors. He worked with flambé glazes and won many awards for the work. In 1928 he was appointed Potter to Her Majesty the Queen, and the new designation became part of his mark. The firm is still working although William Moorcroft died in 1945.

The characteristic flowers used by Moorcroft appear on this 6-inch-diameter vase.

James Macintyre
(Moorcroft)
1898–c. 1904
printed brown

James Macintyre
(Moorcraft)
printed signature
used with other
marks, 1898–1935
impressed signature
used c. 1930–c. 1949

MOORCROFT

James Macintyre
(Moorcraft)
impressed
used with "Burslem,"
1913–c. 1921
used with "Made in
England" c. 1921–
present

*Moorcraft
paper label
c. 1930– 1949*

England—Poole Potteries

The Poole Pottery was started by Jesse Carter in 1873 in Poole, England. The company specialized in architectural ceramics, but soon began to make other pottery. In 1908 the company was incorporated as Carter and Company; in 1920 it became Carter & Co., Ltd., and had a subsidiary called Carter, Stabler and Adams. The name Poole Pottery, Ltd. was taken in 1963.

Collectors today are interested in the potteries of all the firms from Poole. Unusual glazes and designs were used.

Jesse Carter, his sons Charles, Ernest, and Owen, and friends John Adams, Harold Stabler, and his wife Phoebe, managed the potteries. Poole Potteries is still working.

Carter & Co.
1873–1921
incised or printed

Carter, Stabler
& Adams
1921–
incised or printed

Carter, Stabler
& Adams
1921–1925
"Ltd." added to
mark, 1925–1952

Carter, Stabler
& Adams
1956–

England—Rowland and Marsellus Company

Rowland & Marsellus

Rowland and Marsellus Company is a mark that appears on historical Staffordshire wares dating from the late nineteenth and early twentieth centuries. It is believed to be a mark used by the British Anchor Pottery Company of Longton, England. Many American views were pictured on the plates. Often a retail store name appeared with the Rowland and Marsellus mark. One special type of plate is called a "rolled edge" by dealers. It has a central design showing a building or scene, then several other related scenes in cartouches on the rolled-over edge of the plate.

England—Royal Doulton

The name "Royal Doulton" is a collector's nickname for the products of Doulton and Company made after 1902, when the word "Royal" became part of the company mark.

The Doulton company traces its history back to John Doulton of Fulham, England, who worked as a potter's apprentice from 1805 to 1812. In 1815, he became a partner in Jones, Watts, and Doulton, a

Royal Doulton
impressed or printed mark on decorated stoneware, 1879–1902; china after 1884; "England" added after 1891

Royal Doulton
impressed or printed mark, 1885–1902; "England" added after 1891

Royal Doulton
first "Royal" Doulton mark; printed or impressed mark, 1902–1922, 1927–1932; "Made in England" added after 1930

Royal Doulton
printed on Burslem pieces, 1922–1927

Royal Doulton
printed or impressed on Lambeth pieces, 1922–1956

Royal Doulton
printed on Burslem earthenware pieces, 1932–present; "Bone China" added underneath, 1932–1959; "English Fine Bone China" added underneath, 1959–present; "English Translucent China" added underneath, 1960–present

Putted by. Doulton. &Co
Royal Doulton
"Potted" mark,
before 1939

Royal Doulton
"A" mark, internal
factory mark, c. 1950

Royal Doulton
current mark (notice
shortened lines
between the words
"Royal Doulton" and
"England"), since
1960s

pothouse in Lambeth, England. John Doulton continued in the pottery business with a succession of other potters, including his sons Henry, Frederick, and John, Jr. Doulton and Company was formed in 1853 by the three brothers and the father. The company had several potteries and made a variety of wares, including stoneware, silicon ware, Carrara ware, marqueterie ware, majolica, kingsware, Sung, Chang, flambé, bone china, pottery, and porcelain. The firm became Doulton and Company, Limited, in 1899. The words "Royal Doulton" were used after 1902. The factory is still working and still making the figurines, character jugs, and animal figures so popular with collectors today.

Royal Doulton figurines have been made in thousands of models. The first two figures here from "In an Eastern Market" are "Abdullah" and "Carpet Seller." The third is the American Indian figure "Calumet."

The style of decoration known as japonisme was used at the Royal Worcester factory. This tea set has the 1881 mark. The decoration is gold applied to resemble Japanese lacquer.

England—Royal Worcester

Worcester porcelains were made in Worcester, England, from about 1751. The firm went through many different periods and name changes, which appeared in the marks.

The Flight period was from 1783 to 1792; the Barr and Flight and Barr period, 1792 to 1807; the Barr, Flight and Barr period, 1807 to 1913; the Flight, Barr and Barr period, 1813 to 1840; the Kerr and Binns period, 1852 to 1862. It became the Worcester Royal Porcelain Company Ltd. in 1862. Today collectors refer to the porcelains made after 1862 as Royal Worcester. Figurines, dinner sets, and other tablewares of the best quality

The snake-decorated ewer was a popular form at the Royal Worcester factory about 1890. This vase is 11¾ inches high, decorated in beige tones and gold.

Royal Worcester standard mark, 1862–1875

Royal Worcester standard mark, 1876–1891; letter underneath changed every year

Royal Worcester standard mark, 1891–1963

Royal Worcester revised mark, 1959 on, used with year marks

have been made. The markings on the Royal Worcester give almost an exact indication of age. The standard Royal Worcester printed mark was used for 1862 to 1875. A two-digit numeral was added to the mark in 1873, such as "74" for 1874, "75" for 1875, etc. Letters were also used from 1867 to 1890.

Another standard printed mark was used from 1876 to 1891. Letters were used beneath this mark from 1876 to 1891.

England—Royal Worcester Spode

Josiah Spode established a pottery at Stoke-on-Trent, England, in 1770. The firm has changed ownership but the name "Spode" appears in many of the company marks. Josiah Spode was succeeded by his son, then his grandson. In 1833 the firm was purchased by a former partner, William Taylor Copeland, and a Spode salesman, Thomas Garrett. Copeland & Garrett made porcelains, earthenwares, and introduced Parian ware. Copeland took over sole ownership in 1847. W. T. Copeland & Sons continued until a 1976 merger, when it became Royal Worcester Spode.

COPELAND

& GARRETT

Copeland & Garrett
printed, c. 1833

Copeland & Garrett
c. 1833

W. T. Copeland
& Sons
printed, c. 1885

W. T. Copeland
& Sons
printed, c. 1894

COPELAND
SPODE
ENGLAND

SPODE
COPELAND CHINA
ENGLAND

W. T. Copeland
& Sons
printed, c. 1900

W. T. Copeland
& Sons
printed, c. 1920

W. T. Copeland
& Sons
printed, c. 1940

ENGLAND

ROYAL WORCESTER SPODE

W. T. Copeland &
Sons
printed, 1970

Royal Worcester
Spode
printed, 1976–
present

England—Shelley Potteries

Shelley Potteries
c. 1925–1940

Shelley Potteries
c. 1945

The first known potter in the Shelley family was Michael, who was working in Staffordshire, England, by 1780. The family continued as potters through the nineteenth century. In 1872 Joseph B. Shelley joined James F. Wileman in Wileman & Company at the Foley China Works, Longton, England. The company was renamed Shelley in 1925. In 1966 Allied English Potteries took over the pottery, and it merged with the Doulton group in 1971.

The name "Shelley" appears in marks as early as 1910 and is still in use.

The pottery had many unusual Art Nouveau and Art Deco patterns of tablewares. The director of the firm from 1896 to 1905 was Frederick Rhead, a member of a family of artists connected with many potteries in England and the United States.

England—Susie Cooper

Susie Cooper began her career as a ceramic designer in 1925 when she was hired by the Staffordshire pottery firm of A. E. Gray & Company. She stayed with them until 1932, when she formed Susie Cooper Pottery, Ltd. In 1950 she formed Susie Cooper China, Ltd., and expanded her production to include china as well as earthenware. The firm was amalgamated with Tuscan China in 1958, then in 1966 was acquired by Josiah Wedgwood & Sons, Ltd.

Gray's Pottery
1925–1932

Susie Cooper
Pottery Ltd.
c. 1932

Susie Cooper
Pottery Ltd.
1932–

Wedgwood
1966–

England—Wedgwood

As a young boy Josiah Wedgwood was apprenticed to his brother as a potter. In 1752 he left his brother and joined another potter in business. Josiah was an innovator and experimented with types of clay, glazes, and

Emile Lessore was a famous artist working at Wedgwood. This shell-shaped cream-colored dish was made about 1860.

Signs of the zodiac decorate this three-color jasper vase made by Wedgwood potteries. The body of the vase is lilac-colored. It is part of the collection at the Buten Museum of Wedgwood in Merion, Pennsylvania.

---

designs to create many new types of dishwares. After two partnerships he opened his own business in 1759 in Burslem. Wedgwood pottery sold well; several new types, including creamware, were popular and the pottery was a financial success. Wedgwood and Bentley was formed in 1769, lasting until the death of Thomas Bentley in 1780. The list of Josiah Wedgwood's products includes agate wares, basalt wares, metallic glazes, jasper ware, pearl ware, cane ware, bone china, stone china, Parian, majolica, and more. The firm became Josiah Wedgwood and Sons in 1827, and Josiah Wedgwood and Sons, Ltd., in 1895.

WEDGWOOD

Wedgwood

impressed mark; "England" added 1891; "Made in England" added after 1900

Collectors have trouble dating Wedgwood for several reasons. Many of the twentieth-century pieces are made in the same patterns and from the same molds as the eighteenth-century pieces. Jasper ware has been one type of Wedgwood made for the past two hundred years in very similar designs. The Wedgwood mark is often the name of the firm incised in either upper or upper and lower case letters. The word "England" was added to the mark in 1891, the words "Made in England" by 1898. Often ads offer Wedgwood as "MIE," meaning the mark includes the words "Made in England."

WEDGWOOD

Wedgwood

c. 1900–

The impressed marks that are used are often difficult to read, so be sure to look carefully at the bottom of any piece of Wedgwood. There is a date/letter system that was used to mark Wedgwood from 1860 to 1930.

It consists of three letters indicating month, potter, and year of production. In 1907 the factory began to use a number 3 instead of the first letter, in 1924 they started using a 4 instead of the first letter. The actual date was put on the piece after 1930. Complete tables listing all of the date/letter codes can be found in any good book about Wedgwood or English porcelain marks (see Bibliography).

France—Massier

Clement Massier built a factory in Golfe-Juan, France, in 1881 and began to make pottery with an iridescent glaze. He made art pottery marked with his name, initials, or town name. One of his students was Jacques Sicard, who later worked at the Weller pottery in Ohio, making a very similar iridescent glazed ware. Clement Massier died in 1917. His son Jerome continued working at the pottery.

The art pottery of Massier was often decorated with a gold luster. This vase, made about 1900, has gold insects and flowers on a gold background.

Bronze, green, and gold luster were used on this vase. It is marked "Clement Massier" in gold on the bottom.

France—Quimper

Tin-glazed, hand-painted pottery has been made in Quimper (pronounced "Com pere"), France, since the late seventeenth century. Three firms worked in Quimper and the names and marks have changed because of marriages and mergers. The earliest firm, founded in 1685 by Jean Baptiste Bousquet, was known as HB Quimper. Another firm, founded in 1772 by Francois Eloury, was known as Porquier. The third firm, founded by Guillaume Dumaine in 1778, was known as HR or Henriot Quimper. All three firms made similar wares decorated with designs of Breton peasants and sea and flower motifs. The Eloury (Porquier) and Dumaine (Henriot) firms merged in 1913. Bousquet (HB) merged with the others in 1968. The group was sold to an American family in 1984. The United States holding company is Quimper Faience Inc., located in Stonington, Connecticut. The French firm has been called Societe Nouvelle des Faienceries de Quimper HB Henriot since March 1984.

HB *Quimper*	***AP***	***IR***	*HenRiot* *QuimpeR*
Quimper	**Quimper**	**Quimper**	**Quimper**
Bousquet, mid-nineteenth century	**Eloury (Porquier), c. 1860**	**Dumaine (Henriot), c. 1886–1926**	**Dumaine (Henriot), after 1926**

These two views of a Quimper pitcher show the unsophisticated peasant designs favored by the factory. The piece is marked "France." It is 5½ inches high.

France—Utzschneider and Company (Sarreguemines)

Utzschneider and Company, a porcelain factory, made ceramics in Sarreguemines from 1770. Transfer printed wares and majolica were made in the nineteenth century.

Utzschneider & Co.

Utzschneider & Co.

Utzschneider & Co.

Utzschneider & Co.

Germany—Goebel Hummel

The F. W. Goebel factory was founded in 1871 by Franz and William Goebel in Oeslau, Germany. In 1935, Goebel put the first "M. I. Hummel" figurine on the market when the Goebel factory, in collaboration with Berta Hummel (then Sister Maria Innocentia) and the convent she had entered, made the first Hummel figurines.

Limited edition plates were started by the company in 1971. The firm is still working. The figurines were not made in limited numbers and can be reintroduced by the firm at any time. For this reason collectors are even more concerned about marks on Hummels than on most figurines. The mark is a guarantee of age. Collectors and dealers often discuss the Hummel figurines in terms of the nicknames given to the marks. This makes it confusing for the amateur trying to understand the ads or books. The marks are listed here with these nicknames.

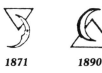

1871   1890   1900   1914–1920

Goebel
early Goebel marks and crown marks

Goebel Hummel "Wide crown" printed blue or black, incised, 1923–1949 1969–1971

Goebel "Narrow Crown" printed blue or black, incised, 1937– 1945

"Little Fiddler" is the name of this Goebel Hummel figurine. It is 8 inches high.

Goebel Hummel
*signature used
on some
models, 1949*

**W. Germany
West Germany**

Goebel Hummel
*added to mark after
1949; printed black
underglaze, stamped
overglaze*

**U.S. - Zone
Germany**

Goebel Hummel
*added to mark, 1946–
1948; printed black
underglaze, stamped
overglaze*

Goebel Hummel
*"incised bee" or "full
bee" 1950–1955
incised underglaze;
some also stamped
black, blue, green, or
magenta; often used
with a crown mark*

Goebel Hummel
*"small bee"
1956
underglaze
black or blue*

Goebel Hummel
*"high bee"
1957
underglaze
black or blue*

Goebel Hummel
*"low bee" or "baby
bee"
1958
underglaze black or
blue*

Goebel Hummel
*"vee bee"
1959
underglaze black or
blue*

Goebel Hummel
*"new bee" or
"stylized bee"
1960–1972
underglaze black or
blue*

Goebel Hummel
*"vee over gee"
1972–1979
blue underglaze*

©by
W. Goebel
W. Germany

Goebel Hummel
*"three line mark"
1964–1972*

Goebel

Goebel Hummel
1979–1991

Goebel
Germany

Goebel Hummel
1991–present

*This figurine by
Goebel Hummel
was named "Big
Housecleaning."*

Germany—Hutschenreuther

The Hutschenreuther Porcelain Company of Selb, Germany, was established in 1814. The firm is still working.

Hutschenreuther

Germany—KPM

Frederick the Great of Prussia encouraged the formation of a porcelain manufactory in Berlin in 1751. It closed in 1757 but was reopened in 1761, only to go bankrupt in 1763. Frederick the Great bought the factory and it became the Konigliche Porzellan Manufaktur, or KPM. The name was changed to Staatliche Porzellan Manufaktur in 1918, and although production ceased during World War II the firm is still working. The firm's nineteenth-century dinnerwares, lithophanes, and porcelain plaques are popular with collectors today.

The initials "KPM" can be confusing because other German companies used the same letters in their marks. Krister Porzellan Manufaktur, Kister Porzellan Manufaktur, and Kranichfelder Porzellan Manufaktur had KPM marks in the late nineteeth and early twentieth centuries.

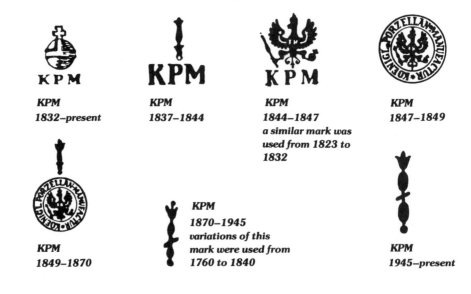

Germany—Rosenthal

The Rosenthal porcelain factory was established in 1879 by Phillip Rosenthal near Selb, Bavaria. At first it was only a decorating shop, but by 1886 it was manufacturing fine tableware.

Several branches were opened. The firm is still in business making china, figurines, Christmas plates, limited edition plates, and giftwares.

Rosenthal & Co.
(Selb & Kronach,
Bavaria)
1891–1907

Rosenthal & Co.
Kronach, Bavaria,
1893–1935;
underglaze green

Rosenthal & Co.
Kronach, Bavaria,
branch
c. 1900, overglaze,
gold
used on figurines and
vases

Rosenthal & Co. AG
1907–1933 (with
Selb, Bavaria)
1934–1956 (with
Selb, Germany)

Rosenthal AG
Selb, Bahnhof,
Plossberg branch
1917–1952,
underglaze green

Rosenthal & Co.
Kronach, Bavaria
1935–1956,
underglaze green

JOHANN HAVILAND
R
BAVARIA

Rosenthal AG
Haviland, Bavaria
branch
hotel dishes
since 1937

Rosen✕thal
GERMANY

Rosenthal AG
1957–present
also on annual
Christmas plate
through 1974

Santa Claus-shaped pieces were made by Royal Bayreuth. This 8-inch-high water pitcher matches the other pieces, including a 6¼-inch pitcher, a creamer, a match holder, two sizes of humidors, a wall vase, a hatpin holder, an ashtray, and candlesticks.

Germany—Royal Bayreuth

The Royal Bayreuth porcelain factory was founded in 1794 in Tettau, Bavaria. It continues today as Royally Privileged Porcelain Factory Tettau GMBH, producing dinnerware and limited editions. The name Royal Bayreuth is still used on pieces sold in the U.S.

Turn-of-the-century lines were the Rose Tapestry, floral, scenic, and portrait china, as well as the Sunbonnet Babies, Beach Babies, and Snow Babies series. Figural and souvenir items were made c. 1885–1915.

Not all pieces were marked. Marks were applied both by decal and rubber stamp. The crest mark was changed slightly over the years by each manager of the factory. Many versions are known.

Royal Bayreuth
"crest mark"
c. 1870–c. 1914
printed blue

Royal Bayreuth
"old Tettau mark"
c. 1957 –
printed blue

Royal Bayreuth
c. 1919
printed green
thought to be used on exports to United Kingdom

Royal Bayreuth
"U.S. Zone"
1946–1949
reissues

Royal Bayreuth
mark on Christmas plate series, started in 1972

Royal Bayreuth
current marks on dinnerwares, printed

The devil and cards design is one of the most popular Royal Bayreuth designs. A three-dimensional devil is the handle of this card-filled dish. The pattern was made about 1890. A few pieces have been reproduced in the 1970s.

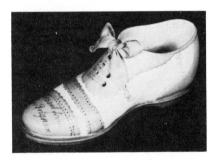

"Present from New Brighton" is written on the toe of this shoe by Royal Bayreuth. It was sold as a souvenir.

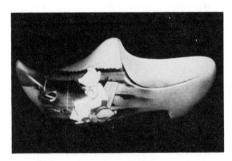

The Sunbonnet Babies were a popular pattern at the Royal Bayreuth factory. This shoe with the decoration of a girl fishing is less than 4 inches long.

Germany—Royal Bonn

Royal Bonn is the name used on nineteenth- and twentieth-century ceramic from the Bonn China Manufactory established in 1775 in Bonn, Germany.

Royal Bonn

Germany—Royal Rudolstadt

The Rudolstadt Pottery was established in Thuringia, Germany, in 1721. The wares seen today are porcelains made by Ernst Bohne (& Söhne) after 1854. The New York and Rudolstadt Pottery Company started in Rudolstadt, Germany. The words Royal Rudolstadt were added to the R. W. Crown mark. Late nineteenth- and early twentieth-century pieces are most often found today.

This Royal Rudolstadt vase has gold and pastel decorations on a cream-colored body.

Germany—RS Prussia

Three members of the Schlegelmilch family made porcelain in Germany in the nineteenth and early twentieth centuries. Their work is known to today's collectors as RS Prussia, RS Germany, RS Poland or RS Tillowitz.

Erdmann Schlegelmilch established a factory in Suhl, Thuringia (1861– c. 1925). His brother Reinhold began his factory in Tillowitz, Silesia (1869–c. 1917). Oscar Schlegelmilch, a nephew, began a factory in Langewiesen, Thuringia (1892–c. 1950).

The RS Prussia wreath mark was used by both Erdmann and Reinhold. The place name below the wreath varied according to the political upheavals of the era.

Reinhold Schlegelmilch, Tillowitz, Germany

RS Prussia
light green

RS Prussia
green

RS Prussia
blue or green

RS Prussia
red "Poland,"
with initials in
green wreath

Erdmann Schlegelmilch, Suhl, Germany, 1861–1925

RS Prussia
red Prussian star with
initials in green wreath

RS Prussia
light green

R S Prussia
dark green gold or
light green gold

RS Prussia: Marks shown are only those including the "RS"; others were used, most included initials or the name "Schlegelmilch"

This 14-inch tankard by RS Prussia is one of the more expensive pieces made by the factory.

This tray decorated with a lady and dog is 14 by 10 inches. It has the RS Germany steeple mark on the bottom.

It is known that "RS Prussia" appeared on plates issued in 1906; "RS Germany" appeared on plates issued in 1913. Recent reproductions with the RS Prussia wreath mark are known.

Germany—Schmid Hummel

The Goebel Hummel pieces were made from designs drawn by Berta Hummel (Sister Maria Innocentia) while she was a member of a convent. In 1971 another firm, Schmid Brothers, Inc., gained the rights to produce works based on the designs Berta Hummel made before she entered the convent. These drawings belonged to her mother, who was paid royalties for their use. The Schmid Hummel works include a limited edition annual plate started in 1971, music boxes, pictures, candles, and other gift items. In 1977 the firm decided to make only limited edition Hummel pieces, and other limited lines were presented.

Schmid Hummel

Holland—Gouda

Gouda Pottery has been made in Gouda, Holland, since the 1700s. Pieter Van der Want founded the Plateelbakkerij/Zennith in 1749. The family continued to be interested in the pottery business in the Gouda area to modern times. Several companies were founded by descendants. The Zennith pottery remained in the family until 1898, when one de-

"Betty" is the name of this 4-inch Gouda vase.

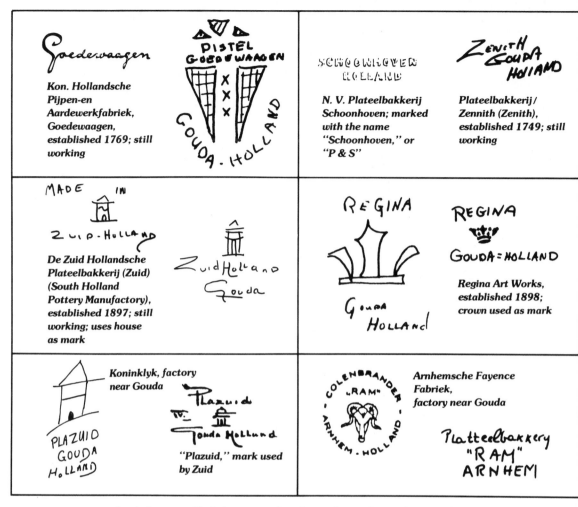

Goedewaagen Kon. Hollandsche Pijpen-en Aardewerkfabriek, Goedewaagen, established 1769; still working	**PISTEL GOEDEWAAGEN GOUDA - HOLLAND**	**SCHOONHOVEN HOLLAND** N. V. Plateelbakkerij Schoonhoven; marked with the name "Schoonhoven," or "P & S"	**ZENITH GOUDA HOLLAND** Plateelbakkerij/Zennith (Zenith), established 1749; still working
MADE IN ZUID-HOLLAND De Zuid Hollandsche Plateelbakkerij (Zuid) (South Holland Pottery Manufactory), established 1897; still working; uses house as mark	**ZuidHolland Gouda**	**REGINA GOUDA HOLLAND**	**REGINA GOUDA=HOLLAND** Regina Art Works, established 1898; crown used as mark
PLAZUID GOUDA HOLLAND Koninklyk, factory near Gouda	**Plazuid Gouda Holland** "Plazuid," mark used by Zuid	**COLENBRANDER "RAM" ARNHEM - HOLLAND** Arnhemsche Fayence Fabriek, factory near Gouda	**Plateelbakkery "RAM" ARNHEM**

Gouda factories. Each factory produced porcelain with one of two marks.

Blue and white Phoenix bird beaker.

scendant, Gerrit Frederick Van der Want, formed the Regina factory. Another family member, Otto Adrianus Van der Want, kept the Zennith pottery. His son expanded the factory with another plant.

The potteries of Gouda and nearby cities made blue and white delftwares, pipes, and after 1890 a distinctive, colorful Art Nouveau-decorated ware.

Collectors group all pottery marked with the name "Gouda" into one class, although many factories were making these wares.

Many of the Gouda marks include a variety of information. The name of the pattern, the name of the workshop, the initials of the artist who did the decorating, the symbol for the plant, and the number representing the factory code for the shape of the piece may be included.

Ireland—Belleek

Belleek Pottery Limited has made Belleek pottery in County Fermanagh, Ireland, since 1863. The characteristic creamy yellow mother-of-pearl-like glaze used on the pottery has been given the generic name Belleek. Since 1929 only this Irish firm may use the word "belleek" as part of the trademark. Some wares with the same nacreous glaze are also colored with pastels. The firm is still working. Collectors often refer to the marks by the nicknames "first mark," "second mark," etc.

Belleek
"first mark"
1863–1891
printed black
1868–1883
printed blue with
English registry mark

Belleek
"second mark"
1891–1926
printed black

Belleek
"third mark"
1927–1941
printed black

Belleek
"fourth mark"
1946–1955
printed green

Belleek
"fifth mark"
1956–1965
printed green
® added

Belleek
"sixth mark"
1965–present
printed green

EUROPEAN POTTERY AND PORCELAIN
OTHER FACTORIES AND MAKERS OF INTEREST

(Dates in parentheses are birth and death dates of the artist. Others are working dates of the pottery.)

Pottery and Location	Dates of Manufacture	Pottery and Location	Dates of Manufacture
Arte Della Ceramica Florence, Italy	1896–1906	Boch Frères La Louvière, Belgium	1841–present

The Boch Frères factory of Belgium made this 14-inch-high vase. It is yellow, blue, orange, and ivory.

This Longwy vase is covered with a thick enamel decoration of blue, green, yellow, and rose.

This Rozenburg vase is decorated in the Art Nouveau manner. It is 16 inches high.

Pottery and Location	Dates of Manufacture	Pottery and Location	Dates of Manufacture
Chaplet, Ernest Choisy-le-Roi, France	(1836–1909)	Haga Purmerend, Holland	1894–1907
Dalpayrat, Pierre-Adrien Bourg-la-Reine, France	1876–1888	Haviland & Co. Limoges, France	1842– present
Deck, Theodore France	(1829–1891)	Hoffmann, Josef Vienna, Austria	(1870–1956)
Delaherche, Auguste France	(1857–1940)	Keramische Werkgenossenschaft Vienna, Austria	1911–1920
Doat, Taxile Sèvres, France United States	(1851– c. 1940) 1875–1905 1909–1911	Longwy France	1798– present
Galle, Emile Nancy, France	(1846–1904) 1874–1935	Rörstrand Stockholm, Sweden	1726– present
Gmundner Keramik Gmunden, Austria	1909–1922	Rozenburg The Hague, Holland	1899–1914
Gustafsberg Gustafsberg, Sweden	1827– present		

163

Pottery and Location	Dates of Manufacture	Pottery and Location	Dates of Manufacture
Sèvres Sèvres, France	1756–present	Wiener Kunstkeramische Werkstätte Vienna, Austria	c. 1908–
Van de Velde, Henry Clemens Germany	(1863–1957)	Wiener Werkstätte Vienna, Austria	1903–1932
Villeroy & Boch Mettlach, Germany	1836–present	Zsolnay Pécs, Hungary	1862–present
Wiener Keramik Vienna, Austria	1905–1912		

Zsolnay pottery is often covered with an iridescent glaze. This vase, of Art Nouveau-inspired shape, has a gold glaze. It was made about 1900.

BIBLIOGRAPHY

General

Jacobson, Gertrude Tatnall. *Haviland China.* 2 vols. Des Moines: Wallace-Homestead, 1979.

Mettlach, 1885–1909 (facsimile catalogs). Wheeling, Illinois: Hans J. Ammelounx, 1975.

Schwartzman, Paulette. *A Collector's Guide to European and American Art Pottery with Current Values.* Paducah, Kentucky: Collector Books, 1978.

Belleek

Degenhardt, Richard K. *Belleek: The Complete Collector's Guide and Illustrated Reference.* Huntington, New York: Portfolio Press, 1978.

Bing & Grondahl

Owen, Pat. *The Story of Bing & Grondahl Christmas Plates, 1895–Present.* Dayton: Viking Import House, 1962 (with yearly additions).

Gouda

Moody, C. W. *Gouda Ceramics: The Art Nouveau Era of Holland.* Berkeley, California: Mike Roberts Color Production, 1970.

Hummel

Ehrmann, Eric. *Hummel: The Complete Collector's Guide and Illustrated Reference.* Huntington, New York: Portfolio Press, 1976.

Hotchkiss, John F. *Hummel Art II.* Des Moines: Wallace-Homestead, 1981.

Luckey, Carl F. *Hummel Figurines & Plates.* 3rd ed. Florence, Alabama: Books Americana, 1980.

Clubs: Goebel Collectors Club, 105 White Plains Rd., Tarrytown, New York 10591; Hummel Collectors Club, 1261 University Dr., Yardley, Pennsylvania 19067

KPM

Baer, Winfred. *Berlin Porcelain.* Washington, D.C.: Smithsonian Institution Press, 1980.

Quimper

Mali, Millicent S. *Quimper Faience.* Pennington, New Jersey: Privately printed, 1979.

Taburet, Marjatta. *La Faience de Quimper.* Paris: Sous le vent, 1979 (written in French).

Royal Bayreuth

Raines, Joan and Marvin. *A Guide to Royal Bayreuth Figurals.* New York: Privately printed, 1973.

———. *A Guide to Royal Bayreuth Figurals.* Book 2. New York: Privately printed, 1977.

Salley, Virginia Sutton and George H. *Royal Bayreuth China.* Portland, Maine: Privately printed, 1969.

Royal Copenhagen

Owen, Pat. *The Story of Royal Copenhagen Christmas Plates, 1908–Present.* Dayton: Viking Import House, 1961 (with yearly additions).

Plates from the Royal Copenhagen Porcelain Manufactory. Copenhagen: Royal Copenhagen Porcelain Manufacturers, 1970.

200 Years of Royal Copenhagen Porcelain. Washington, D.C.: Smithsonian Institution Press, 1976.

RS Prussia

Schlegelmilch, Clifford J. *Handbook of Erdmann and Reinhold Schlegelmilch Prussia-Germany and Oscar Schlegelmilch Germany, Porcelain Marks.* Flint, Michigan: Privately printed, 1973.

Sorensen, Don C. *My Collection.* Los Angeles: Privately printed, 1979.

8

Japanese Pottery and Porcelain of the Nineteenth and Twentieth Centuries

Understanding early Japanese porcelains is a lifelong task, but the average collector in America can comfortably handle the problems of collecting and recognizing the porcelain from the nineteenth and twentieth centuries.

Japanese pottery and porcelain creates a particular handicap for the Westerner. Even though the pieces are signed, the signatures are in Japanese characters. If you could read Japanese you would find that the signature often says something like "Made in Kyoto, Japan," or "In the style of . . . ," or it could be an exact copy of an earlier mark on a piece made in a similar style.

The most successful way for a beginning collector to study Japanese porcelains is to concentrate on one of the several major styles such as Satsuma or Imari ware. After a while you will gradually begin to understand the artists' subtleties of style, and the various levels of quality.

Books can help with this study only in a limited way. Some dictionaries of ceramics and encyclopedialike books of porcelains have definitions and pictures. Perseverance is needed! Magazine articles have appeared that attempt to tell about nineteenth-century Japanese wares, especially Satsuma. Some of these articles can create new problems. The terms used in England and the United States have slightly different meanings. In England, the word *Satsuma* means pottery or porcelain made in the Satsuma area. In the United States it usually means a very special type of crackle-glazed ware with an identifiable decoration of flowers, or figures.

There are several types of Satsuma, as the design gradually changed from the early 1800s to the present, but the basic cream-colored clay and crackle glaze remains. There are even pieces of Satsuma that were decorated in the United States by American women. These were made during World War I and for a few years into the 1920s.

Another problem of understanding Japanese ceramics is the difference in thinking between the modern Western ceramicists and the Oriental ceramicists. If a design or glaze or shape was considered beautiful it was often copied by the Oriental artist, line for line, even to the mark. This was considered an accepted practice and not a type of faking. When you find a piece of Oriental porcelain or pottery you must always remember that the writing in the mark does not always indicate the truth; you may have a later, exact copy. The Japanese, Chinese, and Koreans borrowed freely from each other's designs. The Europeans copied the Oriental work and, the Oriental artists made pieces to suit the European taste.

Types of Wares

Note that often the name represents both a geographic area and a porcelain pattern. *The definitions here are those in common usage and may differ from those accepted by scholarly sources.*

Arita

See Imari.

Banko Ware

This term has several meanings in the everyday language of antiques collectors and dealers. Some misuse the term for Korean ware. (Korean ware is the heavy-glazed pottery from Korea. It usually has a thick orange red glaze with three-dimensional figures of people, gods, mountains, etc., as part of the design. This ware is also called Poo ware in some parts of the country.) The most common usage of the term *Banko ware* in printed literature refers to a ceramic made in the middle of the nineteenth century by a potter named Banko Kichibei (1736–1795). He copied the work of several famous Japanese potters of the day. About 1868 another potter took the name Banko. He purchased the seals of the old Banko pottery and began making identical wares. Most familiar are small reddish brown stoneware teapots with decorative, animal-shaped knobs, and pots of the glazed gray clay. True marbleized wares were made in several colors of clay. These pieces often had the Banko mark, a small incised oval with Japanese characters. Other incised or raised decorations were added to the clay by pressing it into a mold or by using a stamp. The knobs of teapots and sugar bowls were trimmed with a touch of gold. Strangely, the knobs were made to turn freely, although there seems no reason for this.

Eggshell Porcelain

The Chinese and Japanese potters sometimes made very thin porcelain wares called eggshell porcelain. They did indeed resemble the shell of an egg because of the thin, fragile appearance.

Hirado Ware

Another of the kilns near Arita (see Imari) made wares for the Prince of Hirado from 1751 to 1843. These unmarked porcelains were blue and white with fine modeling. Ornamental figures and a good quality celadon were also made. Some pieces were marked. The quality was not maintained after 1843.

Imari

"Imari" and "Arita" mean the same thing to the average collector or dealer. Arita is a port in Japan. Porcelain was made there from about 1616. At first pieces were potted by some Korean potters, but many famous Japanese artists worked at the kilns. The first porcelains were made for the Dutch market in the 1658–1750 period. The Dutch suggested an overall brocade design that would be popular throughout Europe. It was a porcelain with a blue underglaze and iron red and gold decoration that has become known as Imari. The design became so popular that it was copied by the Chinese, English, and many European factories. There were several techniques used in making the various types of Imari but they are all called by the same name by the average collector if it has the brocade pattern.

This Imari plate has Prunus trees and scrolls in blue and orange. It was made in the eighteenth century.

Much of the Imari was marked after 1896. Natural cobalt was used for the blue colors before that time. The blue from the natural cobalt oxide is much darker. The Japanese Imari wares degenerated to less finished decoration and uneven colors by the 1868–1900 period.

Kakiemon

There is both Kakiemon porcelain and Kakiemon style, so any definition must explain the differences. The third of the kilns near Arita was that of the Sakaida Kakiemon family. They made a multicolor enamel-decorated porcelain ware with asymmetrical decorations. Red, blue, green blue, and yellow were favored, with some use of gold. Kakiemon porcelains were popular with the European market and in the 1640s the Dutch imported many pieces. By the eighteenth century the popular Kakiemon porcelain patterns were being copied in China and Europe. These pieces are known as Kakiemon style.

The potters at Kakiemon have continued and Kakiemon the 12th, born in 1879, was also a potter.

Korean Ware. See Banko
Kutani

The kilns in the Kutani province worked from about 1639 to the beginning of the 1700s. The porcelains made there are called old Kutani *(Ko Kutani)*. Green Kutani *(Ao Kutani)* is the most famous. The porcelain has a deep green glaze with designs of birds, flowers, and landscapes. Some pieces were entirely covered with green and yellow glaze with no undecorated porcelain showing. Most collectors will find only the porcelains from nineteenth-century Kutani kilns.

The nineteenth-century work at the kilns started about 1824. Revived Kutani *(Sailo Kutani)* was made from that time. A red and gold brocade design was used on some of these wares called red Kutani. Eggshell porcelains were also made. Many of these pieces were marked with the Japanese symbols for "Kutani."

To confuse the collector even more, "Kutani" has been used to describe a number of other nineteeth-century porcelains, earthenwares, and stonewares. These may or may not be marked "Kutani."

Made in Japan

From 1921 to 1940 the porcelains imported from Japan were marked "Made in Japan." Wares resembled the Nippon and pre-Nippon pieces. Noritake was made at this time. In general the porcelains were of mediocre quality with minimal handwork. Luster and gold were used. Many pieces copied the popular European porcelains.

Nabeshima Ware

Kilns were started by the Prince of Nabeshima near the region of Arita in the seventeenth century. The kilns continued into the twentieth century.

Early pieces included celadons, blue and white porcelains, and porcelains with floral enamel decorations on white. The color covered over half the piece. The early pieces were carefuly drawn and colored. Later the overglaze enamels were applied with less care and slightly overlapped the blue underglaze lines.

Nagasaki Ware

In the second half of the nineteenth century a coarse Imari-patterned porcelain was made in the Nagasaki district. It is sometimes called Nagasaki ware although it is merely a special type of Imari.

Nippon

The word *Nippon* is the Japanese word for "Japan" or "the land of the rising sun." The McKinley Tariff Act was passed in the United States in October 1890. It required the country of origin to be marked on wares brought into the United States. The Japanese wares were marked "Nippon." The first of these pieces began appearing in 1891. The law was changed in 1921 so that "Japan" had to be used instead of "Nippon." "Nippon" was continued in use as part of a trade name.

The marks appearing on Nippon are confusing if used to identify anything but the years of manufacture. The marks were used by factories, decorating firms, or exporting or importing agents. Many of the marks are small symbols and English words. Japanese characters were not used because the wares were made specifically for export to the United States and the American customer. Often only one piece in a set of dishes was marked, so there are many unmarked examples of Nippon.

The earliest Nippon wares were made in small quantities by family potters. The pieces were usually hand-decorated. As is often true, the best work was that done earliest in the period. At first Nippon was like the earlier Japanese potteries, similar in design and body shape. The Oriental designs and spacing of flowers were used as often as the European-inspired borders and geometrics. Small raised dots of glaze called jewels, used as the decoration, were popular on the early Nippon pieces. Shapes of plates, cups, vases, and bowls were inspired by the Oriental designs at first but by 1920 were often direct copies of European shapes. Early pieces were made with separate handles and knobs that were attached with slip. Later the handles were part of the mold and articles for table use were made in one piece. The careful hand-applied decorations gradually disappeared and simpler designs or decals were used. Much Nippon was

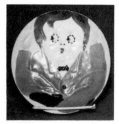

This cartoon figure with the blown-out features is typical of one type of Nippon ware made in the 1930s and 1940s.

Decorations on these Nippon porcelains range from Wild West cowboys to Egyptians on camels to painted flowers. Many of the scenes are European, although the porcelain was made in Japan.

decorated with gold. One type of Nippon featured three-dimensional nuts or fruits molded into the piece and decorated to appear real. Some pieces had *moriaga*, or raised white decorations, some had enamel "jewels." Late examples could resemble Royal Bayreuth of Germany, Pickard of the United States, Royal Doulton of England, Haviland of France, or other porcelains.

Noritake

Porcelain marked "Noritake" was made in Japan after 1904 by Nippon Toki Kaisha, or the Noritake Company Limited. It was a company that manufactured porcelains for export. Dinnerware sets, industrial porcelains such as insulators and spark plugs, and other commercial porcelains were made. Many all-white sets were exported to be decorated in other countries. The factory suffered much damage during World War II but was rebuilt. The firm is still working.

The early Noritake ware had "Nippon" as part of the mark, as required by United States law. The "M" in a wreath or the words "Noritake-Nippon" were most common because the name Noritake does not appear on the wreath mark. (The "M" stands for Morimura, the brothers who opened the New York City office.) Collectors sometimes do not realize that the ware is by the Noritake firm. Other marks include the "RC" (Royal Ceramic) used about 1911, and several later marks, including the name "Noritake" and the words "Made in Japan" or "Occupied Japan." The green "M" in a wreath mark was used until about 1920, then it was red. The "M" in a wreath mark was changed after 1941 to an "N" in the wreath.

Noritake decorations could be naturalistic, stylized, or geometric. There was much hand-painted decoration, but decals, luster, and goldwork were also used. The Azalea pattern was made for the Larkin Soap Company from about 1916 to 1941. Full dinner sets were made and marked with the mark in use at the time.

Occupied Japan

Collectors seem to favor easily dated pieces. The words "Occupied Japan" or "Made in Occupied Japan" were added to porcelains from 1945 to 1952. Pieces could be marked "Japan," "Made in Japan," or "Occupied Japan." Those marks also appeared on metalwork, toys, lacquer, paper, glass, and other items to be exported. Most wares were made after 1948. Collectors will buy anything marked "Occupied Japan" but it is the porcelains that were made in quantity. Most of the marked pieces seem to be figurines made to imitate almost anyone else: Hummel of Germany, Royal Doulton of England, Wedgwood of England, Delft of Holland, French bisque, eighteenth- or nineteenth-century English figurines, Ohio pottery, and almost any other style imaginable. Quality varied from pieces made for the living room to the dime-store novelties of crude detail depicting off-color humor or racial slurs.

Many souvenirs of the United States were made and it is not uncommon to find a plate decorated with Niagara Falls, or a figurine of a cowboy that is marked "Occupied Japan."

Phoenix Bird China

The Phoenix is a mythological bird that was consumed by fire, then rose from the ashes in youthful freshness after nine days. It is a symbol known in many cultures. The Phoenix was popular as a design on blue and white porcelains of the nineteenth and twentieth centuries. Full sets of dishes were made. The dishes were sold in dime stores, gift shops, or given as premiums. Over thirty different potteries in Japan and some in England made this pattern.

Phoenix Bird is sometimes confused with a variation of the pattern, called "flying turkey." The turkey has a tucked-in right wing and elaborate feathers.

These patterns were made as late as the 1940s and after.

Raku

Raku pottery has been continually made from 1580. It has a thick glaze, uneven surface, and is not symmetrical. There is always an unglazed section of the base that shows the clay. The glaze is red or black, green, or cream. It appears very primitive but is much desired in Japan.

Satsuma

Satsuma is another word with several meanings. Pottery was made in the Satsuma province from the beginning of the seventeenth century. Korean potters were brought to Japan to make the pottery. Early pieces were made from brown or reddish brown paste. Glazes were dark and the decorations simple. The crackle-glazed cream-colored ware we call Satsuma today was made for export to Europe about 1825. The ware was decorated with very detailed drawings of flowers and trees, and later pieces included people. The first designs were floral designs spaced in the

Japanese manner, asymmetrical with much open space. No human figure appeared on the early pieces. By the middle of the nineteenth century pieces had overall patterns, diapering, or elaborate designs of birds, flowers, landscapes, mythical animals, or human figures. The designs became more and more elaborate.

Cobalt blue was used in the first half of the 1880s. Decorations were crowded. Dragons, plants, animals, and people were added in the raised design. By 1905 colors had become darker and gold was used. The "thousand face" pattern appeared about 1880. This was an overall design of faces. As the century progressed the faces became fewer and larger while the backgrounds became darker. The "immortals" were shown on some

Japanese figures appear on this late nineteenth-century Satsuma teapot.

Characteristic Japanese figures and overall geometric designs with gold trim decorate this 9½-inch-high vase, which collectors would call Satsuma.

pieces as a group of men with halos. By the end of the nineteenth century the design became very dark and the "glowing immortals" had a sinister appearance. About 1915 raised white slip was used to make three-dimensional lines that resembled toothpaste. A dark brown background was used in the 1920s, while a slightly redder brown background was popular during the 1930s.

Many of the scholarly experts consider the nineteenth- and twentieth-century pieces to be erroneously called Satsuma. Whatever the technical definition is, it is true that a collector going to a shop will find a variety of wares from the light cream crackle glaze to the dark-glazed pieces with crude designs, all called Satsuma.

To add to the confusion the wares were made in these patterns through the nineteenth and twentieth centuries by many artists and many factories and not just at the original Satsuma kilns. The word *Satsuma* appears in English on some of the later wares that should probably be classified as Nippon.

TERMINOLOGY

Lithophane: A translucent panel of porcelain molded so that a design appears when the panel is held to the light. It was made first in Paris in 1827; a few are still being made. Japanese lithophanes were popular in the late nineteenth century. Usually the base of a cup was a lithophane that showed a young woman when the empty cup was held to the light.

Blown-out: A design in which parts of the pattern are molded in three dimensions; for example, raised nuts on a flat dish. Nippon was often made in this way.

Japanese Coralene: Glass beading applied to a pottery piece as part of the decoration. Patented in 1909.

Moriaga (also spelled Moriye, Moriya, Moriage): Japanese pottery with a raised overglaze decoration. It looks like squeezed toothpaste has been applied to the piece. The word *moriaga* means "squeezed." This style of decoration was popular from about 1870 to 1900.

BIBLIOGRAPHY

Andacht, Sandra. *Satsuma: An Illustrated Guide.* Des Moines: Wallace-Homestead, 1978.

Chandler, Ceil. *Made in Occupied Japan.* Texas: Chandler's Discriminating Junk. (Paper reprint New York: Crown, 1976.)

Cox, Warren E. *The Book of Pottery and Porcelain.* New York: Crown, 1949.

Florence, Gene. *Collector's Encyclopedia of Occupied Japan Collectibles.* Paducah, Kentucky: Collector Books, 1976.

Joseph, Marie A. *Occupied Japan Collectibles.* Whitesboro, New York: Privately printed, 1972.

Klamkin, Marian. *Made in Occupied Japan: A Collector's Guide.* New York: Crown, 1976.

Lima, Paul and Cindy. *The Enchantment of Hand Painted Nippon Porcelain.* Silverado, California: Silverado Studios, 1971.

Loendorf, Gene. *Nippon Hand Painted China.* Valley City, North Dakota: Privately printed, 1975.

Melvin, James and Florence and Bourdeau, Rodney and Wilma. *Noritake Azalea China.* 1980 ed. Danbury, Connecticut: Privately printed, 1980.

Meyer, Florence. *The Colorful World of Nippon.* Des Moines: Wallace-Homestead, 1971.

Robinson, Dorothy. *Nippon Hand Painted China.* New York: Crown, 1973.

Sato, Masahiko. *Arts of Japan 2: Kyoto Ceramics.* New York: John Weatherhill, 1973.

Stitt, Irene. *Japanese Ceramics of the Last 100 Years.* New York: Crown, 1974.

Clubs: Nippon Club, 23 Roberta Lane, Syosset, New York 11791; Occupied Japan Club, 18309 Faysmith Ave., Torrance, California 90504; Phoenix Bird Collectors of America, 18608 Chelton Dr., Birmingham, Michigan 48009

Publication: Orientalia Journal, P.O. Box 94, Little Neck, New York 10363

9

Jewelry and Metalwork after 1880

The jewelry of the Art Nouveau and Art Deco periods has a characteristic "look." Once seen, the designs are easily remembered. Pieces made in the United States and Europe are very similar, as the designers borrowed freely from one another. The very stylized flowers of the silver jewelry of Georg Jensen of Denmark, the ladies with flowing hair of the Art Nouveau pieces from France, the Byzantine look of the English wares, were all copied. The only country to make a slightly different style of work was Russia. The designs there were influenced by the factory of Peter Carl Fabergé. He directed a staff of goldsmiths and silversmiths who made Russian-style jewelry and decorative objects in an opulent style. The famed Fabergé Easter eggs are considered the high point of this work. The quality of any piece of Russian silverwork or goldwork is evident to the average collector with little knowledge. For the average collector the chances of finding a piece of Fabergé is remote. The mark on the piece adds so much to the value that it is prudent to memorize the Cyrillic letters ФАБЕРЖЕ just in case. For any other Russian marks, see the books listed in the Bibliography.

Boucheron of Paris made this silver and gold compact mounted with enamel and jewels about 1940.

Art Nouveau designs were popular from 1880 to about 1910. During the years they were popular, metalwork was made in this style by only a small group of craftsmen. In the United States most silver and pewter was made in the accepted Victorian shapes. Pewter was not a popular metal; it was silverplated Britannia ware that had most of the market. At the turn of the century, from about 1900 to 1910, the Arts and Crafts movement influenced the designs of the metalworkers. Of special interest at that time was copper, hammered and designed to represent the handcrafted look of the movement.

Jules Brateau made pewter of this type in France. This plate, marked on the face, was made about 1900.

Smoking accessories were popular in the Art Deco period. These ashtrays, made of gold, enamel, and real minerals like nephrite and agate, were sold by Cartier of Paris in the 1930s.

The following tables list the maker, date, country, mark, and medium used by metalworkers and jewelry designers of the 1880–1930 period. Those included in the list put a name on the piece, although sometimes the name is that of a store or a designer. Silver, copper, and jewelry were often made by the same designers and firms.

The bronze figurine makers are not included. For information on these, see the series of books *Bronzes, Sculptors & Founders* by Harold Berman, Abage/Publishers, Chicago, Illinois. Not all American companies are included in the table, only important ones working in these styles. For other silvermakers' marks see the *Encyclopedia of American Silver Manufacturers* by Dorothy Rainwater, Crown, New York, 1975.

Parentheses enclose the birth and death dates of the artist. Other dates given are approximate working dates of the factory or artist. Name in parentheses are other workers or designers connected with the factory. No more than one mark is used for each listing although the makers often used a variety of marks.

METALWORKERS AND JEWELRY DESIGNERS, 1880–1930
Austria

Workshops, Artists, & Locations	Dates	Artists' Factories & Related Information	
Czescha, Carl Otto (Czeschka) Vienna	(1878–1960)	Metalwork, furniture (Wiener Werkstätte)	
Gringold, Emil	c. 1900	Jewelry	

Workshops, Artists, & Locations	Dates	Artists' Factories & Related Information
Hagenauer Werkstätte Vienna	1898–1956	Metalwork (Carl Hagenauer [1872–1928], Karl Hagenauer [1898–1956], Otto Prutscher, Josef Hoffmann
Hauptmann, Franz	c. 1900	Jewelry
Hoffmann, Josef Vienna	(1870–1956)	Jewelry, metalwork designer (Wiener Werkstätte)
Hofstetter, Josef	c. 1900	Jewelry
Hossfeld, Josef Vienna	1900–1930s	Silver (Wiener Werkstätte)
Kallert, Karl Vienna	1900–1930s	Silver (Wiener Werkstätte)
Koch, Konrad Vienna	1900–1930s	Metalwork (Wiener Werkstätte)
Krupp, Arthur Vienna	1900–1930s	Silver
Kurzer & Wolf Vienna	1900–1930s	Jewelry, silver
Lightblau, Ernst Vienna	c. 1920	Silver (Wiener Werkstätte)
Likarz, Maria Vienna	(1893–)	Jewelry, metalwork (Wiener Werkstätte)
Mesner, F.	c. 1900	Jewelry
Moser, Koloman Vienna	(1868–1918)	Jewelry, glass, metalwork (Wiener Werkstätte)
Pêche, Dagobert Vienna	(1887–1923)	Metalwork (Wiener Werkstätte)
Pflaumer, Eugen Vienna	1900–1930s	Jewelry (Wiener Werkstätte)

Workshops, Artists, & Locations	Dates	Artists' Factories & Related Information	
Pollak, J. Vienna	c. 1920	Silver (Wiener Werkstätte)	
Prutscher, Otto Vienna	(1880–1961)	Jewelry (Wiener Werkstätte)	
Roset & Fischmeister	c. 1900	Jewelry	
Scheidt, Georg Adam Vienna	c. 1900	Jewelry, silver	G·A·S·
Schonthoner, V.	c. 1900	Jewelry	
Unger, Elsa	c. 1900	Jewelry	
Veit, Frederich Vienna	c. 1930	Silver	
Wagner, Anna	c. 1900	Jewelry	
Wiener Werkstätte Vienna	1903–1932	Metalwork, jewelry, ceramic, furniture (C. O. Czescha, J. Hoffmann, J. Hossfeld, K. Kallert, K. Koch, M. Likarz, K. Moser, O. Prutscher, E. Wimmer, J. Zimpel)	WIENER WERK STÄTTE WW
Wimmer, Eduard Josef Vienna	(1882–1961)	Designer (Wiener Werkstätte)	
Zimpel, Julius Vienna	(1896–1925)	Metalwork, jewelry (Wiener Werkstätte)	

France

Workshops, Artists, & Locations	Dates	Artists' Factories & Related Information	
Aucoc, Andre Paris	1821–c. 1900	Gold, silver, jewelry (R. Lalique, L. Aucoc)	
Bablet, Paul Paris	(1889–)	Jewelry	
Bapst & Falize	1871–1892	Jewelry, gold, silver	B + F
Belperron, Suzanne Paris	c. 1920–1930	Jewelry	

Workshops, Artists, & Locations	Dates	Artists' Factories & Related Information
Bigot, Alexandre Paris	(1862–1927)	Metalwork, ceramic
Boin-Taburet	c. 1925	Silver
Boucheron Paris, Biarritz, London, New York	1858–present	Jewelry (F. Boucheron [1830–1902], O. Loeuillard, L. Rault, J. Debut, J. Brateau, L. Hirtz)
Brandt, Edgar Paris	(1880–) 1900–1930	Metalwork, brass, iron, copper
Brateau, Jules	c. 1900	Pewter (Boucheron)
Cardeilhac Paris	1802–1951	Silver (Vital-Antoine Cardeilhac, Ernest Cardeilhac, Edward Cardeilhac)
Cartier Paris, London, New York	1869–present	Jewelry (L. F. Cartier, A. Cartier, L. Cartier, P. Cartier, J. Cartier)
Chaumet, Joseph Paris	(1854–1928)	Jewelry
Christofle, L'Orfevrerie St. Denis	1839–present	Silver, silverplate (Charles Christofle, Henry Bouilhet, E. Reiber, J. M. Olbrich)
de Ribaucort, Georges	(1887–1907)	Jewelry
Desbois, Jules	c. 1900	Jewelry
Despres, Jean	c. 1920	Silver
Editeur, F. V.	c. 1900	Jewelry
Epinay de Briort, Prosper	(1836–)	Jewelry, sculpture
Falguieres, G. Paris	c, 1900	Jewelry

Workshops, Artists, & Locations	Dates	Artists' Factories & Related Information	
Falize, André Paris	c. 1900	Jewelry	
Feuillatre, Eugene Paris	(1870–1916)	Silver, jewelry, enamel, sculpture (R. Lalique)	FEUILLATRE
Fonesque & Olive Paris	c. 1900	Jewelry	F·O
Fontana et Cie Paris	1840–1930s	Gold, jewelry (J. Fontana, A. Templier, C. Fontana, P. Fontana)	
Fontenay, Eugene Paris	(1823–1887)	Jewelry	
Fouquet, Alphonse Paris	(1828–1911)	Jewelry	
Fouquet, Georges Paris	(1862–1957) 1891–	Jewelry	G. FOUQUET
Fouquet, Jean Paris	(1899–)	Jewelry	
Froment-Meurice, Emile Paris	(1837–1913)	Gold, jewelry	FROMENT MEURICE
Gaillard, Ernest Paris	(1836–)	Silver	
Gaillard, Lucien Paris	(1861–1910)	Silver, jewelry	L Gaillard
Gautrait, L. Paris	c. 1900	Jewelry	L GAUTRAI
Georges-Jean, Les Les Essarts– Le-Roy	c. 1900	Copper, enamel	Georges-Jean LES ESSARTS LE ROY S. et O.
Grasset, Eugene Paris (Maison Vever)	(1841–1917)	Jewelry	
Hirne Paris	1880–1900	Jewelry (AF Thesmar)	Hirnè.

Workshops, Artists, & Locations	Dates	Artists' Factories & Related Information
LaCloche Paris	1897–	Jewelry, enamel (Fernand LaCloche, Jules LaCloche, Leopold LaCloche, Jacques LaCloche)
R. LALIQUE Lalique, René Paris	(1860–1945)	Jewelry, silver, glass
Liard Paris	c. 1902	Silver, jewelry
Lienard, Paul Paris	c. 1905	Jewelry
La Maison Moderne Paris	c. 1889	Jewelry (Meier-Graefe)
Margeant, E.	c. 1900	Jewelry
Mucha, Alphonse Maria Paris	(1860–1939)	Silver, jewelry
Plissen & Hartz Paris	c. 1905	Jewelry
Poillerat, Gilbert	1920s	Lamps, ironwork
Puiforcat, Jean Paris	(1897–1945)	Silver
Robin, Maurice & Cie Paris	1900–1930s	Jewelry, silver
Saint-Yves Paris	c. 1910	Jewelry
Sandoz, Gerard	c. 1925–1930	Silver
Soyer Fils Paris	c. 1900	Silver, enamel
Templier, Raymond	c. 1930	Jewelry
Tetard, Frères	c. 1920	Silver
Thesmar, André-Fernand Paris	(1843–1912)	Jewelry, enamel, metalwork

Workshops, Artists, & Locations	Dates	Artists' Factories & Related Information
Van Cleef & Arpels Paris	1959–present	Jewelry
Vever, Ernest Metz, Paris (Maison Vever)	1848–	Jewelry
Vever, Henri Paris (Maison Vever)	(1854-1942)	Jewelry
Vever, Paul Paris (Maison Vever)	(1851–1915)	Jewelry (E. Grasset)
Zorra, L. Paris	c. 1900	Jewelry

VEVER PARIS

Germany

Baack, Siegmund Hamburg, Berlin	c. 1895	Silver, gold, jewelry
FTB Berlin	c. 1900	Pewter

F.T.B.

This German silvered pewter tea and coffee set was made in Cologne about 1900. It is marked "Kayserzinn."

186

Workshops, Artists, & Locations	Dates	Artists' Factories & Related Information
Behrens, Peter Munich	(1868–1940)	Metalwork
Edelzinn. See Hueck. Eduard.		
Fahrner, Theodor Pforzheim	(1868–1928)	Silver, jewelry
J. Friedmann's Nachfolger (D&M Lowenthal) Frankfurt-am-Main	c. 1900	Jewelry, silver (M. Christiansen)
Gross, Karl Munich	(1869–)	Jewelry, pewter, silver designer
Hueck, Eduard Lüdenscheid, Westphalia	1864–	Pewter (Richard Hueck, Peter Behrens, Albin Muller, Josef Olbrich)
J. P. Kayser Sohn Krefeld-Bochum	1885–c. 1910	Pewter (H. Leven, Otto Schulze)
Kayserzinn. See J. P. Kayser Sohn.		
Koch, Robert	c. 1900	Jewelry
Leonhardt & Fiegel Berlin	c. 1900	Silver
Lettre, Emil Berlin	(1876–1954)	Jewelry, silver
Mory, Ludwig Munich	1883–	Pewter (Rudolf Hoffmann, Fritz Mory)
Muller, Albin Darmstadt	(1871–1941)	Pewter (Eduard Hueck)
Nürnberger Metall-und- Lackierwarrenfabrik Nürnberg	1895–1934	Pewter, tin toys (C. Bing)

Workshops, Artists, & Locations	Dates	Artists' Factories & Related Information	
Olbrich, Josef Maria Darmstadt	(1867–1908)	Designer of pewter (Eduard Hueck), silverplate (C. Schroeder), silver (Christofle), jewelry (D&M Loewenthal, Theodor Fahrner)	
Orion Nürnberg	c. 1890	Pewter	Orion 213
Orivit. See Schmitz, F. H. Osiris. See Walter Scherf & Co.			
Pauser, Joseph Bremen	c. 1900	Silver (Henry Van de Velde)	J.P.
Riemerschmid, Richard Munich, Nürnberg	(1868–1957)	Designer, silver, ceramic	
Rückert, M. J. Mainz	c. 1900	Silver, flatware (Peter Behrens)	RÜCKERT
Walter Scherf & Co. Nürnberg	c. 1901	Pewter (F. Adler)	OSIRIS
Schmitz, Ferdinand Hubert (Rheinisch Bronze-geisserei) Köln-Ehrenfeld	1901–	Pewter, silver	ORIVIT
Schroeder, C. B. Düsseldorf	c. 1900	Silver, flatware (Josef Olbrich)	CBS 90
Strobl, A. Munich	c. 1900	(E. Wollenweber)	
Sy & Wagner Berlin	Wagner (1826–) Sy (1827–1881)	Gold, silver, silverplate, flatware and tableware (Emil Wagner, Francois Sy)	SY & WAGNER.
Thiede, Oskar	c. 1900	Silver	

Workshops, Artists, & Locations	Dates	Artists' Factories & Related Information
Treskow, Elizabeth Cologne	c. 1900	Silver
Vereinigte Werkstätten Munich	c. 1900	Jewelry (Peter Behrens, Richard Riemerschmid)
Vogt, A. Pforzheim	c. 1902	Jewelry, metalwork (H. Christiansen)
Von Cranach, Wilhelm Lucas Berlin	(1861–1918)	Gold, jewelry
Von Mayrhofer, Adolf	c. 1920	Silver
Wagenfeld, Wilhelm Bremen, Berlin	(1900–) c. 1930–	Designer, chromium-plated metal, copper, glass
Wende, Theodor Darmstadt	c. 1900	Silver
Werner, Louis	c. 1900	Jewelry
Werner, O. M. Berlin	c. 1900	Jewelry (J. H. Werner)
M. H. Wilkens & Sohne Bremen, Berlin	c. 1900	Silver, jewelry (H. Vogeler, Martin Heinrich Wilkens)
Eduard D. Wollenweber Munich	c. 1900	Silver, jewelry
Württembergische Metallwarenfabrik Geislingen	1853–present	Pewter, silverplate, glass, Ikora metal (Wilhelm Wagenfeld)

Great Britain

Adam, Francis	(1878–1961)	Wrought iron, jewelry
Adams, Robert London	(1917–present)	Jewelry
Adie Brothers Birmingham	1879–	Silver, silverplate (Percy Adie, Tony Adie)

Workshops, Artists, & Locations	Dates	Artists' Factories & Related Information	
Aitken, William Birmingham	c. 1905	Arts and crafts	
Allen, Kate	c. 1900	Jewelry	
Antrobus, Philip, Ltd. London	1810–	Jewelry	
Artificers' Guild London	1901–1942	Silver, copper, metalwork (Nelson Dawson, Montague Fordham, Edward Spencer, John Paul Cooper)	
Ashbee, Charles Robert London	(1863–1942)	Silver, jewelry, furniture	
Asprey & Company, Ltd. London	1781–present	Jewelry	
Attenborough, Richard London	c. 1850–1862	Gold, silver, jewelry	
Baker, Oliver	c. 1900	Jewelry	
Benham & Froud London	c. 1900	Copper (Christopher Dresser, designer)	
Benson, J. W. London	1874–present	Jewelry	

The London Guild of Handicraft made furniture, books, jewelry, and other decorative pieces in the Art Deco style. This 1901 silver dish was made by Charles Robert Ashbee.

Workshops, Artists, & Locations	Dates	Artists' Factories & Related Information
Benson, William Smith London	(1854–1924)	Metalwork, Art Nouveau–style lamps of brass, copper, silver plate (designed wallpaper, furniture, etc., for Morris & Co.)
Birmingham Guild of Handicraft Birmingham	1890–present	Metalwork, jewelry, silver (Arthur Dixon, Montague Fordham, Claude Napier Clavering, E. R. Gittin)
Blackband, William Thomas Birmingham	(1885–1949)	Jewelry
Boyton, Charles & Son London	c. 1900–1940	Silver
Bragg, T. and J. Birmingham	1844–	Gold, jewelry, enamels (Thomas Perry Bragg, Thomas Bragg, John Bragg)
Brogden, John	1842–1885	Gold, jewelry (Watherston & Brogden, 1842–1864) (Brogden & Garland, 1826–1835)(Garland & Watherston, 1835–1841)
Bromsgrove Guild of Applied Art	1890–	Walter Gilbert, Arthur Gaskin, Georgina Gaskin, Joseph Hodel
Burges, William	(1827–1881)	Jeweler, architect, designer
Carr, Alwyn C.E. London	(1872–1940)	Silver, wrought iron (Ramsden & Carr, 1898–1918)
Century Guild	1881–1888	Society of workers. Metalwork, textiles, furniture (Arthur H. Mackmurdo, Herbert Horne); copper, brass, pewter (George Esling, Kellock Brown, Frederick Shields, Clement Heaton, S. Image)
Child & Child London	1880–1916	Jewelry, enamels
Comyns, William & Sons London	1848–present	Silver

Workshops, Artists, & Locations	Dates	Artists' Factories & Related Information	
Connell	c. 1890–1910	Silver (William Connell, d. 1902; George Connell)	
Cooper, John Paul Westerham	(1869–1933)	Silver, copper, jewelry	
Courthope, Frederick	1880–1930s	Silver	
Cuzner, Bernard Birmingham, London	(1877–1956)	Silver, jewelry (Liberty & Co., Birmingham Guild of Handicraft)	
Cymric. See Liberty & Co., Haseler, W. H., & Co.			
Dawson, Edith Robinson London	c. 1900	Jewelry, enamel	
Dawson, Nelson London	(1859–1942)	Jewelry, silver, metalwork, enamel (Artificers' Guild)	
Dixon, James & Sons Sheffield	1806–present	Silver, silverplate, Britannia metal (Christopher Dresser)	
Dresser, Christopher	(1834–1904)	Designed for many companies	
Elkington & Co. Birmingham	1824–present	Silver, silverplate, metalwork, enamel (Jean Puiforcet, C. Dresser)	
Emanuel, Harry London	1860–	Gold, jewelry	
Evers-Swindell, Nora	c. 1900	Jewelry	
Fisher, Alexander London	(1864–1936)	Silver, jewelry, enamel	
Fisher, Kay	(1893–)	Jewelry, silver	
Garrard R. and S. London	1802–1952	Silver, gold, jewelry (Robert Garrard, James Garrard, Sebastien Garrard)	

	Workshops, Artists, & Locations	Dates	Artists' Factories & Related Information
AJG	Gaskin, Arthur Joseph Birmingham	(1862–1928)	Metalwork, jewelry (Liberty & Co.)
G	Gill, Eric	(1882–1940)	Silver, engraver
CG	Giuliano, Carlo London	c. 1860–1895 (d. 1895)	Jewelry
	Gleadowe, R.M.Y.	c. 1930	Silver
G&SC L!	Goldsmiths' & Silversmiths' Co. London	1890–1952	Silver, jewelry (William Gibson, Harold Stabler)
G HL'D	Guild of Handicraft London	1888–1907	Silver, jewelry, furniture, leather, books (Charles Robert Ashbee, L. F. Day)
	Hancocks & Co. London	1898–present	Jewelry
J.H&C	Hardman, John & Co. Birmingham	1838–	Ecclesiastical silver, jewelry
	Harris, Kate	c. 1890–1910	Silver (W. Hunter & Sons)
	Hart, George London, Chipping Campden	(1882–)	Jewelry, silver (Guild of Handicraft)
	Haseler, W. H. & Co. Birmingham	1870–1927	Silver, jewelry, Cymric silver, Tudric pewter (Liberty & Co.)
W·H·H	Heaton, Clement (Heaton's Cloisonne Mosaics, Ltd.) England Switzerland United States	(1861–1940) 1890s 1912–1940	Jewelry, stained glass, enamels (Century Guild)
RGH	Hennell Limited (R. G. Hennel & Sons) (Hennel, Frazer & Haws) London	1735–present 1839	Jewelry

Workshops, Artists, & Locations	Dates	Artists' Factories & Related Information	
Hodgkinson, Winifred	c. 1900	Jewelry	
Horne, Herbert Percy	(1864–1916)	Metalwork, wallpaper, textiles (Century Guild)	
Horner, Charles Halifax	1885–present	Mass produces enameled silver, jewelry	C.H.
Hukin & Heath Birmingham	1879–1953	Silver, silverplate (C. Dresser, A. Harvey)	JWH JTH
Hunt & Roskell London	1840–1939	Silver, silverplate, jewelry (Mortimer & Hurst, John Mortimer, Samuel Hurst, Alfred Benson, Henry Webb, E. Cotterill, G. A. Carter, A. Brown, A. J. Barrett, E. H. Baily)	IM ISM
Hutton, William & Sons Birmingham	1800–1920s	Silver, silverplate, pewter, copper (Hutton & Houghton, 1818–1820, T. Swaffield Brown, K. Harris)	
Instone, Bernard Birmingham	c. 1928	Silver	

Silver decorations were added to this copper pitcher made by Gorham about 1885.

"Martelé" was a trademark used by the Gorham Company. This 19-inch-high vase was made in 1899.

Liberty and Company of Birmingham, England, made a variety of silver and pewter tablewares, jewelry, and other objects in the Arts and Crafts style. **Front row,** *a Cymric silver and enamel coronation spoon made in 1901.* **Back row, left to right:** *Arts and Crafts candlesticks by F.A.E. Jones, Ltd. of Birmingham, made in 1904; a pair of bud vases made by Elkington and Company of Birmingham in 1906; a silver and enamel coaster marked "Cymric," made by Liberty and Company in 1905.*

	Workshops, Artists, & Locations	Dates	Artists' Factories & Related Information
(A.E.J.)	Jones, Albert Edward Birmingham	c. 1904	Silver, jewelry (Liberty & Co.)
K S I A	Keswick School of Industrial Art Keswick	1884–1899	Jewelry, silver, copper
	King, Jessie M. Glasgow, Scotland	(1876–1949)	(Designer, Liberty & Co.)
L & C	Liberty & Co. London	1875–present	Silver, pewter, furniture, ceramic, fabrics, etc. (W. H. Haseler & Co., Bernard Cuzner, Albert Jones. Arthur Gaskin, A. Knox), used marks: Tudric, Cymric
	McBean, Isabel	c. 1900	Jewelry
	MacDonald, Frances Glasgow, Scotland	(1874–1921)	Metalwork, jewelry

Workshops, Artists, & Locations	Dates	Artists' Factories & Related Information	
Mackintosh, Charles Rennie Glasgow, Scotland	(1868–1928)	Furniture, architecture, silver, jewelry	
MacKintosh, Margaret MacDonald Glasgow, Scotland	(1865–1933)	Metalwork, jewelry	MARGARET ACDONALD ACKINTOSH
Mackmurdo, Arthur Heygate	(1851–1942)	Metalwork, furniture, wallpaper	M
McNair, J. Herbert Scotland	(1868–1955)	C. R. Mackintosh	
Marks, Gilbert Leigh Croyden, Surrey	1878–1902 (1861–1905)	Silver, metalwork, pewter, copper (G. Frampton)	GM
Martineau, Sarah Madeleine Liverpool, Cambridge	(1872–)	Silver, jewelry	
Latino Movio assistant to Marks	c. 1902		
Morris, May	(1862–1938)	Jewelry (Women's Guild of Arts)	
Murphy, Harry G. London	(1884–1939)	Jewelry, silver (Henry Wilson, Emile Lettre)	
Murrle, Bennett & Co. London	1884–1915	Jewelry	MBo

This pewter biscuit box is marked "Tudric." It was made by Liberty and Company after 1903.

Newman, Mrs. Philip London	c. 1870–1910	Jewelry (John Brogden)	Mrs. N
Partridge, Fred T.	c. 1900–1908	Jewelry, metalwork (Guild of Handicraft)	PARTRIDGE

	Workshops, Artists, & Locations	Dates	Artists' Factories & Related Information
J.P.	Pearson, John Cornwall	c. 1900	Silver, metalwork, copper (Guild of Handicraft)
	Phillips, Robert London	(–1881)	Jewelry (Carlo Giuliano, Carlo Doria)
	Pickett, Edith	c. 1900	Jewelry
H.P.&CO.	Powell, John Hardman London	(1827–1895)	Jewelry, enamel
CARR·OMAR MADE ME 1898 RAMSDEN & AUTH	Ramsden & Carr London	1898–1919	Jewelry, silver
OMAR RAMSDEN ME FECIT	Ramsden, Omar London	(1878–1939)	Jewelry, silver
	Rathbone, Richard Llewellyn Benson Liverpool, London	(1864–1939)	Copper, silver, jewelry
W.B.R	Reynolds, William Bainbridge London	(1855–1935)	Silver
	Robinson, Fred J.	c. 1900	Jewelry
GES	Sedding, George Elton London	(1882–1915)	Jewelry, silver, copper
	Silver, Rex London	(1879–1965)	Pewter, silver (Liberty & Co.)
	Simpson, Edgar London	c. 1896–1910	Jewelry, silver, metalwork
	Sparrow, Sidney James London	c. 1906	Silver
EDWARD SPENCER DEL	Spencer, Edward London	(1872–1938)	Metalwork (Artificers' Guild)
HS	Stabler, Harold Keswick, London	(1872–1945)	Jewelry, metalwork, silver, (Goldsmiths' & Silversmiths' Co., Wakely & Wheeler; Keswick School of Industrial Art)

The English silversmiths Ramsden and Carr made all sorts of tablewares and jewelry. These silver and enamel pendants with chains were made in 1905.

Starkie Gardner & Co. London	c. 1900–1940	Silver, metalwork, wrought iron	**SG**
Stone, Robert E. London	(1903–)	Silver, jewelry	
Talbot, J. M.	c. 1900	Jewelry	
Traiguair, Phoebe	c. 1900	Silver	
Tudric. See Liberty & Co., Haseler, W. H. & Co.			
Verzay, David	c. 1900	Jewelry	
Wilson, Henry J. London	(1864–1934)	Metalwork, jewelry (Art Workers' Guild)	HW

United States

Alvin Corp. Providence, Rhode Island	1928–present	Silver	ALVIN MFG. CO.
Batchelder, Ernest California	(1875–1957)	Copper, ceramics	

Workshops, Artists, & Locations	Dates	Artists' Factories & Related Information
Bailey, Banks & Biddle Philadelphia, Pennsylvania	1832–present	Jewelry
Bellis, John O. California	–c. 1910	Silver
Berry, Albert Seattle, Washington	1918–1972	Copper, brass, fossilized ivory mounts
Benedict Mfg. Co. Syracuse, New York	1900–1930s	Copper, silverplate
Black, Starr & Frost New York, New York	1876–1929, 1962–	Jewelry, Black, Starr, Frost-Gorham, Inc. 1929–1940; Black, Starr & Gorham, 1940–1962
Blackington, R. & Co. North Attleboro, Massachusetts	1862–present	Jewelry, silver (W. Ballou, R. Blackington)
Bradley & Hubbard Meriden, Connecticut	c. 1895–1930	Brass, lamps
Buffalo Arts & Crafts Shop Buffalo, New York	1900–1915	Copper, silver, metalwork
Caldwell, J. E. & Co. Philadelphia, Pennsylvania	1848–1919	Jewelry, silver
Carence Crafters Chicago, Illinois		Silver, jewelry, copper, brass, pewter
Chicago Arts & Crafts Society Chicago, Illinois	c. 1898	Copper, silver, brass
Clewell, Charles Canton, Ohio	c. 1899–1955	Copper, bronze, pottery
Colonna, Edward Newark, New Jersey Dayton, Ohio Paris, France	(1862–)	(S. Bing, Associated Artists)

BENEDICT

R ⟨→B⟩ Co

J. E. C. & CO.

Workshops, Artists, & Locations	Dates	Artists' Factories & Related Information	
Copeland, Elizabeth Boston, Massachusetts Detroit, Michigan	c. 1916	Silver	
Copper Craftsman Studios Laguna Beach, California	c. 1920	Copper	
Craftsman Workshop Syracuse, New York	c. 1900–1915	Copper (Gustav Stickley)	
D'Arcy Gaw San Francisco, California	c. 1910	Copper (Dirk Van Erp)	
Dixon, Harry San Francisco, California	(1890–1967)	Copper (Dirk Van Erp)	
Dominick & Haff Newark, New Jersey New York, New York	1872–1889	Silver, jewelry	**D. & H.**
Donaldson, Douglas California	(1882–1972)	Silver, jewelry	**D D**
Durgin, William B. Co. (Gorham) Providence, Rhode Island Concord, New Hampshire	1853–present	Silver	
Eaton, C. F. Santa Barbara, California	1900–1930s	Copper	
Fish, E.T.C. Tioga, Pennsylvania	1900–1930s	Copper	
Foster, Theodore W. & Brother Co. Providence, Rhode Island	1873–1951	Jewelry, silver	**F. & B.**
Friedel, Clemens Pasadena, California	(1872–1963)	Silver	

Workshops, Artists, & Locations	Dates	Artists' Factories & Related Information
 Gebelein, George Boston, Massachusetts	(1878–1945)	Silver
Germer, George E. New York, New York Boston, Massachusetts Providence, Rhode Island	(1868–1936)	Jewelry, silver
Glessner, Frances M. Chicago, Illinois	(1848–1922)	Silver
Gorham Corp. Providence, Rhode Island	1865–present	Silver, silverplate, bronze, metalwork, jewelry, copper, gold
Heintz Art Metal Shop Buffalo, New York	c. 1906–1935	Silverplate, copper, brass (Heintz Bros. Mfg.)
Jaccard Jewelry Co. St. Louis, Missouri	1829–present	Jewelry
Jarvie, Robert R. Chicago, Illinois	(1865–1940)	Silver, metalwork, copper
Jennings Brothers Mfg. Co.		Bronze, glass, copper
Kalo Shop Chicago, Illinois	1900–1970	Silver, copper, jewelry (Clara Barck Welles)

The Kalo Shop of Chicago, Illinois, made this tea and coffee set about 1925.

Workshops, Artists, & Locations	Dates	Artists' Factories & Related Information	
Kerr, William B. & Co. Newark, New Jersey	1855–1906	Silver, jewelry	
Kipp, Karl East Aurora, New York	1912–1915	Copper (Roycroft, Toukay Shop)	
Kirk, Arthur Nevill Detroit, Michigan	(1881–1958)	Jewelry, silver	
Kirk, Samuel Baltimore, Maryland	1815–present	Silver	S. KIRK & SON
Koehler, Florence Chicago, Illinois	(1861–1944)	Jewelry (Chicago Arts & Crafts Society)	
Kopper Kraft Shop Silver Crest, New York	1920s(?)	Copper	
Marcus & Co. New York, New York	c. 1900	Jewelry, copper, silver	
Marshall Field & Co. Chicago, Illinois	c. 1904–1950	Jewelry, silver, brass, bronze	MADE IN OUR CRAFT SHOP MARSHALL FIELD & CO.
Mauser Mfg. Co. New York, New York	1890–1903	Silver	M
Oakes, Edward Everet Boston, Massachusetts Detroit, Michigan		Jewelry, silver	
Old Mission Kopper Craft San Francisco, California	c. 1910	Copper	
Raymond Averill Porter	c. 1912	Copper	
Potter Studio Cleveland, Ohio	c. 1899– c. 1927	Brass, copper, jewelry, silver (Potter & Bentley, c. 1927–1929) (Potter & Mellen, 1929–present)	
Preston, Jessie Chicago, Illinois	c. 1900–1918	Jewelry, metalwork, silver	
Reed & Barton Taunton, Massachusetts	1890–present	Silver, silverplate, jewelry	Trade Mark R Sterling
Roycroft East Aurora, New York	1895–1938	Copper, lamps, furniture (D. Hunter, E. Hubbard, K. Kipp, Leon Varney)	

	Workshops, Artists, & Locations	Dates	Artists' Factories & Related Information
	Shiebler, George & Co. New York, New York	c. 1890	Silver
	Shreve & Co. San Francisco, California	1852–present	Jewelry, silver (George C. Shreve, S. S. Shreve)
	Smith Metal Arts Co. Buffalo, New York	c. 1920	Silver, copper; marked silvercrest
	Spaulding & Co. Chicago, Illinois	1888–present	Silver, silverplate, jewelry (Henry A. Spaulding)
	Stickley, Gustav Syracuse, New York	(1857–1942)	Copper, furniture (Craftsman Workshop)
	Stone, Arthur J. New Hampshire Detroit, Michigan Gardiner, Massachusetts	(1847–1938)	Silver (Stone Associates: Alfred Wickstrom, David Carlson, George Blanchard, Charles Brown, Arthur Hartwell, Herbert Taylor, George Erickson, Herman Glendenning, Edgar Caron, Earl Underwood)
	Sweetser Co. New York, New York	c. 1900–1915	Silver, gold
	TC Shop Chicago, Illinois	1910–1923	Jewelry, silver
	Tiffany & Co. New York, New York	1834–present	Silver, metalwork (Charles Louis Tiffany, 1812–1902)
	Tiffany Studios New York, New York	1879–1936	Metalwork, pottery, glass (Louis Comfort Tiffany, 1848–1933)
	Tookay Shop East Aurora, New York	1912–1915	Copper (Karl Kipp)
	Trautmann, George H. Chicago, Illinois	c. 1910–1912	Copper lighting fixtures

The Art Nouveau style was used by very few American firms making silver, but this vase by George Shiebler and Company of New York favored that style. The vase was made about 1890.

Unger Brothers Newark, New Jersey	1881–1910	Silver, jewelry (Herman Unger, Eugene Unger)	
Van Erp, Dirk Oakland and San Francisco, California	(1860–1933)	Copper (D'Arcy Gaw, Harry Dixon)	
Varney, Leon East Aurora, New York	(1895–1935)	Copper, silver (Roycroft)	
Weber, Kem New York	c. 1928	Silver	
Webster Co. North Attleboro, Massachusetts	1869–present	Silver (George K. Webster)	WEBSTER △ 925 COMPANY ⟁ STERLING
Whiting, Frank. M. Co. North Attleboro, Massachusetts	1878–c. 1960	Silver	

Silver spoons were made in myriad fanciful shapes in the United States. **Left to right:** *A spoon by Unger Brothers, c. 1905; spoon by Whiting Manufacturing Company, Providence, Rhode Island, before 1904; spoon by Gorham Company, 1875; teaspoon by Unger Brothers, 1904–1910.*

	Workshops, Artists, & Locations	Dates	Artists' Factories & Related Information
WHITING MFG CO NEW YORK STERLING	Whiting Mfg. Co. North Attleboro, Massachusetts Newark, New Jersey Bridgeport, Connecticut Providence, Rhode Island	1866–present	Silver, jewelry
WINN	Winn, James H. Chicago, Illinois California	(1866–1940)	Jewelry

Others

	Altenloh Brussels, Belgium	c. 1930	Silver

Workshops, Artists, & Locations	Dates	Artists' Factories & Related Information	
Amstelhoek Amsterdam, Holland	1894–	Silver (J. Eisenloeffel, Christian Van dar Hoef, W. Hoeker)	
Andersen, David Norway	1876–present	Silver (Carl Johansgate)	
Anderson, Just Denmark	(1884–1943)	Silver	
Ängman, Jacob Sweden	1876–1942	Silver (Guldsmeds Aktiebolaget, GAB)	
Begeer, Cornelius Amsterdam, Holland	c. 1900–1925	Silver (Carel Begeer, 1883–1956)	
Bernodotte, Sigvard Denmark	1931–1947	Silver (J. Eisenloeffel)	

The style of this teapot made by Georg Jensen in 1905 is still popular. The 4½-inch silver pot has a bone handle.

Workshops, Artists, & Locations	Dates	Artists' Factories & Related Information
Bindesbøll, Thorvald Denmark	(1846–1908)	Jewelry, architecture, furniture
Birks, Henry & Sons Montreal, Canada	1879–present	Silver, jewelry (H. Birks, 1840–1928)
Bojesen, Kai Denmark	c. 1930	Silver
Bolin, W. A. Sweden Russia	1895–present	Jewelry (Carl Edward Bolin, William James Bolin)
Bollin, Moyens Denmark	c. 1900	Jewelry
Bonebakker & Sons Holland	1767–present	Jewelry

BIRKS

Jewelry was also made by Georg Jensen, silversmith. This back-comb was made in the early 1900s.

Georg Jensen of Copenhagen made this large footed bowl about 1930.

Workshops, Artists, & Locations	Dates	Artists' Factories & Related Information
Bulgari Rome, Italy	1881–present	Jewelry (George Bulgari, Constantino Bulgari, Giorgio Bulgari, Sotiri Bulgari)
Castellani, Alessandro Rome, Italy	(1824–1883)	Jewelry
Castellani, Augusto Rome, Italy	(1829–1914)	Jewelry
Cohr, Carl M. Denmark	1863–present	Silver
Dragsted and Michelsen Denmark	c. 1930	Silver
Dubois, Fernard Belgium	(1861–1939)	Jewelry, silver, silverplate
Dubois, Paul Belgium	c. 1900	Jewelry
Eisenloeffel, Jan Amsterdam, Holland	(1876–1957)	Silver (Amstelhoek)
Fisker, Kay Denmark	c. 1930–	Silver
GAB. See Ängman, Jacob.		
Guldsmeds Aktiebolaget Sweden	1907–present	Silver (Jacob Ängman, Sven Arne Gillgreen)
Hansen, Hans Denmark	1906–present	Flatware, hollow ware, jewelry
Heisse, Christian F. Copenhagen, Denmark	20th century	Silver, assay mastermark
Hingelberg, Frantz Denmark	1897–present	Silver, jewelry
Hoeker W. Netherlands	c. 1905–	Jewelry (Lambert Nienhaus)

Workshops, Artists, & Locations	Dates	Artists' Factories & Related Information
Hoosemans, Franz Brussels, Belgium	c. 1900–	Silver, gold
Jensen, Georg Copenhagen, Denmark	(1866–1935)	Jewelry, silver
Llaurenson, Laurent Denmark	c. 1930	Silver
Magnussen, Eric Denmark	(1884–1961)	Jewelry
Masriera, Luis Barcelona, Spain	(1872–1958)	Jewelry
Michelsen, Anton Copenhagen, Denmark	1841–present	Jewelry, silver
Møller, Inger Copenhagen, Denmark	(1886–1966)	Jewelry
Nielsen, Evald Denmark	(1879–1958)	Hand-hammered silver
Nielsen, Harald Denmark	c. 1930	Silver
Nienhaus, Lambert Netherlands	(1873–1960)	Silver, jewelry (W. Hoeker)
Nilsson, Wiven Sweden	(1870–1942)	Jewelry
Orania (Urania?) Netherlands	c. 1900–1910	Pewter
Rodhe, Johan Denmark	c. 1830	Silver
Saarinen, Eliel Finland	(1873–1950)	Silver, designer, architect
Slott-Moller, Harald Denmark	c. 1900	Jewelry
Tostrup, Jacob Oslo, Norway	1832–present	Metalwork, applied art

Workshops, Artists, & Locations	Dates	Artists' Factories & Related Information	
Urania. See Orania.			
Van den Eersten & Hofmeijer Amsterdam, Holland		Jewelry, silver	
Van De Velde, Henri Clemens Belgium	(1863–1957)	Jewelry, furniture, bronze, silver, architecture, porcelain, metalwork, ceramics	
Van Strydonck Brussels, Belgium	c. 1900	Jewelry	
Wolfers Frères Brussels, Belgium	1812–1910	Jewelry	
Wolfers, Marcel Brussels, Belgium	c. 1920	Jewelry (Phillipe Wolfers)	
Wolfers, Phillipe Belgium	(1858–1929)	Jewelry, metalwork, sculpture, ceramics	

BIBLIOGRAPHY

Amaya, Mario. *Art Nouveau.* New York: Dutton, 1966.

Anscombe, Isabelle and Gere, Charlotte. *Arts & Crafts in Britain and America.* New York: Rizzoli, 1978.

Arts and Crafts in Detroit, 1906–1976: The Movement, The Society, The School. Detroit: Detroit Institute of Art, 1977.

Arwas, Victor. *Liberty Style.* New York: Rizzoli, 1979.

Baker, Lillian. *Art Nouveau & Art Deco Jewelry: An Identification & Value Guide.* Paducah, Kentucky: Collector Books, 1981.

Sarah Campbell Blaffer Gallery. *Vienna Moderne, 1898–1918* (exhibition catalog). Houston: University of Houston, n.d.

Brady, Nancy Hubbard. *The Book of the Roycrofters.* East Aurora, New York: House of Hubbard, 1977.

Brunhammer, Yvonne et al. *Art Nouveau Belgium-France.* Houston: Institute for the Arts, Rice University, 1976.

Clark, Robert Judson. *The Arts and Crafts Movement in America, 1876–1916.* Princeton: Princeton University Press, 1972.

Darling, Sharon S. *Chicago Metalsmiths.* Chicago: Chicago Historical Society, 1977.

Elzea, Rowland and Betty. *The Pre-Raphaelite Era, 1848–1914.* Wilmington: Wilmington Society of the Fine Arts, 1976.

Frankart, Inc. *Handbook for the Season 1930–1931.* Tecumseh, New Brunswick: Privately printed, 1981.

Garner, Philippe. *The Encyclopedia of Decorative Arts, 1890–1940.* New York: Van Nostrand Reinhold, 1979.

Georg Jensen Silversmithy: 77 Artists, 75 Years. Washington, D.C.: Smithsonian Institution Press, 1980.

Gere, Charlotte. *American & European Jewelry, 1830–1914.* New York: Crown, 1975.

Hamilton, Charles F. *Roycroft Collectibles.* San Diego: A. S. Barnes & Co., 1980.

Haslam, Malcolm. *Marks and Monograms of the Modern Movement, 1875–1930.* New York: Scribner's, 1977.

Hawley, Henry. *Fabergé and His Contemporaries.* Cleveland: Cleveland Museum of Arts, 1967.

Hughes, Graham. *Modern Silver Throughout the World, 1880–1967.* New York: Crown, 1967.

———. *Modern Jewelry.* New York: Crown, 1963.

Janson, Dora Jane. *From Slave to Siren: The Victorian Woman and Her Jewelry from Neoclassic to Art Nouveau.* Durham, North Carolina: Duke University Museum of Art, 1971.

Johnson, Diane Chalmers. *American Art Nouveau.* New York: Abrams, 1979.

Klamkin, Marian. *The Collector's Book of Art Nouveau.* New York: Dodd, Mead, 1971.

McClinton, Morrison Katharine. *Collecting American 19th Century Silver.* New York: Scribner's, 1968.

Mackay, James. *Turn-of-the-Century Antiques.* New York: Dutton, 1974.

Moore, M. Eudorah; Andersen, Timothy J.; and Winter, Robert W. *California Design, 1910.* Pasadena: California Design Publications, 1974.

Naylor, Gillian. *The Arts and Crafts Movement.* London: Studio Vista Publishers, 1971.

Rainwater, Dorothy T. *Encyclopedia of America Silver Manufacturers.* New York: Crown, 1975.

Revi, Christian. *The Spinning Wheel's Complete Book of Antiques.* New York: Grosset & Dunlap, 1949.

Ross, Marvin C. *The Art of Karl Fabergé and His Contemporaries: Russian Imperial Portraits and Mementoes, Imperial Decorations and Watches.* Norman, Oklahoma: University of Oklahoma Press, 1965.

Sallee, Lynn. *Old Costume Jewelry, 1870–1945.* Florence, Alabama: Books Americana, 1979.

Scheffler, Wolfgang. *Werke Um, 1900.* Berlin: Kunstgewerbe Museum, 1966.

Scott, Jack L. *Pewter Wares from Sheffield.* Baltimore: Antiquary Press, 1980.

Smith, Carolyn A. and Hixon, Peggy R. *The Mystery Era of American Pewter, 1928–1931.* Oklahoma City: Universal Press, 1979.

Club: Roycrofters at Large Association, Erie City, East Aurora, New York 14052

Publication: The Magazine Silver, 1619-A S.W. Jefferson St., Portland, Oregon 97201

10

Glass, from Carnival and Depression to Modern

Twentieth-century glass has become increasingly popular as the prices for Victorian art glass, historic flasks, and pressed glass patterns have soared. Collectors are turning to various types of household glasswares that were the products of the early 1900s. A myriad of firms in America made good quality glasswares for use in the home. Most of the glass was mass-produced machine-made commercial ware that was made in full sets for the dinner table, or items used by florists. When a design became popular other manufacturers made similar pieces. It is virtually impossible to determine whether an unmarked etched glass goblet was made by Cambridge, Heisey, Fostoria, McKee, or any other firm of the same period without carefully studying the old catalogs, ads, and actual marked pieces. It would be nice to find an easy key to identification, but the more research is done the more complex the problem appears. Some of the glasswares are typical of just one firm, but most of them were freely copied and recopied.

A collector should choose the wares of one factory. Study their old catalogs in depth and then scour the flea markets and house sales for some of the unrecognized examples. Following are some twentieth-century glassmakers.

TWENTIETH-CENTURY AMERICAN FACTORIES OF INTEREST

Akro-Agate

Akro-Agate Company

Are you old enough to remember glass marbles? If you were young after 1911, chances are that you played with marbles made by the Akro-Agate Company. The company was established in 1911 in Akron, Ohio, by three men, George Rankin, Gilbert Marsh, and Horace Hill. Their trademark pictured a crow flying through the letter *A*. (A crow as in *Akro.*) At the beginning they bought their marbles, boxed them, and sold the boxes to retail outlets. In 1914 they moved the firm to Clarksburg, West Virginia, where they began manufacturing their own glass marbles. Marbles were their only product until 1932, when the company started making agate glass or solid-color ashtrays, figurines, bowls, garden pots, and other pieces. In 1942, they started making children's toy glass tea sets. They later added novelty packaging glasswares to their line. The firm went out of business in 1951 and their molds, trademark, and other assets were sold to the Master Glass Company of Clarksburg, West Virginia. It is our understanding that all of the old molds have been destroyed.

Cambridge Glass Company

Cambridge Glass Company paper label

The Cambridge Glass Company (do not confuse with the earlier New England Glass Company of Cambridge, Massachusetts) was officially organized in 1873, but no glass was made until 1902. Arthur J. Bennet of New York City was hired to run the plant. It was called the National Glass Company, but was located in Cambridge, Ohio. By 1907, the firm went bankrupt and Mr. Bennet purchased the plant, naming it the Cambridge Glass Company about 1910. Early pressed pieces resembled cut glass. The firm made Carnival glass and many types of glass stemware, tableware, and novelties. Colored glass was made, including Crown Tuscan (pink opaque), Rubina, Carmen (red), avocado (yellow green), ivory, primrose (yellow opaque), milk glass, jade, ebony, violet, amethyst, blue, royal blue, amber, azurite, and Amberina (shaded). Designs kept pace with the tastes of the buyers and went from pseudo-cut-glass patterns to linear Art Deco pieces. Animal figurines, swan bowls, figural flower holders, etched crystal, colored stemware, and stemware with nude lady stems were well known.

Cambridge Glass Company used several marks, including a "C" in a triangle (c. 1915–1930), the words "near cut" (1904–1940s), and the paper Cambridge sticker (c. 1935–).

The company was sold to Mr. Bennet's son-in-law, W. L. Orme, in 1939; it went out of business in 1958. The molds were sold to the Imperial Glass Company and many of the old pieces have been reproduced.

No. 865. Wine 2¼ oz.
Packed 40 doz. in a barrel.

No. 866. Wine, 2¼ oz.
Packed 40 doz. in a barrel.

No. 667. Wine, 2¼ oz.
Packed 45 doz. in a barrel.

No. 671. Wine, 1¾ oz.
Packed 50 doz. in a barrel.

No. 670. Wine, 2 oz.
Packed 50 doz. in a barrel.

No. 668. Wine, 2 oz.
Packed 45 doz. in a barrel.

Page from a 1903 Cambridge Glass catalog showing wineglass patterns.

Caprice 66
13 in. Bowl, crimped, 4 Ftd.

Caprice 151
5 in. 2 Handle Jelly

Caprice 133
6 in. Low Ftd. Bonbon, Square

Caprice 1338
3 lite Candlestick

A page from a 1949 catalog for the Cambridge Glass Company. Although the pattern is shown in the 1949 catalog, it may have been in production for many years before that date.

A Cambridge Glass Crown Tuscan ashtray held by a figure of a nude woman.

A Crown Tuscan Cambridge vase in Diane pattern.

A jug from a 1949 Cambridge Glass catalog.

A Cambridge Glass ram's head bowl of lavender glass.

Duncan and Miller Glass

George Duncan bought the Ripley and Company Glass Factory in Pittsburgh, Pennsylvania, in 1865. He formed the firm of George Duncan and Sons with Harry Duncan, James Duncan, and his son-in-law, Augustus Heisey. The company became known as the Duncan and Heisey Company sometime between 1886 and 1889. The United States Glass Company was formed in 1891 and it was at that time the Duncan Company joined the United States Glass Company.

James Duncan was unhappy in his new association and in 1894 built a new factory in Washington, Pennsylvania, and called it George A. Duncan and Sons Company. The firm was often incorrectly referred to as Duncan and Miller from 1893 to 1955 because John Miller had been so active in the original management. The firm was finally incorporated as Duncan and Miller Glass Company in November of 1900. The company became a division of the United States Glass Company of Tiffin, Ohio, in 1955, and the use of the Duncan name ceased.

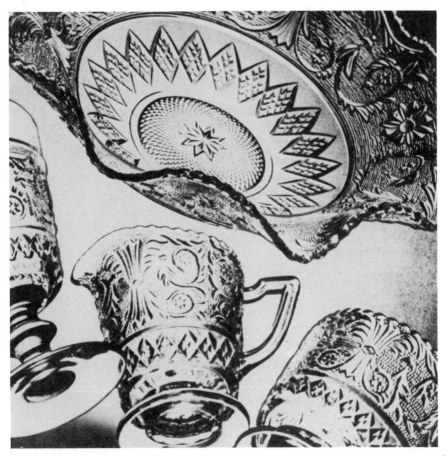

The Early American Sandwich Glass pattern by Duncan and Miller has remained popular. It was first made in 1924. The pattern came in green, crystal, amber. pink, red, or cobalt blue glass.

The glass patterns that they made through the years included all types of pressed, blown, etched, decorated wares, tablewares, vases, gift shop items, or almost any type of glass imaginable. Many of the patterns were produced later by other companies using the Duncan and Miller molds.

Carl Erickson

Erickson glass was made in Bremen, Ohio, by Carl Erickson and his staff from 1943 to 1961. It was free-formed glass. The pieces were marked with the name "Erickson" written with a diamond-point pen.

Fenton Art Glass Company

The Fenton Art Glass Company was founded in Martins Ferry, Ohio, by Frank Leslie Fenton in 1905. At first, the company only decorated the glass made by other companies but by October of 1906 they had their own factory and by January of 1907 they made their first glass. The new factory was located in Williamstown, West Virginia. They made Carnival glass, chocolate glass, and many other types. They introduced a line of "off-hand" glass in 1925 that were pieces made without molds. Although high-priced, they were popular. Even with the popularity, the line was dropped after two years. Hobnail glass, overlay, opalescent, and reproductions of earlier styles of antique glass were made. The company is still working.

Fostoria Glass Company

The Fostoria Glass Company of Fostoria, Ohio, was formed by L. B. Martin in December of 1887. He chose a site with a new gas well, which seemed to be ideal for fuel. Unfortunately, the well went dry after a few years and the firm was forced to move to Moundsville, West Virginia, in 1891. The company made pressed glass, oil lamps, restaurant glass, and other tablewares. Fostoria glass was advertised in all of the popular magazines of the mid-1920s, with colored glass table settings featured. In September 1983, the company was purchased by Lancaster Colony of Columbus, Ohio. The factory closed in 1986.

Several popular patterns by Fostoria. The deep-plate etched ware was introduced in 1915, discontinued in 1925. The blown crystal vases were introduced in 1913, discontinued in 1918. American pattern was introduced in 1915, and was still being made in the 1970s. It was made in blue, canary, green, and amber.

→

Deep-Plate Etched Ware

Blown Crystal

American Pattern

FLORID PATTERN
DEEP ETCHED No. 256

No. 858   5½-ounce Fruit, Optic,
Etched 256
Height 3¼ inches
Top Diameter 3¾ inches

No. 858   5½-ounce Saucer Champagne,
Optic, Etched 256
Height 4⅛ inches
Top Diameter 3⅞ inches

No. 858   9-ounce Goblet, Optic,
Etched 256
Height 6⅛ inches
Top Diameter 3⅛ inches

No. 1227   8-inch Nappy, Optic,
Etched 256
Height 3⅛ inches

No. 1227   4½-inch Nappy, Optic,
Etched 256   Height 1½ inches

Florid pattern was introduced in 1920, discontinued in 1928. This is a picture from an old Fostoria catalog.

Warwick pattern was first made in 1920, discontinued in 1933. It is typical of the cutting used at the Fostoria glassworks.

Fry Glass

Fry glass was made by the famous H. C. Fry Glass Company of Rochester, Pennsylvania, from 1922 to 1933. It included cut glass, but the Fry glass that is in demand is the Foval, or Pearl Art, glass. This was an opal ware decorated with colored trim. It was made from 1926 to 1927.

A page from the Fry catalog showing No. 10.

Heisey Glass

Augustus H. Heisey of Hanover, Germany, was born in 1842, and came to the United States in 1843. He lived in Merritown, Pennsylvania, where he went to school, worked briefly as a printer and took a job as a clerk at the King Glass Company of Pittsburgh, Pennsylvania. He enlisted and fought in the Civil War, returned home in 1865, and went to work again at the King Glass Company. Later he worked as a salesman for the Ripley Glass Company. Mr. Heisey met Susan Duncan, who was the daughter of George Duncan, owner of the Ripley Glass Company, and married her in

The Heisey glass factory was one of the landmarks of Newark, Ohio. In the days before air pollution, a factory gloried in a picture like this one of a smoking chimney, which indicated full production and many jobs.

A. H. Heisey & Co., Inc., after 1901

A. H. Heisey & Co., Inc., paper label

1870. In 1874, Mr. Duncan gave Susan and her brother James each a one-quarter interest in the glass company, which changed its name to George Duncan and Sons.When George Duncan died, Heisey and James Duncan bought the rest of the glass company and became full owners.

The company merged with the U.S. Glass Company in 1893. Augustus Heisey left the firm in 1893 to start his own factory in Newark, Ohio. A. H. Heisey and Company opened in 1896. The early ware was pressed glass that was made to look like the more expensive cut glass. It was not until 1900 that the famous Heisey mark, an "H" in a diamond, was first used.

No. 1200, Cut Block pattern, first made in 1896. This was Heisey's second pattern.

Fancy Loop, or No. 1205, a Heisey pattern of 1897.

By 1905 many patterns of pressed glass were made that were called "colonial" in design. They were made with panels, scallops, and bands in simple fashion. Although some colored glass was made, such as custard, milk glass, emerald green, cobalt, most of the pieces until 1920 were clear. Stemware was first made in 1914 and most of it had etched or engraved designs.

No. 4136, a pretzel jar with Tallyho deep plate etching. This piece is signed.

No. 339, Continental pitcher marked with the "H" in a diamond. It was first made in 1903.

This pattern called Old Queen Anne, was new in 1907.

At the death of Augustus Heisey in 1922 the firm president was his son Edgar Wilson Heisey. The factory began making colored glass until the Depression, when they made only clear glass because it was less expensive. Tangerine, moon gleam (green), flamingo (pink), marigold (yellow amber), hawthorn (plum), alexandrite (orchid changing in electric light), Sahara (yellow), and zircon (turquoise) were made.

E. W. Heisey died in 1942 and his brother T. Clarence Heisey became president. The firm continued adding Heisey figurines, some colored glass, and new patterns of tablewares and stemwares.

The company went out of business in 1957. The Imperial Glass Company of Bellaire, Ohio, bought some of the molds and the rights to the trademark. Some Heisey patterns have been made by Imperial since 1960. After 1968 they stopped using the diamond "H" trademark.

No. 3380, or Old Dominion-shape goblet with Titania etching, made about 1925.

A whiskey decanter in No. 1404, or Old Sandwich pattern. Forty-five items were made in this pattern between 1929 and 1954. It came in crystal, flamingo, amber, Sahara, and cobalt blue.

A ball vase, No. 4045, with No. 469, or Mermaid, etching. The vase was made in 4-, 6-, 7-, 9-, or 12-inch sizes.

A Wabash pitcher with Frontenac etching, made about 1921. It was offered in crystal, moonbeam, or flamingo color.

This Ridgeleigh mustard jar (No. 1469) was one of ninety items made in this pattern between 1935 and the early 1940s. The pattern was offered in crystal, Sahara, and zircon.

Imperial Glass Company

The Imperial Glass Company was founded in Bellaire, Ohio, in 1901. It was not until January of 1904 that their building was completed and glass was first made.

c. 1911

The company made clear pressed glass, and common containers like jelly glasses. In 1910 they started making the iridescent pressed glass that we now call Carnival glass. "Imperial Jewel," or stretch glass, was first made in 1915. Freehand wares (patented Feb. 19, 1920) were made by a group of Swedish glassmakers after 1922. The Depression forced a change in their operation and by 1931 the company became known as the Imperial Glass Corporation. They produced a lower-priced glass that was made to be sold by dime stores or given away as premiums. Much of the glass is now referred to as "Depression glass."

1914–

1914–

Imperial Glass purchased molds from several companies, including Central Glass Company of Summitville, Indiana, A. H. Heisey and Company of Newark, Ohio, and the Cambridge Glass Company of Cambridge, Ohio. It became a division of Lenox, Inc., in 1977, was sold in 1981, and went bankrupt in 1982.

1920–

The company is still working and through the years they have produced an amazing variety of glassware. The marks used by the firm have

used on milk glass since February 1951; discontinued in 1977

used since June 1977

1981–1982

| 1748/13 Lamb | 1748/14 Elephant | 1748/15 Mouse | 1748/16 Parrot |

| 1748/19 Cat | 1748/20 Turtle | 1748/21 Ape | 1748/22 Crow |

Part of a page from an Imperial catalog showing decorated cocktail glasses.

changed through the years. They can be used as an aid in dating a piece of Imperial glass.

Kemple Glass

John E. Kemple started making glass in 1906 at the Fostoria Glass Company of Moundsville, West Virginia. He worked at a number of glasshouses until he opened his own company in 1945. He started making milk glass with his wife, Geraldine, at a factory located in East Palestine, Ohio. Their plant burned in 1956 and Kemple Glass moved to Kenova, West Virginia, in 1957.

The company made milk glass, blue milk glass, slag glass, ruby glass, cobalt blue, black amethyst, green, amber, red, end-of-day, and other colors. Most pieces were molded.

Some of the Kemple glass was made in the McKee Glass Company molds used between 1870 and 1890. The "pres-cut" mark of McKee remained for a while but it gradually wore off in the molds. Other pieces were made from molds by the Indiana Tumbler and Goblet Works, the St. Claire Glass Works, the Phoenix Glass Company, the Mannington Art Glass Company, and the American Glass Company. Some original molds were used. Wherever possible the letter *K* was added to the bottom of the piece to show it was made by Kemple.

When Mr. Kemple died in 1970 the factory closed and some of these molds were sold to Wheaton Industries of Millville, New Jersey.

McKee Glass Company

1904–1930s
McKee Glass
Company

PRESCUT

Samuel and James McKee started making window glass and bottles in their glassworks in Pittsburgh, Pennsylvania, in 1834. In 1850, James McKee joined Frederick McKee and they formed a flint glass manufacturing plant under the name J. and F. McKee. The name was changed to McKee and Brother about 1853. When Stewart McKee joined his brothers in the firm in 1865 the name became McKee and Brothers. The company worked in Pittsburgh until 1889, when it moved twenty-seven miles to Jeannette, Pennsylvania. They joined several other companies and became known as the National Glass Company. The McKees left the group in 1903 and formed the McKee Glass Company. That company became a division of Thatcher Glass Manufacturing Company of Jeannette, Pennsylvania, from 1951 to 1961. It is now part of the Jeannette Glass Company. The firm used the trademark "pres-cut" before 1894. Another one of their marks is a "McK" in a circle.

McKee tumblers from an old catalog.

McKee jug with wisteria cutting.

No. 21 High Footed Bowl

No. 21-2 Claret Tankard

McKee Colonial pattern "Prescut" glass.

New Martinsville-Viking

The New Martinsville Glass Manufacturing Company started working in December 1900. The company bought glass molds from a company in Martins Ferry, Ohio, and started making restaurant glass and lamps. The company had financial problems in 1937, and was purchased and renamed the New Martinsville Glass Company. In 1944 it was renamed the Viking Glass Company.

The early wares made by the factory were art glass such as "peachblow" and opaque glass in many colors. The term *peachblow* referred to a

New Martinsville Carnation, Leaf and Star, and Florene patterns from a catalog published about the time of World War I.

No. 88 Carnation
Fig. 44

No. 711 Ware
Leaf and Star (K)
Fig. 45

No. 720 Florene Pattern
Fig. 46

No. 35 Fern Compote

Combination Ash Tray

Ash Trays

variety of colors that range from white and yellow to pink. The company also made pressed glass in many patterns. Some of the pieces were ruby-stained and gold-flashed and some were decorated with enamel painted designs.

A selection of New Martinsville plates. The ABC plate with the boy has been copied many times.

After the company changed hands in 1937 the type of glassware changed very little. Some new lines were added, including clear glass animals and other clear glass sets. When the company became the Viking Glass Company in 1944, the name was chosen as one that would be suitable for a firm making heavy Swedish-inspired clear glass pieces. The company is still working.

Northwood Glass

The tradition of glassmaking often goes through many generations in a family. The name Northwood can be found in the histories of glass in America and in England. John Northwood of England was an engraver who specialized in cameo glass engraving. He is best known for his copy of the Portland vase. He was the art director at Stevens and Williams and his son John Northwood II worked at the same English glassworks until 1946. Harry Northwood, John Northwood, Sr.'s, oldest son, came to America about 1880. He worked for the glass firm of Hobbs, Brockunier and Company, located in Wheeling, West Virginia. In 1886 he began working for the La Belle Glass Company of Bridgeport, Ohio. Their glassworks closed because of a fire a year later. Mr. Northwood then moved to Martins Ferry, Ohio, where he went to work for the Buckeye Glass Company. He worked with the company for eight years and at the same time was manager and part owner of the Northwood Glass Company. The Northwood Glass Company moved to Ellwood, Pennsylvania, in 1895, and in 1897 it moved to Indiana, Pennsylvania, where the company became the Northwood Glass Works. Northwood joined with a group that formed the National Glass Company in 1891. He left them in 1902 to form his own company, the Harry Northwood Glass Company, in Wheeling, West Virginia. When Northwood died in 1923 the company closed.

Glass made by Northwood during the early years was blown, pressed, colored, or clear. He seemed to be the developer of many colored glasswares. Royal Oak and Royal Ivy were made about 1889. Later, glass decorated with gold or etched designs was made. When the firm worked in Pennsylvania several custard glass patterns were made including Chrysanthemum Sprig and Louis XV. The West Virginia factory was the source of much of the Carnival glass that is found today.

Paden City Glass

David Fisher was the first president of the Paden City Glass Manufacturing Company in Paden City, West Virginia, in 1916. The firm was an immediate financial success and in 1933 Samuel Fisher took over the management from his father. In spite of the Depression the firm continued to prosper.

The glassware made at Paden City was molded in a hand-operated press. Most of the glass was sold to other companies and the designs were made specifically for these firms. Wide borders were used so the other firms could decorate the finished glass. Paden City also made glass from molds that were furnished by other companies. The company put in its own etching and decorating department in 1924 and glasswares with cut or etched designs were offered for sale.

Colored glassware was made and it is said the company made twenty-one different colors of glass ranging from black and white to pastels. Many pieces of Paden City glass were used by firms making silver overlay glass.

The Paden City Glass Manufacturing Company closed in September 1951, and their molds were sold to the Canton Glass Company of Marion, Indiana, and probably to several other companies.

Paden City glass from an old catalog.

Pairpoint Glass

The Pairpoint Manufacturing Company of New Bedford, Massachusetts, originally made silverplated stands and holders for the Mt. Washington Glass Company. In 1894 the Pairpoint Manufacturing Company took over the glassworks of the Mt. Washington Glass Company and began making glass and silver under the new name of the Pairpoint Corporation. The company made pressed, cut, and art glass. They closed in 1929 and remained closed until 1939, when they reopened as the Gunderson Glass Works, Inc. Gunderson closed in 1948, but in 1952 it was reopened and

Pairpoint glass from a catalog issued from 1920 to 1930.

the company joined the National Pairpoint Company, a firm making toys, aluminum windows, and other items in the old Pairpoint plant. The new company was called Gunderson-Pairpoint Glass Works, which lasted until 1957.

The glass operation moved to East Wareham, Massachusetts, in 1957 and closed in 1958. From 1958 to 1970 the Pairpoint Glass Company made glass in a leased plant in Spain. A new Pairpoint factory, which is still working, was built in Sagamore, Massachusetts, in 1970.

Phoenix

The Phoenix Glass Company started working in 1880 in the town of Phillipsburg, Pennsylvania, now known as Monaca. At first they made tu-

A Phoenix vase of green glass with raised bird decoration.

bular glass insulation, kerosene lamp chimneys, and finally electric lighting parts. They began making decorated colored glasswares for use in lighting fixtures about 1886. The Phoenix Glass Company made "sculptured glassware" during the mid-1930s. This line of colored glass was made until the 1950s. The company is still working.

Sinclaire

H. P. Sinclaire & Company

H. P. Sinclaire and Company of Corning, New York, was a glass-cutting firm that worked between 1905 and 1929. They made clear and colored glass. The firm used a mark of an "S" in a wreath. Only a small percentage of their pieces were marked.

Tiffin

Joseph Beatty and Edward Stillman made glass in Steubenville, Ohio, from 1847 to 1850. The factory failed in 1850. In 1851 Alexander J. Beatty bought the factory, and in 1875 he was joined by his sons Robert J. and George. A. J. Beatty and Sons moved to Tiffin, Ohio, in 1888. The company joined with the U.S. Glass Company in 1892 to become factory R. The U.S. Glass Company went bankrupt in 1963 and the Tiffin plant

Tiffin Rose, a pattern introduced in 1941. The name was later changed to Rambling Rose and the pattern has been kept in production.

employees purchased the plant and inventory. They continued running it from 1963 to 1966, when it was sold to the Continental Can Company. Continental sold it in 1969 to Interpace, and in May 1980 the factory was closed.

Tiffin made a variety of wares, including black satin glass in the early days, but specialized in stemware in the last twenty years.

Verlys Glass

Verlys glass was first made in France about 1931. Verlys of America purchased molds from the French company Holophane Francaise in 1935 and they began producing lead glass in the United States. The glass was chemically etched and cut by glass cutters. The American pieces were signed with a diamond-point-scratched name, or the molded name, "Verlys." The French pieces are marked with the molded signature in script "A Verlys/ France," "Verlys/France" or "Verlys/Made in France." The Verlys molds were leased to A. H. Hensey Co. from 1955 to 1957 (unmarked) and were sold to the Fenton Art Glass Co. in 1961 (unmarked).

Verlys, 1935–1951

Mermaids decorate this Verlys smoky topaz vase.

Carnival Glass

The iridescent golden glass that Louis Comfort Tiffany made during the last part of the nineteenth century was made for persons of means. It was expensive and was never made in quantity. Tiffany's designs and coloring influenced the makers of less expensive glasswares, and iridescent glass was made for the masses. Pressed-glass makers could easily make the new colored glasswares by using the same molding techniques.

Northwood Glass Company of Wheeling, West Virginia, was one of the best-known makers of Carnival glass and other types of glass. These pieces, the fernery and two covered compotes, are in the Northwood Grape pattern.

This blue Buddha of Carnival glass was made by an unknown maker.

Pressed glass was made to resemble cut glass. The patterns for iridescent glass were different because the coloring allowed changes. The colored glass was not transparent, so one design could be put on the inside and a different design on the outside. The iridescent coloring also inspired designs with exotic birds or flowers. The glass was first marketed as iridescent glass but the collector of the 1940s referred to it as "taffeta glass," while the collector of the 1960s and later called it "Carnival glass."

Most of the Carnival glass made was manufactured by the Fenton Art Glass Company, from 1905 to the present, of Williamstown, West Virginia; the Northwood Glass Company, 1902–1923, of Wheeling, West Virginia; the Imperial Glass Company, from 1902 to the present, of Bellaire, Ohio; and the Millersburg Glass Company, 1910–1912, of Millersburg, Ohio.

Most Carnival glass collectors specialize by either factory, color, pattern, or object. Full sets of tablewares were made, so a collector can specialize

This Northwood Grape pattern hatpin holder was made of aqua opalescent glass.

Frolicking Bears, a Carnival glass pattern made by an unknown maker. The tumbler and pitcher are purple.

in plates or tumblers, collect a full set in a special pattern, or just seek orange iridescent Carnival. The color of Carnival glass is the color of the original glass before the iridescent color was added. Examine the bottom of a piece of Carnival glass and the original glass color can easily be found. Vivid shades are marigold, amber, cobalt blue, purple, amethyst, red, and green. Pastel colors are white, Clambroth, violet, smoky, peach, aqua, marigold, Vaseline, ice blue, and ice green. Some of the pieces called marigold are exceptions to the rule that the base glass color is the official color name. Clear glass decorated with an orange iridescent-colored surface is sometimes referred to as marigold. Some, but not all, Carnival glass is marked. Some Carnival glass was made in England and Australia.

This "Peoples" vase may have been made by the Millersburg Glass Company of Millersburg, Ohio. This example is marigold.

Carnival glass should not be displayed in direct light if it was made before 1910. The base glass used during that period was made from a formula that will eventually turn purple or brown in the sun. The iridescent finish on the glass might become dull or fade with long exposure to sunlight. The best way to display Carnival is under fluorescent lights. On the following chart, dates in parentheses indicate when Carnival glass was made; dates not in parentheses are the manufacturers' dates.

The "rose pinwheel" Carnival glass bowl with iridescent finish was made of amethyst glass.

CARNIVAL GLASS MANUFACTURERS

Manufacturers and Location	Dates of Manufacture	Manufacturers and Location	Dates of Manufacture
Cambridge Glass Co. Cambridge, Ohio	1901–1958	Indiana Glass Co. Dunkirk, Indiana	1904– present
Dugan Glass Co. Diamond Glass Co. Indiana, Pennsylvania	1913–1930	Jenkins Glass Company Kokomo, Indiana	1901–1932
Fenton Art Glass Co. Williamstown, West Virginia	1905– present (1910–1921)	Millersburg Glass Co. Millersburg, Ohio	1910–
Heisey Glass Co. Newark, Ohio	1896–1956	Northwood Glass Co. Wheeling, West Virginia	1902–1923 (1910–1918)
Imperial Glass Co. Bellaire, Ohio	1902– present (1910–1924)	U. S. Glass Co. Pittsburgh, Pennsylvania	c. 1900

NEW CARNIVAL GLASS MANUFACTURERS

Manufacturers and Location	Dates of Manufacture	Manufacturers and Location	Dates of Manufacture
Elizabeth Degenhart (Crystal Art Glass Co.; Boyd Glass) Cambridge, Ohio	1947– present	Federal Glass Co. Columbus, Ohio	1900–1979

Manufacturers and Location	Dates of Manufacture	Manufacturers and Location	Dates of Manufacture
Fenton Art Glass Co. Williamstown, West Virginia	1905– present (1969)	St. Clair Glass Works Elwood, Indiana	1938– present (1960s)
Hansen Brothers Mackinaw City, Michigan	(1960s)	L. E. Smith Glass Co. Mt. Pleasant, Pennsylvania	1911– present (1971)
Imperial Glass Co. Bellaire, Ohio	1902– present (1962)	Westmoreland Glass Co. Grapeville, Pennsylvania	1890–1984
Indiana Glass Co. Dunkirk, Indiana	1904– present (1971)	Wheaton Industries Millville, New Jersey	1888– present
Jeannette Glass Co. Jeannette, Pennsylvania	1900– present	L. G. Wright Glass Co. New Martinsville, West Verginia	

Depression Glass

The term *Depression glass* has become a catchall name that includes the originally inexpensive glasswares from the time of the Great Depression. The words *Depression glass* first appeared in the antiques trading publications about 1969. Clear and colored glass made in the 1930s originally for sale in dime stores and department stores was included.

The glass was made by tank molding, a newly developed method of making inexpensive glass. Silica sand, soda ash, and limestone were heated in a ceramic tank. Liquid glass was then sent through pipes to an automated pressing mold. The finished glass was the shape of the mold

Moderntone was made in amethyst, cobalt blue, crystal, and fired-on colors. It was made from 1931 to 1942 by the Hazel Atlas Glass Company.

Sharon pattern was made by the Federal Glass Company of Columbus, Ohio, from 1935 to 1939. It has been reproduced.

and decorated with a pattern that was acid-etched or tooled into the mold. The resulting glassware had many flaws and bubbles. Most of the patterns were lacy in appearance to help hide the flaws. To keep food from getting lodged in the patterns the designs were molded on the outside. Many colors were made: pastel pink, blue, and green; clear; and the darker colors, cobalt blue, ruby red, and purple.

Glassware was made in dinner sets, luncheon sets, or other serviceable shapes. A twenty-piece set sold at Sears, Roebuck for as little as $1.99. After the repeal of Prohibition in December of 1933, Depression glass makers had a new market. Cocktail shakers, punch cups, drink glasses, ice buckets, decanters, and other utensils for the service of liquor became popular.

The words *Depression glass* now have a much more complicated meaning than they did in 1969. Through the publications written for the collector the term has come to mean many types of colored glassware made from the late 1920s through the 1970s. Patterns are not only of the lacy type but take many other forms.

Types of Depression Glass

Bubble pattern was made by the Anchor Hocking Glass Company from 1934 to 1965. It was made in dark colors such as ruby red.

Mold-Etched Pattern.   The lacy-patterned Depression glass was one of the earliest types made. Most of the patterns were made from 1929 to 1935. A mold-etched design featuring swags, bows, dancing ladies, birds, or flowers was used. The colors were pastel, the designs delicate, and the finished piece looked rather fragile. These glass pieces were often molded with thinner edges than some of the later pieces. Stemmed goblets were almost unknown. Most patterns were made in sets of dishes for table use. Examples of the lacy patterns are Adam, Cameo, Cherry Blossom, and Madrid.

Flowers, Birds, and Animals.   The patterns used for the glassware changed slightly in character during the mid-1930s. A few patterns such as Apple Blossom and Iris were made by 1929, but most of the other patterns of the period reached their popularity by 1935. This type of glassware was still being made during the 1970s. The designs were often carved into the mold so that a raised portion of the glass formed a flower or fruit. The frosted, lacy look disappeared and the dishes were heavier in weight. Colors such as cobalt blue and royal ruby, and opaque glass as well as pastel colors were used. Clear glass, called crystal, was popular. Patterns that are most popular with collectors include Mayfair or Open Rose, Sharon or Cabbage Rose.

From 1929 to 1933 the Jeannette Glass Company of Jeannette, Pennsylvania, made this Cubist pattern. It has been reproduced.

This pink Adam pattern salad plate is 7¾ inches in diameter. It was made by the Jeannette Glass Company of Jeannette, Pennsylvania, from 1932 to 1934. The same pattern was also made in green.

Geometric. Most of the wares now called Depression glass fall into this general design category. A few geometric patterns were made from the late 1920s but most of the popular designs were not made until the late 1930s or early 1940s. Styles changed and the general look of tableware included heavy, blocky pieces with simple outlines and bold colors. Royal ruby and cobalt blue were especially popular. A few of the patterns such as Hobnail, Ribbon, and Sheraton were copies of the pressed-glass patterns of the 1880 period.

Other patterns were inspired by Art Deco designs or modern art. Glasswares such as Moderne and Cubist were made. Many of the patterns were similar because companies copied the best-selling designs of their competitors. For example, three octagon-based patterns were made—United States Octagon, Imperial Octagon, and Tiered Octagon, each slightly different.

Pseudo–Sandwich Glass. The famous glassworks in Sandwich, Massachusetts, made many pieces of "lacy Sandwich" during the nineteenth century. Many of the Depression glass makers realized that the Sandwich patterns could be copied in more modern glass. About ten pseudo-Sandwich patterns were made that were similar but identifiable if careful attention is paid to the details. Most of the glassware was called Sandwich by the makers and this is still causing great confusion for many collectors. Some of the glass was made to be included as a premium in a box of oatmeal and huge quantities were distributed. This pattern is often referred to as Oatmeal Lace, although it has at least four other names, such as Flower, Early American, Scroll and Star, and Princess Feather. Pseudo-Sandwich pattern Depression glass is still being made.

Pseudo–Cut Glass.   A few patterns were made that resembled the brilliant period cut-glass patterns of the 1880s. They were deliberately made to fool the eye and many customers felt the Depression glass copies were just as attractive. One unusual pattern now classed as Depression glass is Rock Crystal made by the McKee Glass Company during the 1920s and 1930s. It was made to resemble the very expensive earlier period carved glasswares made in Europe.

Opaque.   A new type of glass became popular with the consumer during the late 1930s. Opaque glass was varied. Some of the patterns that appeared in the other colors and types of glass were made of opaque glass similar to the milk glass of the nineteenth century. The companies making the glass patterns gave their colors trade names. Monax was an opaque glass with a tinted edge of pink and blue. Ivrene was ivory, Cremax or Clambroth was a creamy opaque ware, Delphite was blue, Jadite was green, and Milk-white was a dense white.

To further complicate the problem for the collector, several of the opaque Depression glass colors are called by other names by many collectors.

The creamy-colored wares are collected by those who specialize in various types of custard glass. The pink milk glass pieces made by the Depres-

Cameo pattern Depression glass was made by the Anchor Hocking Glass Company of Lancaster, Ohio, from 1930 to 1934. It was made in clear and pastel colors.

sion glass companies are sometimes confused with the more expensive opaque pink wares called Crown Tuscan, which were made by the Cambridge Glass Company.

Enameled or Silk-Screen Decoration.   A new type of design technique was featured on the Depression glass pieces in the 1940s. Existing patterns often had flowers, sailboats, tomatoes, and other designs added to the glass by a white enameling process. The Tom and Jerry sets decorated with the name, or dishwares decorated with colored bands were also part of this group of Depression glass. The designs were not molded and they were not of glass but were added after the glass was made. One of the most famous and one of the first Depression glass pieces of this type was the Shirley Temple glass made from 1934 to 1942.

Molded Figurines. Several companies made small glass statuettes during the 1930–1950 period and they must be included in the general term *Depression glass*. Small poodles, dogs, ashtrays decorated with small modeled figures, and patterns using figures as the stems of compotes or the handles for bowls were made.

The Imperial Dolphin pattern was based on the pressed-glass dolphin pieces of the 1880s that had dolphin handles and stems. A few wares were made resembling physical objects. An oak bucket (Ye Old Oaken Bucket pattern), a bunch of grapes (Grape Cluster Basket), or one of the amusing drink glasses molded like a woman (Bottom's-Up) are just a few of the types that were made.

Utility Wares, Icebox Dishes, Reamers. The Depression glass makers were interested in selling quantities of glass, and all types of glasswares were developed. Canister sets, cheese storage containers, icebox dishes, and lemon reamers were standard items. Measuring cups, feeding dishes, baskets, salt and pepper shakers, bowls, and even coffeepots with molded decoration were also made. Many of the pieces were individually designed and not part of a set. Collectors have been finding many glass items that were kitchenware and not tableware.

Depression glass is a popular field for collectors. Reproductions made to fool the collector have already appeared in several patterns, including Cherry Blossom and Sharon. Madrid pattern was reissued under the name Recollection in 1976 for the giftware market. Depression glass prices, like most other prices, are based on popularity and rarity. As more is known and more collectors appear the prices will change. Quantities of Depression glass can still be found in attics and basements. There are many unknown and unlisted patterns waiting to be discovered and named.

TERMINOLOGY

Akro Agate: Glass made in Clarksburg, West Virginia, from 1932 to 1951. The firm, located in Akron, Ohio, from 1911 to 1914, had been known for making marbles but started making children's dishes. The marbleized glassware is sometimes incorrectly referred to as Akro Agate, meaning a color.

Bottom's-Up: A drinking glass made so it cannot be put down because the bottom is rounded. Often made with the figure of a woman molded across the sides and bottom.

Butter Dish: A covered dish used on the table to hold butter, or a covered storage dish used for butter in the refrigerator.

Chinex: A pattern by the Macbeth Evans Division of the Corning Glass Works from the late 1930s to the 1940s. The ivory-colored glass made with scroll-designed edges was made either with plain or with a colored decal decoration. Sometimes confused with Cremax.

Cremax: An ivory-colored glassware made by the Macbeth Evans Division of the Corning Glass Works in the late 1930s and early 1940s. It is sometimes confused with Chinex but it has a ridged edge. Cremax is also used as a color name for a creamy opaque glass used in some other patterns such as American Sweetheart.

Delphite: Opaque light blue colored glass, sometimes incorrectly called blue milk glass.

Drip-o-Lator or Dripper: An additional piece put between cover and coffeepot. Coffee is put in the top or spreader, hot water is poured in and drips through to the pot to make coffee.

Fired-on Colors: Color applied to glass, then baked under high heat at the factory.

Flashed or Flashed-on: Color added over clear glass.

Grill Plate: A round three-section plate used to serve meat and vegetables in the separate sections. Similar to a modern TV dinner tray.

Ice Lip: A specially shaped lip of a pitcher curved to keep the ice cubes from falling out with the water when the water is poured.

Iridescent: Rainbowlike colors that appear on glassware when the light reflects from it.

Ivy Ball: A round glass vase, which may or may not have a pedestal stem.

Jade-Ite: Opaque light green-colored glass.

Jadite: Opaque light green-colored kitchenware made by the Jeannette Glass Company.

Leftover: A covered dish used to hold leftover food in a refrigerator. Part of the refrigerator sets.

Monax: White-colored glass made by the Macbeth Evans Dicition of the Corning Glass Works, has "fire" on edge, a slightly iridescent coloring.

Opalescent: Opaque white glass that appears to have colors at the edges.

Plate Sizes:	
6 inches—dessert	9 inches—breakfast
7 inches—bread & butter	10 inches—dinner
7–7½ inches—salad	13 inches—chop
8–9 inches—luncheon	

Platonite: Heat-resistant white glass made by the Hazel Atlas Glass Company.

Reamer: A dish and pointed-top cone used to extract juice from lemons, oranges, and grapefruits.

Tilt Jug: Pitcher.

Tumble-up: A glass bottle with a small tumbler turned upside down over the neck to serve as a top and a drinking glass.

Water Server: A covered pitcher kept filled with water in the refrigerator. Part of refrigerator sets.

DEPRESSION GLASS COLOR CHART

Amber	Topaz, Golden Glow	*Opaque*	
Blue Green	Ultra-Marine	*Black*	Black
Clear	Crystal	*Opaque Blue*	Delphite
Cream		*Opaque*	
Opaque	Cremax, Clambroth, Chinex	*Green*	Jadite
		Opaque	
Deep Blue	Cobalt, Ritz Blue, Dark Blue, Deep Blue	*White*	Milk-White, Monax
Green	Springtime Green, Emerald, Imperial Green, Forest Green, Nu-green	*Pink*	Rose, Rose Pink, Rose Marie, Rose Tint, Rose Glow, Nu-Rose, Wild Rose, Flamingo, Cheri-glo
Ivory	Ivrene		
Medium		*Purple*	Burgundy, Amethyst
Blue	Madonna	*Red*	Royal Ruby, Ruby Red, Carmen

MANUFACTURERS OF DEPRESSION GLASS

Company and Location	Dates of Factory	Company and Location	Dates of Factory
Akro-Agate Company Clarksburg, West Virginia	1914–1951	Duncan and Miller Glass Company Washington, Pennsylvania	1893–1955
Belmont Tumbler Co. Bellaire, Ohio	c. 1920?– 1952	Federal Glass Company Columbus, Ohio	1900–1979

Company and Location		Company and Location	
Fenton Art Glass Company Williamstown, West Virginia	1906– present	Macbeth-Evans Glass Company Indiana (several factories); Toledo, Ohio; Charleroi, Pennsylvania; Corning, New York	1899– c. 1987
Hazel-Atlas Glass Company Washington, Pennsylvania; Zanesville, Ohio; Clarksburg, West Virginia; Wheeling, West Virginia	1902–1956		
		McKee Glass Company Jeannette, Pennsylvania	1853–1961
		New Martinsville Glass Manufacturing Company New Martinsville, West Virginia	1901–1944
Hocking/Anchor Hocking Lancaster, Ohio	1905– present		
Imperial Glass Company Bellaire, Ohio	1904–1982	Paden City Glass Manufacturing Company Paden City, West Virginia	1916–1951
Indiana Glass Company Dunkirk, Indiana	1907– present		
Jeannette Glass Company Jeannette, Pennsylvania	c. 1900– present	L. E. Smith Glass Company Mt. Pleasant, Pennsylvania	1907– present
Jenkins Glass Co. Kokomo, Indiana; Arcadia, Indiana	1901–1932	U.S. Glass Company Pennsylvania (several factories); Tiffin, Ohio; Gas City, Indiana	1891–1966
Libbey Glass Company Toledo, Ohio	1892– present		
		Westmoreland Glass Company Grapeville, Pennsylvania	1890–1985
Liberty Works Egg Harbor, New Jersey	1903–1932		

Stained Glass

Stained glass can be found in all sizes, from church windows over 12 feet wide to small hanging panes of decorated stained glass. The very rare stained glass of the twelfth through the seventeenth centuries is not readily available for collectors, but there are quantities of nineteenth-century glass available. Glass painted with enamel paints and glass manufactured in colors were popular.

A large stained-glass advertising sign that once hung in the Centlivre Brewery in Indiana.

Gothic designs became a part of the wealthy American home during the nineteenth century and millionaires built mansions with stained-glass windows. The English designers of the William Morris school made stained-glass windows for homes during the 1860s. It was not until the 1870–1890 period that stained glass reached the height of its popularity. Stained glass was created by craftsmen and not machines. Many important designers such as Louis C. Tiffany and John LaFarge produced thousands of windows. Almost every home of the "well-to-do" was built with a stained-glass window or doorway. Many of the designs of the 1880s were influenced by Japanese or Moorish lines. The Art Nouveau style of design with flowing lines was popular in the northern part of the United States, while the more formal scenes were favored in other parts of the country. The best of the colored-glass windows were out of style by 1919 and the geometric windows with cut "jewels" and faceted clear glass became popular. The machine-made windows of the 1920s were of poor quality and by the 1930s homes with stained-glass windows were out of fashion. It was not until the early 1970s that there was a renewed interest in stained glass.

The quality of the stained glass determines the price. Some of the best windows were made by known artists, but most of the windows that were made for the home were unsigned.

Clear colors, attractive designs, morticed frames, and solid leading are important. Beveled glass, cut jewels, and "rippling" glass add to the value. Church windows and those with religious scenes are still available at comparatively low prices because of the small demand.

American windows with enamel-painted designs are usually not as important as those with designs of colored-glass sections.

Stained glass can be restored but it requires special knowledge. Releading is difficult, and it is usually best to leave the window slightly curved and try to have it braced. Air pollution frequently adds dark sooty mterial to the outside of a window, and this can be removed. Cracks should be repaired with clear epoxy glue or covered with a new strip of leading. Again, it is always best to leave stained-glass repairs in the hands of an expert.

Stained glass was used in wooden fireplace screens and room dividers, and small sections of glass were often hung in windows. Parts of unrepairable windows can still be used this way.

Art Nouveau and Art Deco Glass

The art glasswares of the 1880–1940 period were very different from the Victorian colored wares that preceded them. New techniques, new designs, and influences all changed the look of glass. Color had been the new, exciting, and salable feature of the Victorian wares. Peachblow, iridescent goldwares, Burmese, Amberina, Rubena, spatter, and spangle glass all had a new color to offer. Satin glass, Coralene, Pomona, Mary Gregory, and other glasswares featured new design ideas. The cameo glass of the period after 1870 had a different look. Heavy layers of glass were molded in a single piece and layers of the glass were cut away to make the design. The resulting pieces were heavy in look and in weight. Large vases and lamp bases were popular. Glass was often made with a dull finish and it resembled stone more than the clear crystal of an earlier time. Several new techniques evolved such as pâte de verre (glass paste) or cire perdue (lost wax). Clear glass for table use in the form of goblets or plates was still popular, but it was made by different factories than the art glass of the cameo types. Colored heavy glass with designs formed inside the glass or made in unusual shapes was also popular with the art glassmakers.

The production of the larger firms was commercially successful and their glass was sold in quantity. However, many pieces were hand-finished in such a way that they are almost one of a kind. Smaller firms made individual pieces.

Cameo and other glasswares of this period should be carefully collected. The quality varied from factory to factory and even within the works of one maker.

MAJOR ART GLASS FACTORIES OF INTEREST TO TODAY'S COLLECTORS

Daum Nancy

Mr. Jean Daum started a glassworks in 1875 in Nancy, France. His sons Auguste (1853–1909) and Antonin (1864–1930) continued the factory. They worked in the Art Nouveau style, making glass that was similar to the work of Gallé. Cased glass, enamel-decorated glass, etched or frosted glass, and other types were made. Paul (1890–1944) and Henri (1894–1966) Daum, sons of Auguste, and Michel (1900–), son of Antonin, worked at the glasshouse but began making free-form clear glass. In 1966, the firm began making pâte de verre again, but the designs were by modern artists. The company, now called Cristalleries de Nancy, was run by Jacques Daum (1919–), son of Paul.

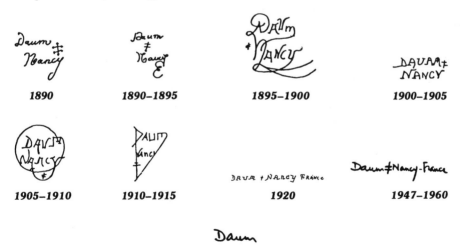

| 1890 | 1890–1895 | 1895–1900 | 1900–1905 |

| 1905–1910 | 1910–1915 | 1920 | 1947–1960 |

| 1960–1971 |

The glass is marked with the Daum signature in various forms. Many of the early pieces were signed on the base with an etched mark, and the signature was often in gilt. The mark became "Daum Nancy" with the cross of Lorraine on the base in about 1910. The word "France" was added after 1919.

A wrought-iron base holds the intaglio-carved shade of this Daum Nancy lamp made about 1925.

Gallé

Gallé glass was decorated in many ways. This enameled vase was made about 1900.

Emile Gallé (1846–1904) worked in Nancy, France. He made furniture, ceramics, and glass. His glass business was established in 1867 in Lorraine, France, and in 1874, he moved to Nancy, France, where he made all sorts of art glasswares including lamps, vases, and tablewares. He developed his own designs for cameo glass and various forms of cased glass. Some pieces were enameled, while others had blown-out decorations. Many pieces were made of opaque-colored glass that was wheel-cut in the cameo style. He also invented several methods by which to use slivers of colored glass in the body of a piece to make a part of the design.

Designs often pictured trees, animals, and insects. The Japanese influence as well as the Art Nouveau styles were apparent in his work.

The factory was managed by Pedrizet-Gallé, a son-in-law, after Emile Gallé died in 1904. It closed in 1931.

Gallé glass was signed with a variety of signatures. He often used Chinese-looking letters that are difficult to read. Some were signed "E. Gallé a Nancy," "Cristallerie d'E.," "Gallé Nancy," "Gallé," or "Emile Gallé." There seems no dating significance to the marks, as they were apparently interchangeable. A star was added to the signature from 1904 to 1914.

Lalique

René Lalique (1860–1945) was a designer of jewelry, silver, glass, and other decorative arts in Paris, France. He started experimenting with glass by 1897. He hired four glassworkers in 1902 and started a workshop using the cire perdue method to make figurines or vases. He also began making

Commercial packaging was an important part of the glass business of Lalique. This powder jar was made for the D'Orsay perfume company. It is marked with the molded words "R. Lalique France."

R.LALIQUE
FRANCE

R. Lalique France

two marks used
until 1945

LALIQUE FRANCE

Lalique France

two marks used
from 1945 to 1960

LALIQUE

Lalique France

two marks used
after 1960

Lalique marks

commercial perfume bottles in small numbers. In 1907, he designed a
bottle for François Coty, but the bottle was made at the Legras and Cie
glassworks. By 1901, he was making bottles for Coty as well as many

*This Lalique vase is called "Amiens."
It is 7⅛ inches high, made of frosted
and clear glass.*

Parakeets are molded in relief against a band of stylized flowers on this opalescent Lalique bowl. It is marked "R. Lalique France."

A glass automobile hood ornament may seem strange today but the Lalique ornaments were very popular. This eagle head is signed "R. Lalique."

other perfume manufacturers. After World War I, Lalique made a variety of quality glasswares, using modern industrial techniques. Lalique made all types of glassware, including tablewares and lamps. His frosted-finish pieces have come to be associated with the name Lalique. Some of the glass was colored—brown, green, blue, gray, yellow, or black. Most of it was made in colorless glass, but there were some pieces made in a pale opalescent glass. Decorations were Art Nouveau or Art Deco.

René Lalique died in 1945 and the firm has continued in business. The mark that had been "R. Lalique" was changed to "Lalique" after his death.

Loetz Glass (Lötz)

A factory was founded in Klostermuhle, Bohemia, in 1836; and about 1840 it was purchased by Johann Loetz (1778–1848). When he died, his wife, Suzanne, continued the glassworks, renaming it Glasfabrik Johann Loetz Witwe (Widow Johann Lietz Glassworks). About 1879, a nephew, Max Ritter von Spaun, took over the management; and the company began making the art glass that is of interest to the collector. At first, the firm made several types of glass that resembled real stones such as onyx, carnelian, agate, aventurine, chalcedony, and jasper. About 1890, the company developed an iridescent gold glass that was similar to the later works of Tiffany. Much of it was sent to the United States. Many other types of glass were developed at the firm. The company went bankrupt in

1911, but they were reorganized in 1913, and made glass until the company closed during World War II.

Most Loetz glass is not signed. Some pieces are marked "Loetz Austria" or with crossed arrows in a circle.

This green and blue iridescent glass vase is typical of the work of the Loetz factory. It was made about 1900 and is signed, although many pieces were left unsigned.

Moser

Koloman, or Kolo, Moser (1868–1918), founded a studio in Karlsbad, Bohemia, in 1900, after working in the art schools of Vienna for a number of years. He made iridescent glass, cameo glass, plus many types of colored glassware.

"Möser/Karlsbad/Made in Austria" is signed on the bottom of this vase with Egyptian motifs.

Ludwig Moser (1833–1916) was a glass engraver in Karlsbad, Bohemia. He founded a company called Ludwig Moser & Sohne in Karlsbad about 1857. They made clear glass pieced with colored glass insets and carved in naturalistic designs. They also made glass with enamel decoration. The company is still working. Most current collectors who ask for Moser glass are referring to the work of this firm.

Steuben

The Steuben Glassworks was founded in Corning, New York, in 1903 by Frederick Carder (1863–1963), Thomas Hawkes (1846–1913), and others. The company made a number of colored glasswares during the early 1900s, including Cluthra, Cintra, peachblow, Aurene (an iridescent ware similar to Tiffany's Favrile), calcite, ivrene, verre de soie, and others. In 1918, Steuben became part of the Corning Glass Works. The firm began making clear glass with blown, cut, or engraved designs. The company was reorganized in 1933 and began making the clear, modern design wares that are still being made. Early pieces were marked with the etched fleur-de-lis and "Steuben." Later pieces are marked with an engraved "Steuben."

common mark, 1903–1932

Steuben

stamped after 1929; engraved with diamond point after 1932

STEUBEN

stamped with acid after 1929; engraved with diamond point after 1932

Aurene was the name for the iridescent gold glass made by the Steuben Glassworks. This vase is signed "Steuben-Aurene."

The black overlay design on the frosted white ground of this Steuben vase is typical of the acid-cut-back cameo technique.

Tiffany

Louis Comfort Tiffany (1848–1933) was responsible for many types of decorative arts in the early twentieth century. He was the son of the owner of the famous Tiffany jewelry store in New York. The family was wealthy and Louis Tiffany decided to become an artist. He studied in Paris and painted watercolors and oils. He met many of the rich and famous through his family's connections and when he returned to America, he became an interior decorator. His firm coordinated or made everything for a room, including furniture, wallpaper, carpet, lights, and accessories. He even did several rooms at the White House in 1883.

While decorating, he became interested in stained-glass windows. He designed several that were made in his workshops. He soon began working with the glass itself and developed many new colors and textures. The

Tiffany made a variety of glasswares. This gold iridescent glass salt dish is typical of the commercial pieces offered to the public.

Tiffany Glass Company was started in 1885 and it was a firm that primarily made stained-glass windows. He founded the Tiffany Glass and Decorating Company in 1892 to make and sell all kinds of glass and to continue the interior decorating. The following year, Tiffany joined with Arthur J. Nash and founded a glass company at Corona, Long Island, New York, that made experimental glass. It was here that the famous iridescent glass called Favrile was developed. Many other types such as agate, millefiori, paperweight, Cypriote, and others were developed during the following years. By 1887, the company was making the bronze or copper metal mounts used for the desk sets and lamps. The company name was changed to Tiffany Furnaces in 1902, but the rest of Louis Tiffany's companies were named Tiffany Studios. Their work continued and the firms made enamel on metal, art pottery, and jewelry. Louis Comfort Tiffany was appointed a vice-president of the family store, Tiffany and Company. In 1920, Tiffany Furnaces became Louis C. Tiffany Furnaces, Inc., and in 1928, the company was sold and the name Tiffany was no longer used. (Of course, the store called Tiffany is still in business today and still sells many items using the Tiffany name.)

The works of Louis Tiffany fell out of favor during the 1920s. The Tiffany Studios went out of business in 1939. It was not until the 1960s that the art world "rediscovered" the designs of L. C. Tiffany.

When buying Tiffany glass or other pieces made by the various firms of the same period, carefully check the name used in the mark. Much of the glass was marked with the etched "L. C. Tiffany" or variations of the signature. Lamp bases and other metal pieces were often marked with the stamped name of the firm. Forgeries are known and fake marks with strange names and combinations of names are to be found. If a piece does not look like Tiffany glass, don't trust the mark!

ART NOUVEAU AND ART DECO ART GLASS MANUFACTURERS AND DESIGNERS OF THE NINETEENTH AND TWENTIETH CENTURIES

Manufacturer/Designer and Location	Dates of Manufacture	Manufacturer/Designer and Location	Dates of Manufacture
Appert Freres Clichy, France	c. 1883	Burgun, Schverer & Cie (Verrerie de Meisentahl, S.A.) Alsace-Lorraine, France	1711– present
Argy-Rousseau Paris, France	c. 1913–1931		
Baccarat (Saint-Anne Glassworks) Baccarat, France	1764– present	Carder. See Steuben.	
E. Bakalowits Sohne Vienna, Austria	1845–1914	Desire Christian-Sohn France	1896–
Les Frères Boutigny Paris, France	1880–1890	James Couper & Sons Glasgow, Scotland	1880s– c. 1900
Philippe-Joseph Brocard Paris, France	(d. 1896)	Albert Dammouse Sèvres, France	1871–1913

Baccarat cameo vase, 10½ inches high.

Manufacturer/Designer and Location	Dates of Manufacture	Manufacturer/Designer and Location	Dates of Manufacture
D'Argental. See Saint Louis ("D'Argental" is mark used by company).		Marcel Goupy Paris, France	1918–1936
Daum Nancy Nancy, France	1875– present	Jacques Grüber Nancy, France	1897–c. 1925
De Vez. See Pantin ("De Vez" is a mark used by the company).		Handel & Co. Meriden, Connecticut	1893–1941
Decorchemont Paris, France	1900–1971	Honesdale White Mills, Pennsylvania	1901–1932
Degué France	?	Imperial Glass Co. Ohio; Pennsylvania	1901– present
Andre Delatte Nancy, France	1921–	Jobling Great Britain	1920s–1930s

Delatte enameled glass vase, 13 inches high.

Manufacturer/Designer and Location	Dates of Manufacture	Manufacturer/Designer and Location	Dates of Manufacture
		Kew-Blas. See Union Glass Co.	
		Kosta Glasbruk Sweden	1742– present
		Lalique Paris, France	1897– present
		Le Verre Francais. See Schneider ("Le Verre Francais" is a mark used by the company).	
Georges Despret Jeumont, France	1884–c. 1914	Legras and Cie St. Denis, France	1864–1920
Durand. See Vineland Glass Manufacturing Co.		Mount Joye (trademark for Legras).	
Fenton Art Glass Co. Martins Ferry, Ohio	1904– present	J. and L. Lobmeyr Vienna, Austria	1859– present
Fostoria Fostoria, Ohio	1899–1917	Loetz (Glasfabrik Johann Loetz Witwe) Klostermühle, Germany	1840–1943
Emile Gallé Saint-Clement, France	1846–1904		

Manufacturer/Designer and Location	Dates of Manufacture	Manufacturer/Designer and Location	Dates of Manufacture
Lustre Art Glass Co. Maspeth, New York	1920–1925	A. Douglass Nash Corporation (Stourbridge Glass Company) Corona, New York	1928–1931
Moncrieff (Monart) Perth Perthshire, Scotland	1880– present	John Northwood (Stevens and Williams; Thomas Webb and Sons) England	(1836–1902)
Monot. See Pantin.		Orrefors Sweden	1898– present
Koloman Moser (E. Bakalowits Sohne) Vienna, Austria	1868–1918	Pantin (E. S. Monot) Pantin, France	1851– present
Ludwig Moser & Sohne Karlsbad, Germany	1857– present	Quezal Art Glass and Decorating Co. (Martin Bach) Brooklyn, New York	1902–1925
Muller Frères Croismare, France	1895–1936		

Muller Frères white, orange, and green cameo vase, 10 inches high.

Pantin cameo vase marked "De Vez," 12 inches high.

Quezal vase of iridescent gold and blue glass, 12¾ inches high.

Manufacturer/Designer and Location	Dates of Manufacture	Manufacturer/Designer and Location	Dates of Manufacture
Sabino, Marius-Ernest Paris, France	1920s–1930s 1960– present	Steuben Glassworks (Frederick Carder) Corning, New York	1903– present
Saint Louis Company (Compagnie des Cristalleries de Saint Louis) Munzthal, France (Germany)	1809– present	Stevens & Williams Stourbridge, England	1847– present
		Louis C. Tiffany Corona, New York	1879–1933
Schneider Epinay-sur-Seine, France	1913– present	Union Glass Co. (Kew Blas) Somerville, Massachusetts	1851–1924
		Val St. Lambert Val St. Lambert, France	1802– present
		Vallerysthal Vallerysthal, France	1836– present
		Verlys, France (Société Anonyme Holophane Les Andelys) France	1931–

Saint Louis goblet signed "D'Argental."

Schneider cameo vase marked "Le Verre Francais," 12 inches high.

Val St. Lambert acid-cut-back vase of lavender on clear glass.

Manufacturer/Designer and Location	Dates of Manufacture	Manufacturer/Designer and Location	Dates of Manufacture
Verlys of America, Inc. Newark, Ohio	1935–1951	Thomas Webb & Sons Stourbridge, England	1837– present
Vineland Glass Manufacturing Co. (Victor Durand) Vineland, New Jersey	1924–1931	WMF (Württemberg Metal Goods Factory) Geislingen, Germany	1853– present
Almaric V. Walter Nancy, France	(1859–1942)		

A. Walter pâte de verre vase, c. 1920, 4½ inches high.

Webb cameo vase, white on brown, 5⅜ inches high.

BIBLIOGRAPHY

General

Arwas, Victor. *Glass, Art Nouveau to Art Deco.* New York: Rizzoli, 1977.

Bloch-Dermant, Janine. *The Art of French Glass, 1860–1914.* New York: Vendome Press, 1980.

Blount, Berniece and Henry. *French Cameo Glass.* Des Moines: Privately printed, 1968.

Duncan, Alastair. *Art Nouveau and Art Deco Lighting.* New York: Simon and Schuster, 1978.

Grover, Ray and Lee. *Art Glass Nouveau.* Rutland, Vermont: Charles E. Tuttle, 1967.

———. *Carved and Decorated European Art Glass.* Rutland, Vermont: Charles E. Tuttle, 1970.

———. *English Cameo Glass.* New York: Crown, 1980.

The Random House Collector's Encyclopedia, Victoriana to Art Deco. New York: Random House, 1974.

Revi, Albert Christian. *American Art Nouveau Glass.* Camden, New Jersey: Thomas Nelson, 1968.

Akro-Agate

Appleton, Bud. *A Guide to Akro Agate Glass.* Silver Spring, Maryland: Privately printed, 1966.

————. *Akro Agate.* Des Moines: Wallace-Homestead, 1972.

Florence, Gene. *The Collector's Encyclopedia of Akro Agate Glassware.* Paducah, Kentucky: Collector Books, 1975.

Papapanu, Sophia C. *Akro Agate Children's Line and Price Guide.* Syracuse: Privately printed, 1973.

Cambridge

Bennett, Harold and Judy. *The Cambridge Glass Book.* Des Moines: Wallace-Homestead, 1970.

Cambridge Glass Company. *The Art of Making Fine Glassware.* Cambridge, Ohio: Privately printed, 1939.

————. *The Cambridge Line.* Cambridge, Ohio: Privately printed, 1958.

————. *1903 Catalog of Pressed and Blown Ware.* Cambridge, Ohio: Privately printed, 1976.

————. *Genuine Hand Made Cambridge.* Cambridge, Ohio: Privately printed, 1956.

National Cambridge Collectors, Inc. *Cambridge Glass, 1949–1953.* Cambridge, Ohio: Privately printed, 1978.

————. *The Cambridge Glass Co.* Cambridge, Ohio: Privately printed, 1976.

Upton, Charles and Mary Alice. *1979 Price Guide to the Cambridge Glass Book.* Cambridge, Ohio: Privately printed, 1979.

Welker, Mary, Lyle and Lynn. *Cambridge, Ohio Glass in Color.* New Concord, Ohio: Privately printed, 1969.

————. *Cambridge, Ohio Glass in Color.* Book 2. New Concord, Ohio: Privately printed, 1970.

————. *The Cambridge Glass Co.: A Reprint of Parts of Old Company Catalogues.* New Concord, Ohio: Privately printed, 1970.

————. *The Cambridge Glass Co.: A Reprint of Parts of Old Company Catalogues.* Book 2. New Concord, Ohio: Privately printed, 1974.

Clubs: National Cambridge Collectors, Inc., P.O. Box 416, Cambridge, Ohio 43725

Museum: Cambridge Glass Museum, 812 Jefferson Ave., Cambridge, Ohio 43725

Carnival Glass

Cosentino, Geraldine and Stewart, Regina. *Carnival Glass: A Guide for the Beginning Collector.* New York: Golden Press, 1976.

Hand, Sherman. *The Collector's Encyclopedia of Carnival Glass.* Paducah, Kentucky: Collector Books, 1978.

Klamkin, Marian. *The Collector's Guide to Carnival Glass.* New York: Hawthorn Books, 1976.

Clubs: American Carnival Glass Association, P.O. Box 273, Gnadenhutten, Ohio 44629; International Carnival Glass Association, RR #1, Mentone, Indiana 46539

Publications: *Carnival Glass News and Views,* P.O. Box 5421, Kansas City, Missouri 64131; *Carnival Glass Tumbler and Mug News,* P.O. Box 5421, Kansas City, Missouri 64131

Daum

Daum, Noil. *Daum, One Hundred Years of Glass and Crystal.* Washington, D.C.: Smithsonian Institution Press, 1978.

Depression Glass

Brady, Ann. *1979 Western Depression Glass Price Guide.* Portland, Oregon: Privately printed, 1979.

Florence, Gene. *Collector's Encyclopedia of Depression Glass.* Paducah, Kentucky: Collector Books, 1979.

Klamkin, Marian. *The Collector's Guide to Depression Glass.* New York: Hawthorn Books, 1973.

Kovel, Ralph and Terry. *The Kovels' Illustrated Price Guide to Depression Glass and American Dinnerware.* New York: Crown, 1980.

McGrain, Pat. *1981 Price Survey.* Frederick, Maryland: Privately printed, 1980.

Stout, Sandra McPhee. *Depression Glass I.* Des Moines: Wallace-Homestead, 1970.

———. *Depression Glass II.* Des Moines: Wallace-Homestead, 1971.

———. *Depression Glass III.* Des Moines: Wallace-Homestead, 1976.

Walker, Mary. *Reamers 200 Years.* Sherman Oaks, California: Privately printed, 1980.

Weatherman, Hazel. *Colored Glassware of the Depression Era 2.* Springfield, Missouri: Glassbooks, 1974.

———. *Colored Glassware of the Depression Era 2: Price Trends.* Springfield, Missouri: Glassbooks, 1977.

Clubs: National Depression Glass Association, Inc., 6100 Martway, #24, Mission, Kansas 66202; National Reamer Collectors Association, c/o Gloria Yates, 277 Highland Ave., Wadsworth, Ohio 44281; Ohio Candlewick Collectors' Club, 613 S. Patterson St., Gibsonburg, Ohio 43431

Publications: *Depression Glass Daze,* P.O. Box 57, Otisville, Missouri 48463; *Depression Glass National Market Appraisal Report,* 2943 Realty Ct., Gastonia, North Carolina 28016; *National Journal,* P.O. Box 3121, Wescosville, Pennsylvania 18106; *Obsession in Depression,* 20415 Harvest Ave. Lakewood, California 90715

Duncan and Miller

Bones, Frances. *The Book of Duncan Glass.* Des Moines: Wallace-Homestead, 1973.

Krause, Gail. *The Encyclopedia of Duncan Glass.* Hicksville, New York: Exposition Press, 1976.

———. *A Pictorial History of Duncan & Miller Glass.* Hicksville, New York: Exposition Press, 1976.

Club: National Duncan Glass Society, P.O. Box 965, Washington, Pennsylvania 15301

Carl Erickson

Knower, Ramona and Franklin. *Erickson Freehand Glass.* Columbus: Privately printed, 1971.

Fenton

Edwards, Bill. *Fenton Carnival Glass: The Early Years.* Paducah, Kentucky: Collector Books, 1981.

Heacock, William. *Fenton Glass: The First Twenty-Five Years.* Marietta, Ohio: 1978. O-Val Advertising Corp., P.O. Box 663, Marietta, Ohio 45750.

———. *Fenton Glass: The Second Twenty-Five Years.* Marietta, Ohio: 1980. O-Val Advertising Corp., P.O. Box 663, Marietta, Ohio 45750.

Linn, Alan. *The Fenton Story of Glass Making.* Williamstown, West Virginia: Fenton Art Glass Co., 1969.

Club: Fenton Art Glass Collectors of America, Inc., P.O. Box 2441, Appleton, Wisconsin 54913

Fostoria

Weatherman, Hazel Marie. *Fostoria, Its First Fifty Years.* Springfield, Missouri: Privately printed, 1972.

———. *The 2nd Price Watch to Fostoria.* Springfield, Missouri: Privately printed, 1977.

Club: Fostoria Glass Society of America, Inc., P.O. Box 826, Moundsville, West Virginia 26041

Fry

Lafferty, James R., Sr. *Fry Insights.* Barstow, California: Privately printed, 1968.

———. *Pearl Art Glass Foval.* Barstow, California: Privately printed, 1967.

Gallé

Garner, Philippe. *Emile Gallé.* New York: Rizzoli, 1976.

Traub, Jules S. *The Glass of Désiré Christian, Ghost for Gallé.* Chicago: The Art Glass Exchange, 1978.

Heisey

Burns, Mary Louise. *Heisey's Glassware of Distinction.* Mesa, Arizona: Triangle Books, 1974.

Bradley, Stephen H. and Constance and Ryan, Robert. *Heisey Stemware.* Newark, Ohio: Spencer Walker Press, 1976.

Coyle, Robert. *The Heisey Animals, Etc.* Book 2. Newark, Ohio: Privately printed, 1973.

Cudd, Viola N. *Heisey Glassware.* Brenham, Texas: Privately printed, 1969.

Emanuele, Concetta. *Heisey Gems.* Sunol, California: Privately printed, 1968.

———. *Heisey Gems II.* Sunol, California: Privately printed, 1969.

Gammon, Don. *Heisey Orchid Etch Glassware.* Cape Girardeau, Missouri: Privately printed, 1977.

A. H. Heisey & Company. *Heisey Hand-Wrought Crystal Catalog and Price List No. 33 (1956).* Chattanooga: Antiques Research Publications, n.d.

———. *Heisey Hand-Wrought Crystal Catalog and Price List No. 32 (1953).* Hanover, Massachusetts: Wind Song Publications, 1978.

———. *Heisey Glassware Catalog No. 75 (1913).* Gas City, Indiana: L. W. Promotions, 1975.

———. *Heisey Glassware Pressed Ware Catalog No. 109.* Gas City, Indiana: L. W. Promotions, 1974.

———. *Heisey's Lead Blown Glassware.* Gas City, Indiana: L. W. Promotions, 1973.

———. *Heisey Glassware Identification and Price Guide.* Gas City, Indiana: L. W. Promotions, 1973.

———. *Salts and Peppers.* (Reprint of 1910 catalog.) Privately printed.

———. *Heisey's Glassware Catalogue No. 76.* Santa Monica, California: Privately printed, 1968.

McDermott, James F. *The Heisey Animals.* Newark, Ohio: Privately printed, 1969.

Ream, Louise W. and Neila and Bredehoft, Thomas. *Encyclopedia of Heisey Glassware: Etchings & Carvings.* Vol. I. Newark, Ohio: Heisey Collectors of America, 1977.

Vogel, Clarence W. *Heisey's Art and Colored Glass, 1922–1942.* Plymouth, Ohio: Heisey Publications, 1970.

———. *Heisey's First Ten Years, 1896–1905.* Plymouth, Ohio: Heisey Publications, 1969.

———. *Heisey's Early and Late Years, 1896–1958.* Plymouth, Ohio: Heisey Publications, 1971.

———. *Heisey's Colonial Years, 1906–1922.* Plymouth, Ohio: Heisey Publications, 1969.

Willey, Harold E. *Heisey's Deep Plate Etching, Etched and Carved, Pressed and Blown, Handmade Glassware.* Newark, Ohio: Privately printed, 1973.

———. *Heisey's Cut Handmade Glassware.* Newark, Ohio: Privately printed, 1974.

Yeakley, Virginia and Loren. *Heisey Glass in Color.* Newark, Ohio: Privately printed, 1970.

———. *Heisey Glass in Color.* Book 2. Newark, Ohio: Privately printed, 1978.

Club: Heisey Collectors of America, Inc., P.O. Box 27, Newark, Ohio 43055

Publication: Heisey Glass Newscaster, P.O. Box 102, Plymouth, Ohio 44865

Museum: Heisey Museum, Newark, Ohio 43055

Imperial

Archer, Margaret and Douglas. *Imperial Glass.* Paducah, Kentucky: Collector Books, 1978.

Ross, Richard and Wilma. *Imperial Glass*. Bellaire, Ohio: Privately printed, 1971.
Club: Imperial Glass Collectors' Society, P.O. Box 4012, Silver Spring, Maryland 20904

Lalique

Arwas, Victor. *Lalique*. New York: Rizzoli, 1980.
Lalique, Marc and Marie-Claude. *Lalique par Lalique*. Lausanne: Edipop, 1977.
McClinton, Katharine Morrison. *Introduction to Lalique Glass*. Des Moines: Wallace-Homestead, 1978.
————. *Lalique for Collectors*. New York: Scribner's, 1975.
Percy, Christopher Vane. *The Glass of Lalique*. New York: Scribner's, 1977.

McKee

Gross, Vicki and Mike. *That Collectible McKee*. Hillsboro, Oregon: Privately printed, 1973.
Stout, Sandra McPhee. *The Complete Book of McKee Glass*. Kansas City, Oregon: Trojan Press, 1972.
————. *Handbook and Inventory Guide to the Complete Book of McKee Glass*. Kansas City, Oregon: Trojan Press, 1972.

New Martinsville

Miller, Everett and Addie. *The New Martinsville Glass Story*. Book 1. Marietta, Ohio: Richardson Publishing, 1972.
————. *The New Martinsville Glass Story*. Book 2. Manchester, Michigan: Rymack Printing, 1975.

Northwood

Hartung, Marion T. *Northwood Pattern Glass in Color, Clear, Colored, Custard, and Carnival*. Emporia, Kansas: Privately printed, 1969.

Paden City

Barnett, Jerry. *Paden City, the Color Company*. Springfield, Missouri: Privately printed, 1978.
Publication: Paden City Partyline, 13325 Danvers Way, Westminster, California 92683

Pairpoint

Padgett, Leonard E. *Pairpoint Glass*. Des Moines: Wallace-Homestead, 1979.
St. Aubin, Louis, O., Jr. *Pairpoint Lamps*. New Bedford, Massachusetts: Privately printed, 1974.

Phoenix

Lafferty, James R., Sr. *The Phoenix*. Privately printed, 1969.

Sinclaire

Farrar, Estelle Sinclaire. *H. P. Sinclaire, Jr., Glassmaker*. Vol. I. Garden City, New York: Farrar Books, 1974.

———. *H. P. Sinclaire, Jr., Glassmaker.* Vol. II. Garden City, New York: Farrar Books, 1975.

Stained Glass

Adam, Stephen. *Decorative Stained Glass.* New York: Rizzoli, 1980.
Halliday, Sonia and Lushington, Laura. *Stained Glass.* New York: Crown, 1976.

Steuben

Gardner, Paul V. *The Glass of Frederick Carder.* New York: Crown, 1971.

Tiffany

Koch, Robert. *Louis C. Tiffany, Rebel in Glass.* New York: Crown, 1964.
———. *Louis C. Tiffany's Art Glass.* New York: Crown, 1977.
———. *Louis C. Tiffany's Glass, Bronzes, Lamps.* New York: Crown, 1971.

Tiffin

Bickenheuser, Fred. *Tiffin Glassmasters.* Grove City, Ohio: Glassmasters Publications, 1979.

Verlys

McPeek, Carole and Wayne. *Verlys of America Decorative Glass.* Newark, Ohio: Privately printed, 1972.

11

Lamps,
Twentieth Century

Lighting changed dramatically with the invention of the light bulb in 1879. One of our present-day sixty-watt light bulbs is equal to the light of twenty-five double-wick whale oil lamps. This meant that electric lamps could be made with shades that would cut or direct the light. The shape of the electric bulb and the nature of a light source with no flame made it possible for the first time to design a lamp with the light source hanging down, or even at an angle.

Tiffany Lamps

Louis Comfort Tiffany designed the first lamp with this new potential in mind. His famous lily lamp had a series of small, down-positioned bulbs that lit a small circle on the tabletop. The first lamps made by Tiffany were used in the Tiffany Chapel and the Church of the Covenant in Boston, Massachusetts. They were large hanging center fixtures. By 1898 Tiffany was making hanging fixtures with leaded glass globes, student lamps, and blown-glass oil lamps.

Lamps with leaded glass shades and bronze bases are bringing the highest prices today. They were not made until 1899, when three of the most famous lamp designs were first made: the Nautilus, Dragon Fly, and the Tyler Scroll lamps. Many types of lamps were made for electric bulbs as well as kerosene and oil. They included table lamps, chandeliers, floor lamps, desk lamps, and student lamps.

Most famous of all American-made lamps are the Tiffany lamps. This lamp was made of gold Favrile glass with a bronze base.

This spider-web leaded-glass, mosaic, and bronze lamp set a world record price for Tiffany lamps in 1980. The 33-inch-high lamp sold for $360,000.

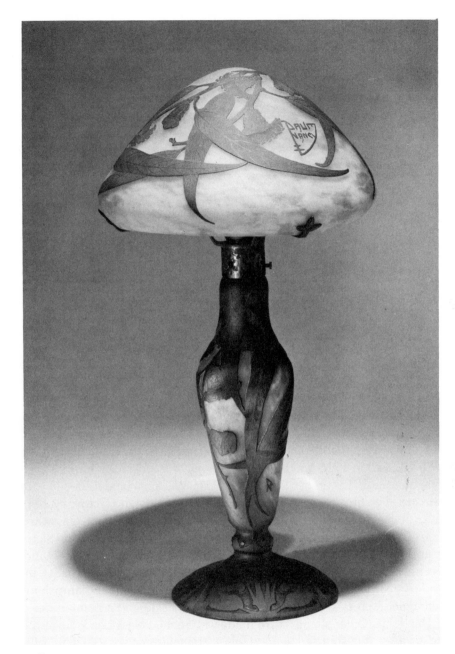

The "Daum Nancy" signature is clearly seen on this red and yellow cameo glass lamp.

The Tiffany Studios made over five hundred different lamp base designs, and almost five hundred lampshade designs.

The bases were usually made of bronze and a few were made with glass accents. There were also pottery bases made by Grueby, Teco, and other potteries. The shades were usually leaded or iridescent Favrile glass as well as other types. Bronze, cut-out silver, or blown or molded glass were also used for shades.

The base of the lamp, or a plate on the base, was stamped with a model number after 1902. The shade was marked with a model number on the metal part of the shade. There was no mark on the glass unless the shade was blown. The lamp left the Tiffany showroom with a shade and base with the identical number. Many "matched" lamps can be found now with different shades. A customer was permitted to choose a lamp base and shade, so the combination could have differed in many ways.

It is possible, but very unlikely, that any unsigned Tiffany lamps were ever made. Tiffany lamps can be found in art museums and famous collections, and the prices began rising dramatically about 1970.

Lamps Other than Tiffany—Handel

Although Tiffany lamps are the most famous, many other glass-shaded lamps were made. Handel lamps made by Philip Handel are considered among the finest.

Adolph Eyden and Philip Handel were glass decorators working under their own names in 1885 in Meriden, Connecticut. In 1893 Handel bought out Adolph Eyden and changed the company name to Handel and Company. He died in 1914 and his widow, Fannie, took over the business. She remarried in 1918, and in 1919 a cousin, William Handel, became the manager. The firm continued under his direction until the factory closed in 1936. It made many types of metalwares, chinawares, and glasswares, such as bottles, vases, and ashtrays. Most of the pieces were signed "Handel," either impressed, on a cloth label, painted or stamped. Handel received a patent for "chipped" glass in 1904. This was a process that made a textured surface on the finished glass. Many Handel lampshades were made with a "chipped" surface on the outside and a painted design on the inside. Other shades were made with refined glass beads furnishing the texture. It also used leaded glass, metal-framed glass, and other techniques.

Sometimes the Handel base was used by another maker to hold a shade. This floor lamp has the Handel bronze base and a Steuben shade.

It is estimated that the company made twenty-five thousand lamps a year for twenty-five years. Many of these were ordinary lamps that sold from $6 up. The highest-priced lamps with leaded glass or reverse-painted glass shades originally sold for $150. Their lamps were made for oil, gas, or electricity. Desk lamps, table lamps, floor lamps, night lights, small shades for wall fixtures and other types of lamps were made.

This Handel lamp has a "chipped ice" painted shade and a bronze base.

Pairpoint

Pairpoint lamps were made from 1890 to 1929 in New Bedford, Massachusetts. The company made glass and plated silver wares as well as lamps. Pressed, cut, and decorated shades were made. There are three

The glass shade of this Pairpoint lamp has the characteristic painting inside the shade. The metal base is stamped with the company name.

The Pairpoint "Puffy" lamp often took strange forms. This shade has raised roses and butterflies.

basic types of Pairpoint shades. Ribbed shades were made with vertical ribs and some occasional floral designs. The second type had a glass shade with a scenic design. The most expensive style today is what collectors refer to as the "blown-out" or "Puffies." The shade is made with a three-dimensional design such as an owl, a Dutch scene, or an orange tree. All of the shades were first frosted and then decorated. Shades can range in size from 3½ inches to 22 inches in diameter. The bases were often made to match the shade, such as a tree trunk for the shade of an orange tree. Bases were usually of metal with a finish of brass, bronze, copper, or silver. Glass was also used, and a few wooden bases are known. The shades were not always signed, which made identification difficult. A few pieces are stamped "The Pairpoint Corporation." Others say "Patented July 9, 1907."

Emeralite

Emeralite lamps were made from 1909 to the 1940s by H. G. McFaddin Company of New York City. They had a brass or bronze base and green

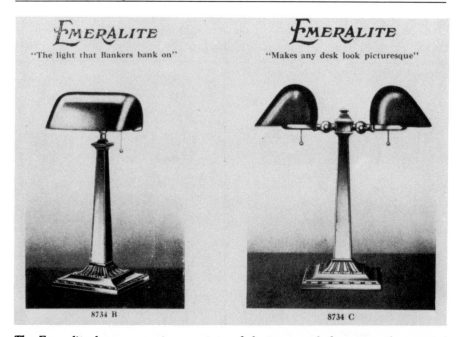

The Emeralite lamp came in a variety of designs, each featuring the special green glass shade. These table lamps were shown in a company catalog of 1916.

glass shade lined with white opal glass. The shade was said to be beneficial to the eyes. Other firms made similar green-shaded lamps. These include Rex-O-Lux, made in the 1920s by the William E. Gray Company of Utica, New York, and Greenalite lamps, made by S. Robert Schwartz of New York City.

Aladdin Lamps

Kerosene lamps became popular after the modern petroleum industry began in 1859. The lamps of the 1890s used round wicks with the air supplied to the flame through a central tube. A German kerosene lamp was made in 1905 with a mantle that fit over the burner to give a better light. The mantle was used in the same manner as in today's gaslight. Victor Johnson of Kansas City, Missouri, saw the German lamp and started a company in Chicago to make and sell lamps. He called it the Mantle Lamp Company of America and his product was the Aladdin Lamp. It gave more light and used less fuel, and became an instant success. Improvements continued and the company made many types of lamps. Kerosene lamps for home use continued to be made at the Aladdin factory in Nashville, Tennessee, until 1968. The company still makes lamps in other countries.

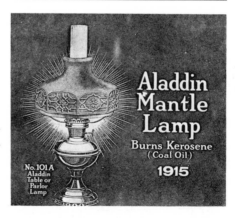

This is Aladdin Lamp No. 101A, shown in a 1915 catalog.

Sixteen United States models of Aladdin lamps were made from 1909 to 1968. A few others were models made in other countries. All styles were made, including table, hanging, bracket, and floor lamps. The most popular lamps with today's collectors are the glass models that were made in the 1930s. A variety of styles were made in amber, peach, white, moonstone, cobalt blue, red, and many other colors.

MANUFACTURERS OF DECORATIVE LIGHTING FIXTURES

Manufacturer and Location	Dates of Manufacture	Comments
Art Glass Manufacturing Company New York, New York	c. 1920	Leaded art glass domes
Albert Berry Seattle, Washington	1918–1972	Copper, slag glass shades, Indian designs
Bradley & Hubbard Meriden, Connecticut	c. 1895– c. 1920	Pierced-metal and bent-glass piano and banquet lamps
W. B. Brown Company Bluffton, Indiana		Mission wood chandeliers, domes, portables
Buffalo Lamp Buffalo, New York		
Chicago Gas Appliance Chicago, Illinois	c. 1910	Leaded-glass, pierced-metal, and bent-glass shades
Cincinnati Artistic Wrought Iron Company Cincinnati, Ohio		Leaded-glass, pierced-metal, and bent-glass shades
Classique Lamps		Copper
Cleveland Window Glass Company Cleveland, Ohio	c. 1906	Leaded art glass domes
Continental Art Glass and Brass Company New York, New York	c. 1910	Electric and gas hanging fixtures; gas, electric and oil lampshades
Craftsman, Gustav Stickley Syracuse, New York	1900–1915	Copper, glass or copper shades
Crown Novelty Company New York, New York	c. 1911	Portables, glass shades
Della Robbia Studios New York, New York	c. 1911	Venetian glass shades
Duffner & Kimberley New York, New York	c. 1895 1906–1926	Leaded-glass shades, pierced-metal, and bent-glass shades
Eagle Glass and Manufacturing Company Wellsburg, West Virginia	c. 1912	Reed and ribbon-patterned glass shades
Emeralite (H. G. McFaddin Co.) New York, New York	1909–1940s	Green glass shades
Fostoria Glass Specialties Co. Fostoria, Ohio	1899–1917	Art glass shades

Manufacturer and Location	Dates of Manufacture	Comments
Faries Manufacturing Co. Decatur, Illinois	1880–1930s	Verdelite line, similar to Emeralite
Frankart, Inc. New York, New York	1920s–1930s	Green metal, Art Deco, nude women
Frankelite Company Cleveland, Ohio	c. 1907– present	Figural-type Art Nouveau boudoir lamps
Fulper Flemington, New Jersey	1858–1929	Pottery, lamps, doll heads
John L. Garvey New York, New York	c. 1900	Gas globe lamps
Giannini & Hilgart Chicago, Illinois	1899– present	Leaded shades, windows, mosaics
Goodwin & Kintz Winsted, Connecticut	c. 1910	Gas and electric portables, electroliers, newels
Greenalite (S. Robert Schwartz) New York, New York	1920s	Green glass shades
L. Grosse Art Glass Company Pittsburgh, Pennsylvania	c. 1892	Stained glass windows and ornamental panels
Handel Meriden, Connecticut	1885–1936	Chipped surface, reverse painted, leaded and metal framed glass
Haskins Glass Company Wheeling, West Virginia	c. 1912	Cut and etched shades and globes
Helmschmeid Manufacturing Company Meriden, Connecticut	1904–1934	Pierced-metal and bent-glass shades
Horn & Brannen Lamp Co.		Reverse painted shades, puffies
Jefferson Company Chicago, Illinois	c. 1920	
Jefferson Glass Co., Ltd. Canada		
Jefferson Lamp Co. Follansbee, West Virginia		
Edward Kennard, Bigelow Studios Boston, Massachusetts		
Kimberly Company New York, New York	c. 1912	
Kiss Brothers Manufacturing Company Meriden, Connecticut	c. 1920	Pierced-metal overlaid art glass
Kramerlite Company, Inc. New York, New York	c. 1921	Pierced-metal and bent-glass shades

This pottery-and-stained-glass lamp was made by Fulper Pottery about 1915–1925. The 16½-inch-high lamp has the name stamped on the base.

Manufacturer and Location	Dates of Manufacture	Comments
L & S Lamps Shade Company Alloway, New Jersey	c. 1925	Shades for Durand glass
Lion Electric Company Brooklyn, New York	c. 1920	Pierced-metal and bent-glass shades
Lustre Art Glass Long Island, New York	c. 1920	Blown glass shades
MLC		

MacBeth-Evans
  Pittsburgh,
  Pennsylvania
	c. 1899–after 1913	Lamp chimneys, shades, globes

McCully & Miles Chicago, Illinois	c. 1908	Art glass shades and domes, opalescent glass

Mantle Lamp Company
  Chicago, Illinois
  Nashville, Tennessee
	1909–1968	Aladdin lamps

Edward Miller &
  Company
  Meriden, Connecticut
	1890s
	c. 1920
		Oil lamps
		Pierced-metal, mosaic, and bent-glass shades

Moe-Bridges Company Milwaukee, Wisconsin	c. 1926+	Pierced-metal and bent-glass shades

Moran & Hastings
  Manufacturing Company
  Chicago, Illinois
  Milwaukee, Wisconsin
  San Francisco,
  California
	c. 1912	Pierced-metal and bent-glass shades

A. Douglas Nash Co. Corona, New York	1928–1931	Art glass shades
William R. Noe & Sons New York, New York	c. 1921	Metal and glass shades
Nuart	c. 1921	Like Frankart
Old Mission Kopper Kraft San Francisco, California	c. 1910	Copper, mica shades

Pairpoint
  New Bedford,
  Massachusetts
	1890–1929	Pressed, cut, and decorated shades, "Puffies"

H. J. Peters Company Chicago, Illinois	c. 1914	Tiffany style; brushed brass

Manufacturer and Location	Dates of Manufacture	Comments
Pittsburgh Lamp, Brass and Glass Co. Pittsburgh, Pennsylvania	c. 1890–1920	Oil lamps, painted shades
Plume & Atwood Manufacturing Company Waterbury, Connecticut	c. 1920	Oil lamps
H. E. Rainaud Company Meriden, Connecticut	1916–1930	Metal bases, glass and metal shades
Rex-O-Lux (William E. Gray Co.) Utica, New York	c. 1920	Green glass shades
Rochester Lamp Company New York, New York	1884–	
Royal Art Glass Company New York, New York	c. 1925	Table lamps, juniors, bridge lamps and novelties; reverse painted on glass shades, pierced metal
Roycroft East Aurora, New York	1895–1938	Mission style, handwrought copper shades and bases, metal and wood bases with glass or fabric shades
Salem Brothers		
Sampson & Allen Lynn, Massachusetts	c. 1911	Pierced-metal and bent-glass shades
Albert Sechrist Manufacturing Company Denver, Colorado	c. 1910	Glass shades
Shapiro & Aronson New York, New York	c. 1916	Fixtures and portables
Steuben New York, New York	1907– present	Art glass shades
Suess Ornamental Glass Co. (Max Suess) Chicago, Illinois	c. 1886– 1893 +	Leaded shades
Louis Comfort Tiffany Corona, New York	1878–1933	Blown and leaded glass globes, and bronze
George Trauttman Chicago, Illinois	c. 1912	

Manufacturer and Location	Dates of Manufacture	Comments
Unique Art Glass and Metal Company Brooklyn, New York	c. 1910	Electric and gas portables, art glass, bent and mosaic glass
U.S. Art Bent Glass Company Hartford, Connecticut Pittsburgh, Pennsylvania	c. 1910	Art and bent-glass shades
Verona Artistic Metal Furniture Chicago, Illinois	c. 1925	Marked "Verona, Chicago, Ill."
Vineland Flint Glass Co.	1897–present	Art Glass Shades
John C. Virden Company Cleveland, Ohio	c. 1932	Ornate pressed glass and metal chandeliers
Weintraub Brass Manufacturing Company New York, New York	c. 1911	Hand-cut filigree brass lined with Tiffany glass
R. Williamson & Company Chicago, Illinois	1885–1917+	Leaded glass, newels, etc.

Many lamps of this period are unmarked and cannot be attributed to any special maker. This metal and slag glass lamp was made about 1910; maker unknown.

Little is yet known about these companies and their wares, but as collector interest grows and prices continue rising, researchers will begin to fill in the many gaps in information that exist today.

BIBLIOGRAPHY

Courter, J. W. *Aladdin: A Collector's Manual & Price Guide Eight.* Simpson, Illinois: Privately printed, 1980.

———. *Aladdin: The Magic Name in Lamps.* Des Moines: Wallace-Homestead, 1971.

1916 Emeralite Catalog. Washington Mills, New York: Gilded Age Press.

1910–1913 Emeralite Catalog. Washington Mills, New York: Gilded Age Press.

1923 Esrobert Catalog. Washington Mills, New York: Gilded Age Press.

1920 Milhender Catalog of Jefferson & Pittsburgh Lamps. Washington Mills, New York: Gilded Age Press.

Paton, James. *Lamps: A Collector's Guide.* New York: Scribner's, 1978.

Thomas, Jo Ann. *Early Twentieth Century Lighting Fixtures.* Paducah, Kentucky: Collector Books, 1980.

St. Aubin, Louis O., Jr. *Pairpoint Lamps: A Collector's Guide.* New Bedford, Massachusetts: Privately printed, 1974.

Clubs: Aladdin Knight, J. W. Courter, Simpson, Illinois 62985; Rushlight Club, 21 Clair Rd., RFD #4, Vernon, Connecticut 06086

12

Clocks, 1880 to 1950

Designing a clock has always been a challenge. The nineteenth century was a period of invention and new technology, when many clocks were produced with totally new mechanisms, so differently shaped clock cases were necessary.

An eighteenth-century or early nineteenth-century clock had a pendulum with a case that was large enough to cover the space required for the swing of the pendulum. Eli Terry of Plymouth, Connecticut, patented a smaller works for a clock in 1816. The smaller clock could be kept on a shelf or a fireplace mantel instead of the floor or wall. By 1840, clock designers discovered a method of using coiled springs instead of weights to drive the works. Clocks with coil works were even shorter in height.

Shelf Clocks

A series of design changes were also reflected in the furniture preferences of the day. At first, clocks were made with small upright rectangular wooden cases, often with decorated glass doors. Small turrets or steeples were sometimes added to the edges. Many new shapes and materials were developed about 1840 because of the coil- or spring-driven clock. Iron, papier-mâché, white metal, and wood were used for cases. Pillars, scrolls, Gothic arches, dancing ladies, flowers, and a myriad of imaginative sculptured or painted decorations appeared.

Aaron Willard of Massachusetts made this shelf clock about 1805.

Shelf clocks were made in many shapes. Left to right: *A pillar and scroll clock by Eli Terry; an acorn shelf clock by Forestville Manufacturing Company, c. 1849; and another pillar and scroll clock made in Waterbury, Connecticut, about 1825.*

The 1860s saw some drastic changes in furniture design. Incised lines and flat patterns sometimes rubbed with gold were popular. Expensive clocks were made of marble and bronze. When marble was not available, iron or wood was painted to look like it. Cast-iron handles, feet, and trim were painted to look like brass. The designs were similar but the quality of the work varied.

At the end of the nineteenth century came the Egyptian Revival styles. Sphinx heads and mummy cases became the fashionable decorations for clocks.

This Sessions mantel clock, from an old catalog page, was made about 1930.

A simple round-faced mantel clock with an elongated curved wooden case appeared.

Calendar Clocks

The Ithaca Calendar Clock Company of Ithaca, New York, dominated the United States calendar clock business from 1865 to about 1914, when that type of clock lost favor. The clock not only told the time of the day but also the date. Some calendar clocks had to be adjusted by hand when the month had fewer than thirty-one days, while others were made to be accurate for as long as four hundred years. The calendar clock was popular in America, but it was of little interest in Europe. Among the companies that made calendar clocks were the Waterbury Clock Company of Water-

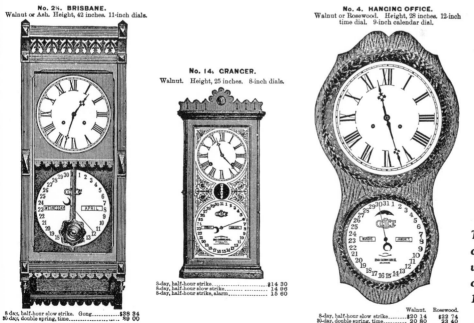

No. 2½. BRISBANE.
Walnut or Ash. Height, 42 inches. 11-inch dials.

No. 14. GRANGER.
Walnut. Height, 25 inches. 8-inch dials.

No. 4. HANGING OFFICE.
Walnut or Rosewood. Height, 28 inches. 12-inch
time dial. 9-inch calendar dial.

8-day, half-hour slow strike. Gong..............$38 34
30-day, double spring, time......................... 49 00

8-day, half-hour strike.........................$14 30
8-day, half-hour slow strike............... 14 96
8-day, half-hour strike, alarm............. 15 60

Walnut.   Rosewood.
8-day, half-hour slow strike........$20 14 $22 74
30-day, double spring, time.......... 20 80   23 40

These Ithaca calendar clocks were offered in a catalog dated 1895.

bury, Connecticut; the Seth Thomas Clock Company of Plymouth, Connecticut; E. Ingraham and Company of Bristol, Connecticut; E. N. Welch Manufacturing Company of Forestville, Connecticut; and the New Haven Clock Company of New Haven, Connecticut.

"Walnuts" and "Oaks"

Elaborately cased clocks were offered in the catalogs of the day as black walnut clocks or embossed oak clocks with elaborate design features. All sorts of curves, scrolls, lines, finials, pillars, and ornamentations were used. The more elaborate the clock the better it sold. "Walnuts" were popular from the late 1870s through 1900. Carved and applied wooden pieces were used on the walnut cases. Decorated glass doors were often added. "Oaks" were in demand from the 1880s until about 1905. They were made by a method similar to the pressed-oak furniture. The wood was actually embossed through the use of steam, pressure, and a mold. The clocks that were the result of the embossed method had decorations that were impossible to make by any other means. One unusual type even pictured prominent men.

"Blacks"

The rectangular marble mantel clocks that had been popular and fashionable remained so from 1880 to about 1920. The expensive marble-and-bronze clock of Europe was copied in less expensive models by the American makers. Iron was painted to look like marble; white metal was coated to appear like bronze, and wooden cases were painted to look like

This Waterbury oak clock was offered for sale in a 1930 catalog, although the style was popular at least fifty years earlier.

WATERBURY CLOCK CO.'S CLOCKS.

Enameled Polished Wood, Imitation Marble, Gilt Engraved, Bronze Ornaments.

COSSACK.

Height, 11⅜ inches; Base, 12 inches; Dial, 5 inches.

8-day, Half-hour Strike Cathedral Gong, ordinary Dial.................................$ 10.50
8-day,   "   "   "   " Porcelain " 12.50

SORRENTO.

Height, 11⅞ inches; Base, 12½ inches; Dial, 5 inches.

8-day, Half-hour Strike, Cathedral Gong, ordinary Dial....................................$ 10.50
8-day   "   "   "   " Porcelain " 12.50

Some less expensive clocks were made of painted wood that looked like black marble. These Waterbury clocks were offered in the same 1895 catalog as the more expensive marble Seth Thomas clocks on the following page.

An 1895 catalog offered these Seth Thomas Company walnut clocks. All had gold-decorated dials and elaborate wooden cases.

marble. Incised lines were rubbed with gold or gilt and that was often the main decoration. This type of clock was sturdy with a good eight-day movement. Some even had alarms or bells.

Octagon Drop or Schoolhouse Clocks

The schoolhouse clock was a popular style of wall clock that was used in offices, homes, and schools from about 1885 until the 1930s. Most of the clock cases were made of golden oak, rosewood, walnut, mahogany, or pressed oak. Some have been found made of pine, cherry, or other woods. The drop below the face of the clock was either four- or five-sided.

Some mantel clocks were made of black marble. These rectangular Seth Thomas clocks were in an 1895 catalog. The trim was gold.

The clockworks were eight-day; time only; time and strike; or time and calendar. Excellent reproductions of many of these clocks have been imported from Japan and Korea, and it is virtually impossible to tell the old from the new unless you are an expert. Some experts claim that the octagonal sides of the clockface case are wedged together on old clocks and not on the new ones.

Electric Clocks

The battery-powered electric clock was first available in quantity in the

Electric clocks were first made to run on batteries, about 1870. It was not until the power supply was uninterrupted and available in most homes that the electric clock was made to plug into a wall. That was about 1930. This United Electric Company clock had a bartender with an arm that moved with each tick (c. 1930).

These drop octagon-shaped clocks were made in a selection of woods by the Waterbury Clock Company about 1895.

United States during the 1870s. Alarm clocks, figural clocks, mantel clocks, plus many other types were made with slight variations in design that would accommodate the new type of works.

Alarm Clocks

The idea of using a clock as a waking device is not new. Some early examples of alarm clocks even set off gunpowder charges. The wind-up alarm with a bell was made in quantity from about 1880. The most popular shape by 1900 was a round-faced clock set on small feet and topped by a large half-sphere that served as the bell. Later models had the bell hidden inside the clock. Some of the more fanciful examples of the early alarm clocks were shaped like trains or had moving figures on the dial. The alarm clock has continued in popularity, and many are made using electricity or batteries, but there are still many that must be wound either weekly or daily.

Animated Clocks

Animated dial clocks were made as early as the seventeenth century. They usually had a ship that rocked, or a moon that moved at the top of

Alarm clocks were popular from the 1880s. These Seth Thomas clocks were offered for sale in an 1895 catalog.

the clockface. Any clock that has a lever or escape wheel that moved some part of the face of the clock in addition to the hands is considered animated. Animated clocks were made in the United States, England, France, and Germany. Many of them first started appearing about 1880. The demand has continued through the twentieth century with new designs available each year. Many of the clocks were made as part of a sales promotion, so the name of the clock manufacturer does not always appear. Dial faces picture a lady strumming a mandolin, the turning of a windmill, an organ grinder turning a crank while a bear dances, comic figures with eyes that roll, or even a dancing Mickey Mouse. One hundred of these clocks are pictured and listed in the *Bulletin of the National Association of Watch and Clock Collectors,* August 1967 and August 1978.

Some of the most sought-after recent clocks were made by Lux Clock Company, August Keebler, and Westclox. From the early 1900s to the 1950s these firms made animated clocks in the shapes of dogs, cats, flowers, or clowns. The clocks operated with a key-wind and pendulum mechanism. They are marked.

Figurals and Blinking-Eye Clocks

The strange idea of putting a clock into a case that was shaped like a man seems to have been an 1870 inspiration. Both men and women were depicted; the clock was placed in the stomach of the figure. Some of them had animated features, where the eyes were designed to roll back and forth with each tick of the clock. Most of them were made of black cast iron and manufactured by Chauncey Jerome, who worked in many cities in Connecticut. The idea has survived and examples of Walt Disney figures with rolling eyes and a clock set in the stomach continues. Another strange American clock was the bobbing doll clock, which was made about 1886. The clock was made with a space for a girl on a swing to hang below the face. The tiny doll on a swing was suspended from a spring that moved up and down as the clock ticked. A similar French clock had a cherub swinging under an alabaster clock case. Other types of fantasy clocks have been made, including women who swing pendulums, glass clocks with no obvious mechanisms, skeleton clocks, and water clocks. They were all designed to confound the person who just wanted to know the correct time.

TOPSY

CONTINENTAL

A variety of "winker" clocks were offered in catalogs of the 1870s. These iron clocks, about 16 inches high, all had eyes that moved from side to side.

Figural clocks that moved were popular in the 1870s. This metal banjo player clock was made of iron. His eyes move.

Other types of novelty clocks were popular. These clocks, offered in an 1895 catalog, all had a moving part. Usually an arm moved to suggest motion. The female figures scrubbed clothes or fanned themselves; the male figures mixed medicines or played the banjo.

Twentieth-century souvenir clocks were popular. This white metal clock, finished in bronze, was made to commemorate the 1928 flight of Charles Lindbergh.

A collector can choose from dozens of categories of clocks and myriad prices and styles. It is always important to know that the clock works, as some repairs can be difficult if not impossible.

The Lux clocks were the novelty clocks of the 1930s. The shaped clown face did not move, but while the hands told the time, the tie moved back and forth with each tick. The cat clock had a wagging tail.

Clocks usually need only cleaning. It is always best to find a clock with its original label or with the maker's name so that it can be identified or dated. Chimes, bells, animation, or unique features always add to the value. The case should be in its original condition. If you buy a refinished and repaired clock be sure you know what pieces are not original.

Other unusual clocks were made, some with strangely shaped cases, some with unusual mechanisms. These two clocks were typical of the clocks offered in an 1895 catalog.

BIBLIOGRAPHY

Ehrhardt, Roy. *Clock Identification and Price Guide.* Book 2. Kansas City, Missouri: Heart of America Press, 1979.

Miller, Robert W. *Clock Guide Identification with Prices.* Des Moines: Wallace-Homestead, 1971.

Nicholson, Don and Alice. *Novelty and Animated Wall Pendulette Clocks.* Garland, Texas: Privately printed, 1977.

Palmer, Brooks. *A Treasury of American Clocks.* New York: Macmillan, 1967.

Schwartz, Marvin D. *Collector's Guide to Antique American Clocks.* Garden City, New York: Doubleday, 1975.

Shenton, Alan and Rita. *The Price Guide to Clocks, 1840–1940.* Suffolk, England: Baron Publishing, 1977.

Advertising clocks often appeared in soda fountains and barbershops. This clock is really an ad for Ever Ready razors. It was made about 1900.

Westcot, Alex. *The Standard Antique Clock Value Guide.* Paducah, Kentucky: Collector Books, 1977.
Club: National Association of Watch & Clock Collectors. 514 Poplar St., P.O. Box 33, Columbia, Pennsylvania 17512
Publication: Clockwise, 1236 E. Main St. Ventura, California 93001

13

Toys and Dolls,
Late Nineteenth and
Twentieth Centuries

Lithographed Tin Toys

Toys have always enchanted collectors. The early cast-iron, hand-painted
tin, wooden, ceramic, or paper toys have always been popular. The earliest
American tin toys were made and painted by hand. The industry operated
mainly in Connecticut during the 1840s. Tin toys were made through the
1870s and 1880s, the period of the cast-iron toys, and after. Most American toys were imported from Germany, France, or England by the 1890s.
The lithographed tin toy was a favorite.

Offset lithography was developed during the 1840s, partly for the toy
industry. There were several styles of printing that put a pattern on a piece
of tin and by 1890 the offset method was used by almost everyone.

German toy makers produced many types of toys such as kitchenware, boats, fire stations, cars, and working people. The makers changed the names on toys to match the market and by 1900 over one-third of all German-made toys were sold to America. Many toys were hand-made as late as 1900. Many were still hand-painted or hand-stenciled.

French toys were often quite elaborate, and they were not exported in quantity to America. Manufacturers in the United States were making toys through the years, but it was not until World War I that the industry blossomed. Imaginative toys were produced and many comic-strip- and celebrity-inspired toys were made. Trains, boats, automobiles, housewares, active animals, and people were made. British toy makers were also more active after World War I. The best of their toys seem to date from the 1920s and 1930s.

Lithographed tin toys should be purchased in good to mint condition. Never repaint a metal toy, as it will destroy the value. Some repairs to mechanical parts are possible, but it is best to locate toys in working condition. There are some makers that are of special interest to collectors. These toys are bringing premium prices and include the names Lehmann, Marx, Chein, Unique, Wolverine, and Strauss.

LITHOGRAPHED-TIN TOY MAKERS OF GREAT INTEREST

Many of the makers marked their toys with names of special symbols. To learn more about the markings, see *Toys, Dolls, Automata, Marks and Labels* by Gwen White, and *The Art of the Tin Toy* by David Pressland.

Alps, Tokyo, Japan, 1948–
Alps Shoji, Ltd. made tin toys in Japan after 1948.

Arnold, Nürnberg, Germany, 1906–c. 1960
Karl Arnold founded the company in 1906 and continued working except for the war years. The firm made tin toys, boats, cheap novelty toys, and trains.

Ashahi, Tokyo, Japan, 1950–
Ashahi Toy Company made lithographed tin toys after 1950.

Bandai, Tokyo, Japan, 1950–
Bandai Company, Ltd. made lithographed tin toys after 1950.

Bassett-Lowke, Ltd., Northampton, England, 1899–1953
The firm made scale-model railroads until 1953, when it stopped making toys.

Bing, Nürnberg, Germany, 1863–1932, 1960–
Gebruder Bing was a toy company that was started in 1863. It made boats, key-wind figures, wheeled vehicles, and many other types of toys. The firm went into receivership in 1932 and was split, with some departments sold to other companies. In the 1960s, the name was

acquired by another German toy maker. Its toys were marked "GBN" until 1919, when the mark became "BW."

Bonnet et Cie. See Victor Bonnet et Cie.

Brenco. See J. G. Brenner and Co.

J. G. Brenner and Company, Manchester, England

The company used "Brenco" as a trademark.

Brimtoy, London, England, 1914–c. 1925

Merged with Wells to form Wells Brimtoy. Made tin road vehicles.

Karl Bub, Nürnberg, Germany, 1851–1967

Burnett, Ltd., Birmingham, England, 1914–

Taken over by Chad Valley.

Carette, Nürnberg, Germany, 1886–1917

Georges Carette made tin cars, boats, railways, and planes.

Chad Valley, Birmingham, England, 1820–present

The company started in 1820, making stationery and printed toys. The first catalog was printed in 1897, and its trademark was used for the first time. It made paper construction toys and lithographed tin toys.

Toy rabbit by J. Chein and Company.

Chein Industries, Inc., Burlington, New Jersey, 1903–present

Chein is known for its colorful lithographed tin banks and toys. The company also made tin boxes, including many reproductions of old designs such as the roly-poly tin. The company is still in business, but its manufacturing of toys ended in 1977.

Citroen, France, 1923–c. 1960s?

André Citroen, the motorcar company, made toy cars as advertisements from 1923 to sometime after World War II.

Crescent Toys, Cwmcarn, Wales and London, England, 1922–present

Made toy soldiers, metal toys; later, plastic toys.

Fischer, Nürnberg, Germany, 1908–c. 1930

H. Fischer and Company made tin toys. Many of them were unmarked, like the famous Toonerville Trolley.

Fleischmann, Nürnberg, Germany, 1887–present

J. Fleischmann's most famous toys are the boats made in the 1920s and 1930s. It took over Doll et Cie in 1939 and made model railroads. It still makes model trains.

Gunthermann, Nürnberg, 1887–1965

The company was founded by S. Gunthermann in 1887. After his death, his widow continued the business with her new husband, Adolf Weigel, who was also the firm's manager. The company made horse-drawn vehicles, cars, planes, and tin toys. The firm was acquired by Siemens in 1965. The company used the mark "SG" from 1887 to 1903 and from 1920 to 1965.

From 1903 to 1920, the manager's initials "AW" were added to the "SG" mark.

Haji, Tokyo, Japan, 1951–

Trademark of Mansei Toy Company, Ltd. of Tokyo, founded in 1951.

Hausser, Neustadt, Germany, 1904–present

The company made tin toys, soldiers, and composition figures sold by the name Elastolin. Production ceased during World War II; but after the war, tin toys were made again. Most of the tin toys were discontinued by 1957, but it is still making wooden toys.

Hess, Nürnberg, Germany, 1825–c. 1930

Mathias Hess founded the firm in 1825. Tin and clockwork toys were made until the early 1930s.

Ives, Plymouth, Connecticut, 1886–1930

Edward Ives was making tin toys with his father by the 1860s. In 1872, his firm was Ives and Blakeslee. Clockwork toys, window displays, horse-drawn vehicles, and trains were made. Iron toys were made in the 1880s. The firm went bankrupt and was acquired by the Lionel Corporation in 1930.

JEP, Paris, France, 1899–1965

Trademark of Jouets de Paris, a firm making toy cars until 1965.

Joustra, France, 1934–present

Mark used by Societé d'exploitation du Jouet Joustra, founded in 1934. The firm is still making tin toys. The company made tin toys, clockwork trains on rails after 1905, electric trains by 1914, cars and railroad accessories.

Kingsbury, Keene, New Hampshire, 1895–c. 1945

"Kingsbury" is a name used on toys by Harry Thayer Kingsbury. He bought the Wilkins Toy Company in 1895 and continued making toys under its name until 1919. After that, the Kingsbury name was used. The firm made clockwork toys and wheeled vehicles. It stopped making toys after World War II.

Lehmann, Brandenburg, Germany, 1881–present

Ernest Paul Lehmann founded the company in 1881, making tin containers. It also made clockwork and lithographed tin toys. The company worked until 1949, when the firm was taken over by the Russians. A cousin of the founder started a new factory in West Germany in 1951. It is still making metal toys.

Lineol, Brandenburg, Germany, 1906–1942

In the 1930s the company made horse-drawn military toys, soldiers, and military vehicles with composition figures. The company is now located in East Germany and little is known about its production.

Lines Brothers, London, England, 1858–present

Made clockwork toys and tin cars. "Tri-Ang" trademark used after 1927; "Minic" trademark used on clockwork toys.

Marklin, Göppingen, Germany, 1859–present

The company started making tin toy kitchenwares. It became Marklin Brothers in 1888, and Gebruder Marklin and Company from 1892 to 1907, then Gebruder Marklin & Cie. It made tin boats, trains, and horse-drawn vehicles in the 1890s. Their toys were the German versions of the Meccano toys of Britain. The company is still making toys, including trains.

Martin, Paris, France, 1878–1921

Fernand Martin started his toy factory in Paris in 1878. He made mechanical toys and clockwork toys. Toys were marked "FM." The company was succeeded by Victor Bonnet et Cie.

Marx, New York, 1921–present

Louis Marx started as office boy to Ferdinand Strauss, the toy maker. He became director of the company, but soon started his own firm with his brother in 1921. He made tin toys, electric trains, windup toys, and many others.

Mettoy Company, Ltd., London, England, 1922–present

Henry Ullmann, owner of the German firm Tipp and Company, founded this company in 1930. It made tin toys. Today it makes the die-cast Corgi Toys.

Minic. See Lines Brothers.

MT, Tokyo, Japan, 1924–

Trademark of the KK Masutoku Toy Factory of Tokyo, founded in 1924.

Ernst Plank, Nürnberg, Germany, 1886–1930s

Early toys made by the company were locomotives, clockwork figures, and music boxes. Magic lanterns, optical toys, steam engines, streetcars, and boats were made by 1895. Tin toys were made till the 1930s, when the company was taken over by Schuller Brothers.

Schuco, Germany, 1912–present

Schreyer and Company was founded in 1912. They used the trademark "Schuco" for their toys. The firm made many clockwork toys and cars during the 1920s and 1930s. It is still working.

SH, Toyko, Japan, 1959–

Trademark of Horikawa Toys, Tokyo.

Stephens and Brown Manufacturing Company, Cromwell, Connecticut, 1869–c. 1880

George Brown was one of the most important early toy makers in America. He had his own company, making key-wind and tin toys. In 1869, he joined J and E Stephens as the Stephens and Brown Manufacturing Company. They made many types of tin toys, cast-iron toys, and banks.

Strauss, New York, New York, c. 1900–1920

Ferdinand Strauss was one of the largest producers of toys at the beginning of the 1900s. The company made clockwork, windup, and other tin toys.

Sutcliffe, Leeds, England, 1885–present

The Sutcliffe Company made toy boats in the 1920s, and still makes tin boats.

J. W. Sutcliffe, England, 1882–present

Made tin toys, battleships, and speedboats with clockwork mechanisms. Today it specializes in tin boats.

Taiyo, Tokyo, Japan, 1959–

Trademark of Taiyo Kogyo Company, Ltd., Tokyo.

Tipp and Company, Germany, 1912–1971

Made tin toys until 1933, when owner Philip Ullmann fled to England. The company made military toys from the 1930s to 1942. In 1948, the company was returned to Ullmann and it made tin toys until 1971.

TM, Tokyo, Japan, 1923–

Trademark of Nomura Toys, Ltd., Tokyo.

TPS, Tokyo, Japan, 1956–

Trademark of Toplay, Ltd., Tokyo.

Tri-Ang. See Lines Brothers.

Victor Bonnet et Cie, Paris, France, 1921–

Victor Bonnet et Cie took over the company of Fernand Martin and continued making the same toys. It used the Martin trademark, its own trademark, and sometimes the name "Vebe." It made many tin-wheeled vehicles during the 1940s and 1950s.

W. George Brown and Company. See Stephens and Brown

Manufacturing Co.

Weedon Manufacturing Company, Boston, Massachusetts, 1882–present

William Weedon started a company that made steam engines, fire engines, and other toys.

Wells, London, England, 1923–1950s

Made tin road vehicles in the 1920s and 1930s, resuming production after the war.

Wilkins Toy Co. See Kingsbury.

This tin bird has the German mark "Ges. Gesch" (patented) but no maker's name.

These three tin windup toys are typical of the exuberant look of the lithographed toys of the 1920s in America.

Ferris wheel by J. Chein and Company about 1950.

CARS AND RELATED CAST TOYS

The child's toy auto of the 1920s and 1930s has become a collector's treasure. There is an imaginary dividing line for collectors: cars made before 1940 and cars made after World War II. Metal toy cars were not made in the United States from mid-1942 to late 1945 because of the war. Many of the bronze molds that had been used for the earlier cars were melted for scrap during this period.

The Substance

Most of the cars that were made before 1940 were made of metal, cast iron, aluminum, stamped steel, or alloys. The most common cars were a white metal alloy consisting of lead, tin, and antimony, or a zinc alloy consisting of aluminum, magnesium, copper, and zinc.

A rubber fire truck driven by a comic character.

"Pot" metal was used in the very inexpensive cars. It was a mixture of metal scraps that included pewter, lead, tin, Britannia metal, and even used toothpaste tubes.

Some cars were made of hard rubber or plastic. The rubber cars were inexpensive, realistic scale models of old cars or very streamlined futuristic or imaginative cars. Collectors do not seem as interested in this type of car because rubber hardens, cracks, and ages badly.

A typical pot metal toy car, unmarked.

Plastic was not used until the late 1930s. Bakelite was the first plastic used, but it was too fragile and was replaced by Butyrate in the 1940s.

Heat melted Butyrate, so most manufacturers switched to polystyrene and copolymer styrene. Today, car models are made of metal, plastic, or a combination of the two.

The Method

Miniature metal cars were usually made by stamping, die-casting, or slush-casting. The earliest lightweight metal cars were stamped from sheet steel or tin and either hand-painted or decorated by lithography. European-stamped tin cars date from the early 1890s.

Die-cast toys were made in a closed mold. Molten metal was injected under pressure into a closed mold. The mold came apart into as many as six pieces, and sometimes several castings made one toy. This method gave a toy with a smooth interior. Lettering could also be part of the casting.

Slush-cast toys were made in simple molds into which pot metal was hand-poured, and poured right out again, causing a rough interior surface. No mark could be cast into the inside of a slush-cast toy. Some of the bronze molds for toys were sold to other makers after a factory closed. There are some new slush-cast toys being made in the old molds.

Other methods of making toy cars include sand-casting for aluminum models and centrifugal-casting for metal wheels.

The Value

The value of a toy auto, or almost any toy, is determined by its rarity, desirability, and condition. Collectors rate condition as "mint in box," "brand new" or "mint," "like new," "excellent," "very good," "good," "fair," "poor," or "good only for parts." There can be a difference of opinion on the grading in many cases, so you must be very careful when buying by mail.

It is important to have a complete car. Sometimes the original wheels, headlights, or accessories are missing or have been replaced. This lowers the value.

Any old toy car, from mint condition to broken, has a resale value. Don't throw anything away before checking with a toy collector. Don't repaint, restore, or even clean an old toy. The original paint helps to identify a toy and shows that it is not a reproduction. An expert can tell whether the paint was applied by dipping, spraying, or brushing and will know the correct color for each make and model of car. A repainted car is worth less than half as much as a car with the original finish.

Any car made before World War II is of value, and most of them made after World War II are also being collected. The general rule has been that any car older than the collector is collectible.

Wheels can help to date a car. Before World War II, wheels were open-spoked metal wheels, solid metal disk wheels, solid metal disk wheels with embossed spikes, white rubber tires or metal rims or solid white rubber tires mounted directly on the axles. The general rule is that white rubber tires were used before World War II and black tires after the war. Black plastic wheels have been in use since about 1960.

THE MAKERS

Just as some ceramic factories or silversmiths have become so famous that their wares command extra interest from collectors, some car makers have gained fame. Frequently, the name on the toy is enough to assure a buyer.

Auburn Rubber Corporation

The Double Fabric Tire Corporation was founded in 1913 in Auburn, Indiana. The company made auto tires for full-sized cars. A toy soldier of molded rubber was first made in 1935. After that, the company made many other toys, including a number of wheeled vehicles. The firm name was changed to the Auburn Rubber Corporation and the toy manufacturing part was purchased by the town of Deming, New Mexico. It made toys until about 1968. Toy collectors prize their cars and the large number of Auburn soldiers and ballplayers.

Buddy "L"

Buddy "L" was the name used by the Moline Pressed Steel Company of Moline, Illinois, in 1921. It made toy trucks, fire engines, and other large toy vehicles like concrete mixers and road rollers. Most of them range in length from 21 to 24 inches. The toys were made from heavy steel and were strong enough to hold a child. By the early 1930s, the toys were less sturdy and much lighter in weight. The company changed from the Buddy "L" Corporation to the Buddy "L" Toy Company, and today it uses the name Buddy L (no quotation marks). Its early toys include a variety of trucks, Fords, and construction equipment.

A windup tin toy. The lady walks as she stirs her food in the mixing bowl.

Dinky Toy

Meccano Limited was founded in Liverpool, England, in 1901. The company made construction kits for toys, using perforated metal parts that had to be bolted together. The company began making clockwork trains and later O gauge electric trains after World War I. Later on, it started making OO gauge. In 1933, the Dinky Toy model cars were first announced. Production was curtailed during World War II, but by 1946 new model cars and planes were offered. The company was purchased by Lines Brothers in 1964 and it has continued making toys under the name Dinky Toy.

The firm had owned a French factory since 1924 and it made a special line of French Dinky toys.

The name "Dinky Toy" was molded in relief in the cast metal or stamped in the pressed-metal base after World War II. The same general rules for the changes in wheel design are true for Dinky Toys for American-made toys such as Tootsietoys.

Grey Iron Casting Company

The Grey Iron Casting Company was founded as the Brady Machine Shop in Mount Joy, Pennsylvania, in 1840. The name was changed in 1881. The company was making wheeled vehicles, trains, banks, stoves, and cap pistols by 1903. Best known are its model Fords of the 1920s and after and its many toy soldiers. Grey toys are still being made by John Wright, Inc., of Wrightsville, Pennsylvania, a division of Donsco.

Hubley Manufacturing Company

The Parcel Post Harley Davidson motorcycle was made by Hubley about 1930.

The Hubley Manufacturing Company was founded in 1894 in Lancaster, Pennsylvania. It made iron toys such as circus wagons and mechanical banks. The iron cars that they were making by the 1930s were advertised with the slogan, "They look just like the real ones." The cars were sometimes marked with the company name cast into the body, or with a decal. Many of its molds were donated to the scrap drives during World War II, at which time the company made bomb fuses. After the war, Hubley made die-cast and plastic toys. The company was acquired by Gabriel Industries in 1965 and it is still making toys, including the Gilbert Erector sets.

Kenton Hardware Manufacturing Company

The Kenton Lock Manufacturing Company was started in 1890 in Kenton, Ohio. The name was changed in 1894 to Kenton Hardware Manufacturing Company. The firm made horse-drawn iron toys till the 1920s. It started making them again from 1939 to 1954. Cars stamped "Kenton" were made by 1900. The company also made iron banks.

Manoil Manufacturing Company

The Mon-O-Lamp Corporation was started in 1928 in New York City; and, by 1934, it changed its name to Manoil Manufacturing Company. At first, the company made lamps, banks, picture frames, and other novelties; but by 1934, it concentrated on making toys. It made mostly slush-cast and some die-cast cars that were noted for their futuristic designs. Tires on its early cars were white rubber on red hubs. The postwar models had black rubber tires. The company made many types of lead soldiers and plastic toys.

The Kenton Hardware Manufacturing Company made many toys, including this cast-iron double-decker bus, 6 inches long.

Tootsietoy

The first Tootsietoy was a small limousine that was made in 1911 by the Dowst Brothers Company of Chicago, Illinois. The "Tootsietoy" name was not registered until 1924 and did not appear on the cars until 1926. The name became Dowst Manufacturing Company from 1926 to 1961. A few models were cast without the name until 1931. This means that some of the oldest and most valuable Tootsietoys have no name or marking on the bottom. Tootsietoys are still being made; but since 1961, the name of the company has been Strombecker Corporation.

"Tootsietoy" appeared on toys after 1926. This brougham was from the General Motors series.

Wheels help date Tootsietoys. The early cars had open-spoked turning metal wheels. From 1923 to 1933, they were made with solid metal disk turning wheels; starting in 1927 solid disk wheels with embossed wire spokes were made. White rubber tires on metal rims were introduced in 1933, and by 1937, solid white rubber wheels were used on the axle. Solid black rubber wheels were used on post–World War II models, and black plastic wheels after 1960.

Tootsietoy coupe, Torpedo series.

The style of the car always helps determine dates. Most cars were made in the style of the day. Some of the modern Tootsietoys may have some plastic parts.

Age is not always the best indication of value: scarcity is often the key. The 1932 Funnies series is valuable. It consists of six comic characters, each in a car. LaSalles, the Graham town car, the 1925 panel delivery truck marked "Florist," and the truck marked "Hochschild Kohn and Co." or "J. C. Penney" are the rarest.

Tootsietoy federal milk truck, 3 inches.

Tootsietoy tanker, General Motors series, 3 inches.

Tootsietoy, doodlebug.

OTHER TOY CAR NAMES TO WATCH FOR

A. C. Williams Company, Ravenna, Ohio, made cast-iron and a few nickel-plated cast-iron cars.

Arcade Manufacturing Company, Freeport, Illinois, was founded in 1868 and flourished in the 1920s and 1930s. It stopped manufacturing at the beginning of World War II. Cars were die-cast iron, marked with a decal which has been forged in recent years. Arcade also made toy cast-iron traffic signs and gasoline pumps, marked on the bottom "Arcade Mfg. Co., Freeport, Ill." Arcade cars are considered to have the heaviest casting, the best paint, and the closest resemblance in scale and replica to the real thing. The company also made coffee mills, hinges, and other household goods.

Auburn. See Cars and Related Cast Toys.

Barclay Manufacturing Company, West Hoboken, New Jersey, was a major manufacturer of slush-cast toys from 1921 to 1971, but also did some die-casting in the 1930s. The die-cast cars were sometimes marked "Barclay Made, U.S.A." Toy soldiers were a specialty.

Buddy L. See Cars and Related Cast Toys.

Carette. See list under Lithographed-Tin Toy Makers.

Carter Tru-Scale, Rockford, Illinois, made farm toy models from 1946 to 1971, when the company sold out to Ertl Company.

Chein. See list under Lithographed-Tin Toy Makers.

Citroen. See list under Lithographed-Tin Toy Makers.

Corgi. See Mettoy Company, Ltd. on list under Lithographed-Tin Toy Makers.

Cosmos Manufacturing Company, 1892, merged with Doust in 1926; made Cracker Jack toys and others.

Dent Hardware Company, Fullerton, Pennsylvania, made mainly cast-iron and some cast-aluminum vehicles, including Mack trucks and buses.

Dinky Toy. See Cars and Related Cast Toys.

Ertl Company, Dyersville, Iowa, made die-cast metal farm and construction toy vehicles from 1945 to 1967. It became a subsidiary of Victor Comptometer Corporation in 1967 and is still making trucks, cars, and toys.

Freidag, Freeport, Illinois, made cast-iron models and some aluminum ones. A favorite is the cast-iron American La France pumper fire engine.

Gebruder Bing, Nürnberg, Germany, made tin toys from c. 1895 to 1934. Bing made popular inexpensive, lithographed metal, clockwork-powered cars, including Checker and Yellow taxicabs and five clockwork Ford Model T's, for the American market.

Grey. See Cars and Related Cast Toys.

Hubley. See Cars and Related Cast Toys.

Ives. See list under Lithographed-Tin Toy Makers.

JEP. See list under Lithographed-Tin Toy Makers.

Lithographed and painted tin roadster by Carette of Germany.

Kenton. See Cars and Related Cast Toys.

Kilgore Manufacturing Company, Westerville, Ohio, made cast-iron cars including a Stutz roadster.

Kingsbury. See list under Lithographed-Tin Toy Makers.

Lehmann. See list under Lithographed-Tin Toy Makers.

Maerklin (Marklin). See list under Lithographed-Tin Toy Makers.

Manoil. See Cars and Related Cast Toys.

Marx. See list under Lithographed-Tin Toy Makers.

Matchbox, made by Lesney Products, England, 1949 to present. U.S. factory, 1964–1982; moved to Hong Kong, 1982.

Meccano, a trade name registered in 1907 for toy car kits in England; it later made trains. See Dinky Toy under Cars and Related Cast Toys.

Playtoy, a brand name for Tootsietoy, sold in Woolworth's in 1937.

Rainbow Rubber Company, Butler, Pennsylvania, made rubber cars.

Sun Rubber Company, Barberton, Ohio, made rubber cars.

Tootsietoys. See Cars and Related Cast Toys.

Tin boy on a motorcycle by Lehmann.

"The Wonder Cyclist" by Louis Marx & Co.

Vindex Company, Belvedere, Illinois, was a sewing machine company that made toys. It made collectible farm equipment, a 13-inch racer, and some smaller-scale vehicles. Two 8-inch Auburns and a 10½-inch Packard are known; identified by decals.

Trains

Toy trains were made of tin and cast iron but most of the collector's interest is with the electric train. A train made in 1896 by Carlisle and Finch ran on a track; but the electric train needed the invention of the transformer. Ives, who had been making windup trains, began making electric trains in the early 1900s. Lionel Manufacturing Company was started in 1903 in New York. It made trains and accessories and eventually purchased the Ives company. The Lionel Company was sold in 1968 to A. C. Albert of Connecticut, and it has continued using the name "Lionel."

A Lionel train car.

Trains were made in Standard Gauge, 2⅛ inches between the rails, O gauge, half as big as Standard Gauge, and HO gauge, half as big as O gauge. Also made were OO Gauge about ¾ inch and S Gauge, ⅞ inch between the rails.

A Buddy "L" train engine and cars.

Other names of interest to the train collector are American Flyer (Chicago, 1907–1967, taken over by Gilbert); Carlisle and Finch (Cincinnati, Ohio, 1896–1916); Dorfan Company (Newark, New Jersey, pre-1926– after World War II); Louis Marx (see list under Lithographed-Tin Toy Makers); Revell, Inc., Meccano (London, England, making trains 1920– present).

Schoenhut

Albert Schoenhut, the toy maker, was born in Germany in 1849. He moved to Philadelphia in 1866 as a repairman for toy pianos. He invented a new sounding board made of metal instead of glass for toy pianos. The Albert Schoenhut Company was established in 1872 and incorporated in 1897. In 1935, the company became O. Schoenhut, Inc., named for one of his sons, Oscar, who took over the company. Six sons worked for the firm.

Many types of Schoenhut toys were made. The Humpty Dumpty Circus was patented in 1903. The first pieces included a chair, a ladder, and a clown; but other pieces were added through the years until there were over forty animals, twenty-nine figures, a tent, wagons, and over forty other pieces of equipment. The earliest animals had glass eyes and woolly cloth manes. The painted eyes and carved manes came later. Before 1910, the circus performers were made with two-part heads: a plaster composition face glued to a wooden base. Bisque heads were used between 1910 and 1918; one-part wooden molded heads were used later. A reduced-size circus was introduced in 1923 and a miniature set in 1927.

The toy that started a company, the famous Schoenhut piano.

This Schoenhut goat seems amused.

Toy pianos remained popular and more than forty-two sizes and styles were sold. In 1911, Schoenhut patented a wooden doll that fit into a stand and had jointed arms and legs. The company continued making dolls until 1926. Dollhouses were first offered in 1918. It also made furniture for the dollhouses. Blocks, games (such as pick-up sticks), toy ships, trains, guns, planes, and many other toys were made. Comic character dolls such as

Felix the Cat (1922), Barney Google (1922), and Maggie and Jiggs (1924) were popular toys. O. Schoenhut, Inc. is still working in Philadelphia, Pennsylvania.

The 12-inch alligator by Schoenhut has glass eyes.

The Humpty Dumpty Circus by Schoenhut came in a variety of styles. This set had over a hundred pieces when it was made about 1920.

The "Walking Wallapus" is one of the rare Schoenhut animals.

Celluloid

The Celluloid toy is one of the few types of toys that is generally overlooked by the collector. Little has been written about the makers of these toys.

"Celluloid" is a trademark for a plastic developed in 1868 by John W. Hyatt. Ivory used for billiard balls was expensive and a New York company offered a $10,000 reward for the discovery of a material that could replace ivory. Mr. Hyatt and many other scientists worked on this problem. Celluloid Manufacturing Company, the Celluloid Novelty Company, Celluloid Fancy Goods Company, and American Xylonite Company all used Celluloid to make jewelry, games, sewing equipment, false teeth, and piano keys. Eventually the Hyatt Company became the American Cellulose and Chemical Manufacturing Company—the Celanese Corporation.

The name Celluloid was often used to identify any similar plastic, although the competitors had trade names like "pyralin," "Parkesine," or "cellonite." Celluloid-like products had many good features. They could be molded, were water resistant, were not cold to the touch, and of course were smooth and hard.

Dolls and dolls' heads have been made of Celluloid from the 1880s. By the early 1900s, dolls of Celluloid with tin windup parts could creep, wave arms and legs, or walk. In the 1930s, the German and Japanese toy makers began to mass-produce Celluloid or Celluloid and tin toys. The easily shaped plastic was joined to stronger metal parts, making possible a variety of windup toys. Many of them, when wound, could walk across a table or floor, could swing, or could rotate balloonlike balls for added motion. The Celluloid toy was easily crushed. Because they were so perishable, they are difficult to find. Repairs to Celluloid are almost impossible. To care for a Celluloid toy, just wash it and keep it out of direct sunlight and away from high heat. It can melt and is highly flammable.

OTHER TOYS WORTH SPECIAL NOTICE—PEDAL CARS

Pedal cars became popular soon after real automobiles were produced in quantity in 1901. One or two children could sit in the car, and by pushing the foot pedals make the car move down the sidewalk. The wooden wagon has always been a popular toy; but when motor-driven automobiles appeared, toy manufacturers quickly converted wagons to cars. Pedal cars were made with side doors, nickel-plated lamps and trim, imitation toolboxes and rubber tires.

The pedal cars from the early 1900s to the 1930s are considered the best by collectors. Cars continue to be made in the image of the automobile of the day. Plastic futuristic pedal toys are an invention of the 1970s.

List of American Makers and Location

*American Metal Wheel Co.
Toledo, Ohio

*American National Co.
Toledo, Ohio

*Auto Specialty Manufacturing Co.
Indianapolis, Indiana

*Garten

*Gendron Wheel Co.
Toledo, Ohio

*Before 1930.

*Kirk-Latty Manufacturing Co.
Cleveland, Ohio

Murray Ohio Manufacturing Co.
(Steelcraft)

Outo-Wheel Coaster Co.

Pedalmobile Manufacturing Co.

*Sideway National Co.
Washington, Pennsylvania

*Toledo Metal Wheel Co.
Toledo, Ohio

A 59-inch-long Toledo Metal Wheel Company fire pumper pedal car.

Battery-operated Toys

Most of the battery-operated toys sought after by collectors were made in Japan from 1946 to 1960. The Japanese were faced with a shortage of materials and industries at the end of World War II. Some toy makers even searched the dumps for the tin cans used by the occupying United States Army. The tin was recycled into toys. Many of the early toys were made as part of cottage industries in Japan. A family would make a single part or do some of the assembly, then pass the toy on to a small factory. It has been said that at least thirty-six thousand toys of one design were needed in order to make a profit.

There are seven classes of these toys: battery-operated banks, comic characters, animals, people, novelties and games, space toys and robots, and automobiles. The comic characters, animals, and people seem to be the most ingenious. The best known was Charlie Weaver, who drank a martini while smoke poured from his ears. The smoke for these toys came from a reservoir of oil inside. It was quickly heated with an electric spark, making the smoke. Once the oil was gone, there was no way to open the toy and replace it. Other unusual battery toys include a teddy bear that draws on a pad, an Indian that beats on a drum, a drinking monkey, a smoking Popeye, a pig that flips an egg in a pan, and a man who shaves. A few battery toys of this type are still being made but they are very expensive and often have some plastic parts. There are over four hundred different toys known.

Be sure the toy you buy is in working condition. Most of them are difficult, if not almost impossible, to repair. The batteries frequently leaked, marring the toy.

And Still More Toys

Toy collecting can be endless. Collect by material, such as the tin or Celluloid toys, or collect by type, such as cars and trains. You can even collect by maker or by age or any way that pleases you. What follows is a discussion of some of the toys that have been written about and collected.

Comic Strip Toys

Comic strip toys have a charm of their own. All sorts of toys have been made to resemble famous characters such as the Yellow Kid or Maggie and Jiggs. The toy usually dates from about the time of the strip, but many revivals occur and during the 1980s Mickey Mouse, Popeye, Orphan Annie, Betty Boop, Flash Gordon, Superman, and others are having renewed interest.

Popeye has kept his popularity for many years. This Marx windup toy was made about 1930.

The "Li'l Abner and the Dogpatch Band" windup toy was made about 1945.

Jigsaw Puzzles and Blocks

Jigsaw puzzles and blocks intrigue a different group of collectors. The jigsaw puzzle dates back to 1760 in England. The early puzzles were often maps or other teaching aids. Puzzles were expensive until the development of the jigsaw for cutting and color lithography for the paper pictures. Die-cut puzzles made the prices even lower.

Picture blocks with scenes on each of the six sides have been known from the eighteenth century. Most of those found today were made during the late nineteenth and early twentieth centuries.

Lead Soldiers

Collecting lead soldiers has been a hobby of grown men for centuries. Times have not changed. Prices reflect the difference in quality from hand-finished, hand-painted expensive soldiers made for display to inexpensive lead soldiers originally found in the dime stores.

Robots

The battery-operated mechanical robots popular after World War II have a special group of collectors. These imaginative toys depicting a world yet to come have been singled out even though they are not as old as many other popular toy collectibles. Most of the robots were made in

Still marching are these lead soldiers picturing the twenty-one-piece U.S. Marine Corps band.

Japan, Germany, and the United States. Almost all are made of plastic and metal.

Still Banks

This lithographed tin still bank was made by Chein and Company in the 1940s.

Collectors have paid high prices for mechanical banks for years, but it was not until 1980 that some very rare still banks began to sell for over four figures.

The still bank can be cast iron from the 1880s and after. Tin, glass, plastic, or ceramic types are still being made today. The registering banks, those that resemble a cash register, first made in 1907, are classed separately.

Toy Irons and Trivets

Toy irons and trivets are part of a larger collecting field of toy dishes and miniatures for children.

TWENTIETH-CENTURY DOLL MANUFACTURERS
OF INTEREST

Dolls have been cherished and saved for many reasons. It has been the extra love, care, and careful storage that has made doll collecting so rewarding. A perfectly preserved doll may appear in a box in any attic, along with the almost destroyed metal toys or well-worn stuffed animals. Collectors have searched for and purchased the nineteeth-century dolls for years until now the prices are sometimes in the thousands of dollars for a single rare doll. Twentieth-century dolls seem to be in greater supply with less demand, so there are still many opportunities for the astute collector with a smaller budget. Some of the modern dolls were expensive when new. They remain expensive when they become older and rarer. Some were originally medium- or low-priced and big-volume sellers when new; and these can still be found at reasonable prices. History will note that the first sad doll was Poor Pitiful Pearl (1957), the first true-to-life baby doll was the Bye-Lo (1922), the first teen girl doll was Barbie (1959), and the first anatomically correct male doll was Baby Brother (late 1960s). There were many others; some are best known by the factory name, some for the famous personalities they portray.

DOLL FACTORIES OF NOTE

The Ideal Toy Corporation

Morris Michtom founded the Ideal Novelty and Toy Company in 1907. At first they made only teddy bears. The firm prospered and made character dolls by 1910, sleeping-eye dolls by 1915, a crying doll by 1920, Shirley Temple dolls in 1934, Betsy Wetsy in 1937, and the Magic Skin Doll in 1946. The Ideal Toy Corporation was the first doll company to use plastic.

The company is still working. Their early dolls were marked with the name "Ideal" in a diamond. Later, just the name "Ideal" was used. Some were just marked with numbers and the words "Made in USA." An extensive list of the dolls made by Ideal appears in *Modern Collector Dolls* by Patricia Smith.

Lenci

Lenci dolls were made by a company founded by Enrico and Elena Konig de E. Scavini in Turin, Italy, during World War I. "Lenci" was Elena's nickname. While Enrico was at war, their only child died and Elena began

Amelia Earhart is portrayed in this rare Lenci portrait doll made about 1930. Notice the characteristically stitched fingers on the hand used on Lenci dolls.

filling her days by making dolls. She used felt because Turin was the center of the Italian felt industry. The fabric was steamed and stiffened in a mold that made a three-dimensional seamless face with a firm surface. The details were hand-painted. The bodies were usually jointed felt or felt and muslin. Child, ethnic, lady, personality, and occupational dolls were made, ranging in size from 4 to 48 inches. One distinguishing characteristic was the doll's hand. The third and fourth fingers were stitched together, while the others were separate.

Lenci dolls are marked in several ways. There was an ink signature on the foot, ribbon labels, or cardboard or metal tags.

Composition and plastic were used in the dolls after World War II. Madame Lenci (Elena) died in 1950, but dolls bearing her name are still being made.

Madame Alexander

Maurice Alexander of Russia moved to New York City and married an Austrian named Hannah Pepper in 1891. He opened a doll hospital in 1895, and his family grew to four daughters. Beatrice, his oldest daughter, married in 1912. In 1923, she made a doll that was a portrait of her own daughter. Soon the four sisters formed the Alexander Doll Company, making dolls under the direction of Beatrice, who was called "Madame Alexander." Beatrice's husband, Phillip Behrman, joined the company and they have continued in business.

Their first dolls were rag dolls with mask-type faces and pressed features that were hand-painted. The characters from the book *Little Women* were among their first dolls. Later dolls were based on other book characters. Composition heads were used from about 1935 to 1948, plastic by the 1940s. The cloth dolls had pink cotton bodies, mohair wigs, and cotton clothing. In the 1930s the firm made stuffed animals, using rayon and oilcloth. The dolls were tagged with the name "Madame Alexander."

Ravca

Bernard Ravca started making dolls in Paris, France, on December 27, 1924. He made a doll representing Marguerite of Faust. The doll was realistic and original; and when he decided to make more, he opened his own studio. Each of his dolls had a personality. The early dolls were made using French bread that was just molded and later treated. The dolls often depicted old French peasants. Some of his other early dolls were large

"Cissy Models Her Formal Gown" is the name of this 1957 Madame Alexander doll.

→

The organ grinder doll by Bernard Ravca holds an organ that plays the "Marseillaise." The 14-inch doll was made in 1939.

figures of young people. At the same time, Miss Francis Diecks, a New York-trained artist, was making dolls of actors and actresses. Her dolls were successful and were being sold in all parts of the country. The two doll makers met, fell in love, married, and continued making dolls. The life-sized "Real People" dolls, "American Presidents," "soldiers," "historic leaders of World War II," "Portrait" dolls, and "French Province" dolls are famous among the many dolls made by Bernard Ravca. The "Ballet" dolls, "Presidents' Wives," and "Sprites, Pixies and Fairies" are the most famous made by Frances.

Some of their dolls were made with silk-stocking faces, spun-wool hair, and painted features. The dolls carry bundles of wood or baskets, wear knit sweaters or stockings and printed skirts. Frances Ravca used cotton and silk material on padded wires. Ravca dolls are usually labeled with a separate cloth label that is stitched to the clothing.

Storybook Dolls

Nancy Ann Abbott began making dolls in California in 1941. She imported the doll bodies and made her own heads. Shortly after, she started making the complete dolls. Storybook dolls were made until 1959. Recently, some models have been offered for sale through a division of Giant Consolidated Industries of Salt Lake City, Utah.

The Nancy Ann Storybook dolls were made of bisque, hard plastic, or vinyl.

Vogue Doll Company

The Vogue Doll Company was established by Mrs. Jennie Graves after World War I. She made only doll clothes until the late 1930s; then she imported German dolls. The Ginny doll of 1948 was the first big seller. Other dolls, large wardrobes, furniture, and other doll accessories were made. In 1958, Vogue Dolls acquired Arran Doll Company. Vogue and Arran were purchased by Tonka Corporation in 1973 and the Ginny doll and her friends were kept in production.

DOLLS BEST KNOWN BY NAME RATHER THAN BY MANUFACTURER

Barbie

Barbie* was probably the first teenage doll that was offered for sale in the twentieth century. The 11½-inch doll with small waist and developed bust became a toy best-seller in 1959. She has been recognized as the most successful doll ever made. Mattel, Inc. made the doll with a huge wardrobe of clothes. Soon after, there was a Barbie* "family." Ken,* Bar-

* A registered trademark of Mattel, Inc., used with permission.

bie's boyfriend, was introduced in 1960. Later came little sister Skipper*
and cousin Francis, and friends Midge, Christie,* Stacey, P.J.,* Steffie, and
Kelley. After that came Ricky, Skooter, Fluff, and Tiff, all friends of Skipper; Tutti and Todd, Barbie's tiny twin brother and sister; Casey, Chris,
Allan, Brad, and other friends of Barbie and her family.

Variations and improvements to the family of dolls continued. Wigs
changed, hair grew, Barbie talked, and moved at the waist or knee, and
many other additions or corrections were produced. The first Barbie doll,
the most valuable, had holes in the bottom of her feet. Pegs in a base fit
into the holes so Barbie can stand up. Contrary to popular belief, Barbie
doll's bust has not changed in size from the very first model (except for
minute variations for technological reasons). Barbie and friends had over
a thousand outfits and a selection of real estate and possessions, including furniture for every room, a boat, beach bus, camper, dune buggy,
plane, bicycle, convertible, hot rod, Corvette, gymnast set, tennis, golf,
skating and skiing equipment, dolls, pets and horses, a theater, dress
shop, college campus, schoolroom, playhouse, ice cream stand, pent-
house, ski cabin, beauty parlor, and even an Olympic ski village and much,
much more.

The original Barbie doll was the sensation of 1959 and is still popular with children and collectors. (© Mattel, Inc., 1980)

OTHER TEEN DOLLS

Other teen dolls were also made, but only a few are bringing a premium
price. The most prized are the first Barbie by Mattel, Inc.; Lilli, made in
West Germany; Brenda Starr by Madame Alexander; Joe Namath by
Ideal; G.I. Jane by Hasbro; Yolanda by Madame Alexander; and Wanda
by Madame Alexander.

Bye-Lo Doll

The Bye-Lo baby was designed by Grace Storey Putnam. She had four
copyrights: one in 1922, two in 1923, and one in 1925. Each copyright was
for a slight change in the doll that was modeled after a real three-day-old
baby. The doll was distributed by Borgfeldt; the heads were made by
several factories, while the bodies were made by others. Bye-Lo babies
came in sizes from 13 to 20 inches and they were made with hard or soft
bodies and heads of composition, bisque, rubber, or Celluloid. Almost all
of the dolls were marked with the name "Bye-Lo" or "Grace Putnam."

Kewpies

The Kewpie doll was designed by Rose O'Neill and was patented in
1913. The big-eyed doll with the pug nose, slight smile, tiny blue wings,
and topknot was an immediate success with the public. Kewpies and mem-

bers of the Kewpie family such as Doodle Dog were made by many factories including Borgfeldt, Kestner, Fulper Pottery, Rex Doll Company,
Mutual Doll Company, Cameo Doll Company, and Karl Standfuss. Most
Kewpies are marked with the name "Rose O'Neill" and/or "Kewpie,"
either incised or on a paper label.

These three bisque Kewpie dolls range from 2 to 5½ inches in height. Notice the Kewpie trademark heart on the largest Kewpie, and the wings showing on the "policeman."

Raggedy Ann

Raggedy Ann was patented in 1915 by John B. Gruelle. The doll with
shoe-button eyes and red hair was so successful copies are still being
made. Raggedy Andy was the boy rag doll that was made to accompany
Raggedy Ann.

Celebrity Dolls

Curly hair and an original dress add to the charm of this Shirley Temple doll.

Many dolls have been made to resemble real movie stars, celebrities,
fictional heroes, heroines, or comic characters. The most famous are of
Shirley Temple (1934), Charlie Chaplin (1916), the Dionne Quintuplets
(1935), and Mickey Mouse (1930). Famous advertising symbols have been
made into dolls, including Aunt Jemima (1910), the Kellogg bear (1926),
Sprout (Green Giant, 1960s), Rastus, the Cream of Wheat chef (1922),
the Planters peanut (1960s), and the Campbell Kids by Grace Drayton
(1900). The list is almost endless; because these dolls can be dated easily,
they remain popular with collectors.

The big bow and short hair on this Schoenhut doll indicate she was made in the 1930s.

Mr. Peanut, the cloth doll, came in a variety of styles. This 21-inch doll is a giveaway of the 1960s and 1970s.

The Buddy Lee doll was manufactured to display the Lee uniforms. This Coca-Cola suit was one of the advertising pieces. Other dolls wore overalls, Western clothes, or trainmen's uniforms.

This "half doll" was part of a series of dolls made by W. Goebel Porzellanfabrik, Oeslau, Germany, in 1917. The model was said to represent Jenny Lind, the Swedish singer.

This half figure has a modeled-on costume with hand-painted flower and gold luster trim. Marked with a crown over "N" mark, she was probably made by Ernst Bohne Sohne Porzellanfabrik, Rudolstadt, Germany, in the early part of the century.

OTHER AMERICAN DOLL
MANUFACTURERS OF INTEREST

Manufacturer and Location	Dates of Manufacture	Manufacturer and Location	Dates of Manufacture
A & H Doll Manufacturing Co. Long Island City, New York	1947–1969	Averill Manufacturing Co. New York, New York	c. 1913–1965
Amberg (Louis and Son) New York, New York	c. 1920–	Beatrice Wright's Toy Co. New York, New York	1951– present
American Character Doll Co. New York, New York	1918–1968	Geo. Borgfeld & Co. New York, New York	1881–1914
		Buddy Lee. See H. D. Lee Co., Inc.	
American Doll & Toy Manufacturing Co. Brooklyn, New York	1892–1909	Delux Toy (Division of Topper) Elizabeth, New Jersey	1957–1972
Arranbee (R & B) Doll Co. New York, New York	1922–1958	Eegee's (Goldberger Doll Manufacturing Co., Inc.) Brooklyn, New York	1917– present

Manufacturer and Location	Dates of Manufacture	Manufacturer and Location	Dates of Manufacture
Effanbee (Fleischaker & Baum) New York, New York	1910– present	Mattel, Inc. Hawthorne, California	1945– present
Hasbro Industries, Inc. (Hassenfeld Bros., Inc.) Pawtucket, Rhode Island	1926– present	Remco Industries, Inc. New York, New York	?–1974
		Schoenhut. See page 307.	
E. I. Horsman & Aetna Doll & Toy Co. Columbia, South Carolina	1865– present	Storbel & Wilken Co. Cincinnati, Ohio; New York	1864–1925
Kenner Products, Inc. Cincinnati, Ohio	1945– present	Storybook Dolls. See Doll Factories of Note.	
H. D. Lee Co., Inc. Merriam, Kansas	1920– present	Terri Lee, Inc. Lincoln, Nebraska Apple Valley, California	1946–1958
Louis Marx & Co. (Dunbee-Combex-Marx, 1976) Brooklyn, New York	1921– present	Uneeda Doll Co. New York, New York	1917– present

OTHER DOLLS TO COLLECT

Pincushion Dolls, or China Half Figures

Pincushion dolls are not really dolls at all and they often were not pincushions. Such is the way of names given by collectors. The top half of the doll is made of glazed porcelain or unglazed porcelain called bisque. It is usually a solid form of head, shoulders, and body to the waist. At the bottom edge of the body are several small holes for thread. Porcelain arms may be attached or separate. Separate legs are sometimes made. The rest of the body is made of fabric, usually a very full trimmed skirt stitched through the holes.

The finished lady was sometimes a cozy, made to cover a hot pot of tea, sometimes a dresser doll covering powder boxes, perfume, or clothes brushes. Other dolls held pincushions, bridge tally pencils, thimbles, or were part of lamps or umbrella handles.

Pincushion doll heads come in all sizes from less than an inch to over 9 inches high. The dolls seem to date from the early 1900s through the 1950s. The dolls represent women of the eighteenth through twentieth centuries with pseudo-Marie Antoinettes, Pierrots and Pierrettes, and Flappers. Many were made in the Art Deco style of the 1920s.

Each group of collectors has a special vocabulary. When buying pincushion dolls, watch out for the words *china* or *porcelain*. One idiosyncrasy of the doll world is that the word *porcelain* is reserved for the best-quality ware; *china* is used for medium- or poor-quality examples, even though the words have slightly different meanings in the dictionary or in an article about table dishes.

Try to find pincushion dolls in good condition with original arms and legs. It is best if the fabric skirt is original but this is more difficult to find. Unusual hairdos, hats, and other special features are desirable. Some dolls are marked.

MARKS OF BEST-KNOWN
MAKERS OF PINCUSHION DOLLS

Manufacturer and Location	Dates of Manufacture	Manufacturer and Location	Dates of Manufacture
Dressel, Kister and Co. Passau, Bavaria	1840–1925+	Karl Schneider's Erben Grafenthal, Germany	late nineteenth, early twentieth centuries
Ernst Bohne & Sohne Rudolstadt, Germany	1854–1945		
		W. Goebel Porzellanfabrik Oeslau, West Germany	1871– present
Gebruder, Heubach Lichte, Germany	1820–1925		

Stuffed Toys

Everyone seems to have had a toy stuffed teddy bear to love. This bear was obviously used by a child but he is still wanted by collectors.

There is no discussion of toys in which one could fo. get the teddy bear. "Teddy" was the cuddly toy that it is said was inspired by Teddy Roosevelt's hunting trip in 1902. The newspapers had written about how the president refused to shoot a defenseless bear, and the public was fascinated. Morris Michtom, a clever businessman, began selling the stuffed bears that his wife, Rose, had been making. He called them "Teddy bears." The sales were so great that the Michtoms founded the Ideal Novelty and Toy Company.

The German version of the toy was made about the same time by the

Steiff Company. It had been making stuffed animals since 1880. Many companies made other teddy bears and today there are thousands of collectors who buy just bears. There are even stores that sell just new bears.

To date your bear, you must look in a book that pictures most of the different types. Even then, it may be difficult because the teddy bears have changed little in appearance through the years.

Many other animals have been made into toys. The Steiff Company has always done well with elephants, dogs, and monkeys. They are all collectors' items if they are old enough or rare enough.

The stuffed fabric cat has the patent date 1899 on the foot. It is 9 inches high.

Related to stuffed toys are the cloth dolls made from printed and stitched fabric. The first American fabric made for stuffed dolls was patented in 1886. It was for a Santa Claus doll made by Edward Peck. The Arnold Print Works of North Adams, Massachusetts (1876–1925), made many printed fabrics of animals or dolls that had to be cut out and stuffed. Other firms connected with making or selling fabric dolls were Art Fabric Mills of New York, New York (1899–1910), Elms and Sellon (1910–1911), Selchow & Righter (1867–present), Cocheco Manufacturing Company (1827–1898), and Saalfield Publishing Company, Akron, Ohio (1907–1973). Most of the fabric dolls had the name of the factory printed somewhere. Unfortunately, the name was frequently lost when the animal was cut and stuffed.

Reproductions of several of the dolls are now available. They are often offered through museum gift shops.

Dollhouses and Dollhouse Furniture

All dollhouses have a value. The older and the more complete the furnishings, the more valuable the dollhouse. The earliest dollhouses date from the sixteenth century in Bavaria, but it was not until the eighteenth century that they were in common use. Furniture and dishes were made to scale by some of the finest craftsmen of the day. By the 1870s, most dollhouses were made on a scale of one inch to one foot, although one-eighth or two-fifths scales were also used. The furniture was made in the same scales. Many dollhouses of the nineteenth and twentieth centuries were homemade, but commercially made houses are also of interest to collectors.

A good dollhouse should be furnished to scale and have the appropriate pieces. The furniture can be from an earlier period, in the same way as furniture in a real house. Furniture can frequently date back several generations. Restoration of an old house should be restrained. Wash it, repair the structural problems, repaint as little as possible, and redecorate with appropriate old wallpaper fabrics and paint colors.

**Dollhouses were often handmade one-of-a-kind toys.
This house represents a dwelling of the 1930s.**

SOME AMERICAN COMMERCIAL DOLLHOUSE
MAKERS OF THE 19th AND 20th CENTURIES

Makers and Locations	Earliest Known	Makers and Locations	Earliest Known
Arcade Manufacturing Co. Freeport, Illinois	1926	McLoughlin Brothers New York, New York	1884
R. Bliss Pawtucket, Rhode Island	1895	Rich Toy Co. Clinton, Iowa	1934
Morton Converse Winchendon, Massachusetts	1909	Schoenhut Company Philadelphia, Pennsylvania	c. 1917
		Stirn and Lyon New York, New York	1881
Grim and Leeds Co. Camden, New Jersey	1903	Tootsietoy Chicago, Illinois	c. 1930

BIBLIOGRAPHY

General

Antique Toy World: The Magazine for Toy Collectors Around the World. Chicago.

Arcade Cast Iron Toys. Freeport, Illinois: Arcade Manufacturing Co. (Catalog reprint.)

Bartholomew, Charles. *Mechanical Toys.* Secaucus: Chartwell Books, 1979.

Best, Charles W. *Cast Iron Toy Pistols, 1870–1940: A Collector's Guide.* Englewood, Colorado: Rocky Mountain Arms and Antiques, 1973.

Crilley, Raymond E. and Burkholder, Charles E. *Collecting Model Farm Toys of the World.* Tucson: Aztex Corp., 1979.

Edw. K. Tryon Co. Toy Catalogue, 1927. Oakhurst, New Jersey: Privately printed. (Catalog reprint.)

Gardiner, Gordon and Morris, Alistair. *Price Guide to Metal Toys.* Suffolk, England: Antique Collectors' Club, 1980.

King, Constance Eileen. *Encyclopedia of Toys.* New York: Crown, 1978.

McClintock, Marshall and Inez. *Toys in America.* Washington, D.C.: Public Affairs Press, 1961.

O'Brien, Richard. *Collecting Toys.* Florence, Alabama: Books Americana, 1980.

The Story of Buddy "L." East Moline, Illinois: Moline Pressed Steel Co., 1925.

Thomas, Julian. *Vindex Toys.* Linden, Missouri: Creative Communications, 1976.

Comic Strip Toys

Harman, Kenny. *Comic Strip Toys.* Des Moines: Wallace-Homestead, 1975.

Lesser, Robert. *A Celebration of Comic Art and Memorabilia.* New York: Hawthorn Books, 1975.

Dinky Toys

Gibson, Cecil. *History of British Dinky Toys, 1934–1964.* Windsor, England: Mikansue & Modellers' World, 1976.

Roulet, Jean-Michel. *History of French Dinky Toys, 1933–1978.* Paris: Adepte Editions, 1979.

Truin, Ronald. *Collecting Meccano Dinky Toys.* London: Cranbourn Press. (1928–1940 reprints.)

Irons and Trivets

Hartung, Marion T. and Hinshaw, Ione E. *Patterns and Pinafores: Pressed Glass Toy Dishes.* Des Moines: Wallace-Homestead, 1971.

Politzer, Judy. *Tuesday's Children: Collecting Little Irons and Trivets.* Walnut Creek, California: Privately printed, 1977.

Jigsaw Puzzles and Blocks

Hanna, Linda. *The English Jigsaw Puzzle, 1760–1890.* London: Wayland Publishers, 1972.

Lead Soldiers

O'Brien, Richard. *Collecting Toys.* 2nd ed. Florence, Alabama: Books Americana, 1980.

Publication: Old Toy Soldier Newsletter, 209 N. Lombard, Oak Park, Illinois 60302

Pedal Cars

Antique Toy World Magazine (Chicago), (February-June 1980).

Robots

Boogaerts, Pierre. *Robot.* Paris: Abi Melzer Productions, 1978.

"Robots," *Antique Toy World Magazine* (Chicago), (monthly column).

Schoenhut

Ackerman, Evelyn and Keller, Fredrick E. *Schoenhut's Humpty Dumpty Circus from A to Z.* Los Angeles: ERA Industries, Inc., 1975.

Buser, M. Elaine and Dan. *Guide to Schoenhut's Dolls, Toys and Circus, 1872–1976.* Paducah, Kentucky: Collector Books, 1976.

Manos, Susan. *Schoenhut Dolls & Toys.* Paducah, Kentucky: Collector Books, 1976.

Publication: The Schoenhut Newsletter, 45 Louis Ave., West Seneca, New York 14224

Still Banks

Cranmer, Don. *Banks: Still Banks of Yesterday.* Sharon Center, Ohio: Privately printed, n.d.

———. *Collector's Encyclopedia of Toys-Banks.* Sharon Center, Ohio: Privately printed, 1976.

Long, Ernest and Ida and Pitman, Jane. *Dictionary of Still Banks.* Mokelumne Hill, California: Privately printed, 1980.

Whiting, Hubert B. *Old Iron Still Banks.* Wakefield, Massachusetts: Privately printed, 1968.

Tootsietoys

Lee, C.B.C. "A History of Prewar Automotive Tootsietoys," *Antique Toy World* (Chicago), (May-December, 1972).

Wieland, James and Force, Edward. *Tootsietoys: World's First Diecast Models.* Osceola, Wisconsin: Motorbooks International, 1980.

Trains

Greenberg, Bruce G. *Greenberg's Price Guide to Lionel Trains, 1901–1942.* Sykesville, Maryland: Greenberg Publishing, 1979.

———. *Greenberg's Price Guide to Lionel Trains, 1945–1979.* Sykesville, Maryland: Greenberg Publishing, 1979.

Levy, Allen. *A Century of Model Trains*. New York: Crescent Books, 1974.

Matzke, Eric. *Greenberg's Guide to Marx Trains*. Sykesville, Maryland: Greenberg Publishing, 1978.

Yorkis, Paul G.; Walsh, James D.; Greenberg, Linda F.; and Greenberg, Bruce C. *Greenberg's Price Guide to American Flyer "S" Gauge*. Sykesville, Maryland: Greenberg Publishing, 1980.

Club: Lionel Collectors Club, P.O. Box 11851, Lexington, Kentucky 40578; National Model Railroad Association, P.O. Box 2186, Indianapolis, Indiana 46206; Toy Train Operating Society, 25 West Walnut St., Suite 305, Pasadena, California 91103; Train Collectors Association, P.O. Box 248, Strasburg, Pennsylvania 17579

Dolls—General

Anderton, Johana Gast. *Twentieth Century Dolls from Bisque to Vinyl*. North Kansas City, Missouri: Trojan Press, 1971.

————. *More Twentieth Century Dolls from Bisque to Vinyl*. 2 vols. Des Moines: Wallace-Homestead, 1979.

Hiller, Mary. *Dolls and Dollmakers*. New York: Putnam, 1968.

Smith, Patricia R. *Modern Collector's Dolls*. Paducah, Kentucky: Collector Books, 1973.

————. *Modern Collector's Dolls*. 2nd Series. Paducah, Kentucky: Collector Books, 1975.

————. *Modern Collector's Dolls*. 3rd Series. Paducah, Kentucky: Collector Books, 1976.

————. *Modern Collector's Dolls*. 4th Series. Paducah, Kentucky: Collector Books, 1979.

Club: United Federation of Doll Clubs, P.O. Box 465, Hanover, PA 17331.

Publication: Doll Investment Newsletter, P.O. Box 1982, Centerville, Massachusetts 02632

Barbie Dolls

DeWein, Sibyl and Ashabraner, Joan. *The Collector's Encyclopedia of Barbie Dolls and Collectibles*. Paducah, Kentucky: Collector Books, 1977.

Smith, Patricia R. *An Identification and Value Guide: Teen Dolls*. Paducah, Kentucky: Collector Books, 1977.

Celebrity Dolls

Burdick, Loraine. *Adult Dolls and Star Toys*. Quest-Eridon Books, 1973.

Smith, Patricia R. *Shirley Temple Dolls and Collectibles*. Paducah, Kentucky: Collector Books, 1977.

Publication: Celebrity Doll Journal, 5 Court Place, Puyallup, Washington 98371

Kewpie Dolls

Angione, Genevieve. *All-Bisque & Half-Bisque Dolls*. Camden, New Jersey: Thomas Nelson, 1969.

Leuzzi, Marlene. *Kewpies in Action.* Englewood, Colorado: Privately printed, 1971.

McCanse, Ralph Alan. *Titans and Kewpies: The Life and Art of Rose O'Neill.* New York: Vantage Press, 1968.

Club: International Rose O'Neill Club, P.O. Box 668, Branson, Missouri 65616

Lenci

Coleman, Dorothy S. *Lenci Dolls.* Riverdale, Maryland: Hobby House Press, 1977.

Madame Alexander

Dolls of Madame Alexander at Auction. Annapolis, Maryland: Auctions by Theriault, 1980.

Smith, Patricia R. *Madame Alexander Collector's Dolls.* Paducah, Kentucky: Collector Books, 1978.

Nancy Ann Storybook Dolls

Miller, Margery. *Nancy Ann Storybook Dolls.* Cumberland, Maryland: Hobby House Press, 1980.

Pincushion Dolls

Marion, Frieda. *China Half-Figures Called Pincushion Dolls.* Newburyport, Massachusetts: J. Palmer Publishers, 1974. (Paperback reprint, Paducah, Kentucky: Collector Books.)

Marion, Frieda and Werner, Norma. *The Collector's Encyclopedia of Half-Dolls.* New York: Crown, 1979.

Stuffed Toys

Bialosky, Peggy and Alan. *The Teddy Bear Catalog.* New York: Workman, 1980.

Cantine, Marguerite. *Beggar T. Bear.* Huntington, New York: Privately printed, 1981.

Conway, Shirley and Wilson, Jean. *100 Years of Steiff, 1880–1980.* Berlin, Ohio: Berlin Printing, 1980.

Walker, Frances and Whitton, Margaret. *Playthings by the Yard: The Story of Cloth Dolls.* Wayne, Pennsylvania: Privately printed, 1973.

Club: Good Bears of the World, P.O. Box 8236, Honolulu, Hawaii 96815

Dollhouses

Jacobs, Flora Gill. *Dolls' Houses in America: Historic Preservation in Miniature.* New York: Scribner's, 1974.

———. *Victorian Dolls' Houses and Their Furnishings.* Washington, D.C.: The Washington Dolls' House and Toy Museum, 1978.

Whitton, Blair, ed. *Bliss Toys and Dollhouses.* New York: Dover, 1979.

14

Store Containers, Ads, Brands, and Tin Cans

Advertising and old store collectibles have become one of the most popular areas of collecting. Restaurants want walls filled with ads, country stores are assembled with shelves of old bottles and boxes, and the young collector enjoys the search for the past of the twentieth century.

Design

Design is the key to dating almost any type of antique or collectible. Styles were copied, but a piece of Art Deco designed in the 1920s could not date from an earlier period. Some knowledge of how design in packaging works will help with the study of packaged items and signs. Most packages were designed in a fashion that was just becoming obsolete. The Art Nouveau style was popular in packaging in the early 1900s, about ten years after it had been prominent in the decorative arts. It is best to first learn the difference between Victorian, Art Nouveau, and Art Deco designs in type and borders to help you determine age. The pseudo-Egyptian and the Japonisme movements of the late nineteenth century also span limited time periods. Pictures were used on packages throughout the nineteenth and twentieth centuries. Pictures of company buildings were popular by the 1880s. Medals and awards were used on many packages and they can often help in dating a tin. An attractive female was first used at about the time of the Civil War. Comic figures usually date within a few years of their popularity. Trains, cars, and airplanes help determine the date of labels, as do clothing styles if it appears the styles are trying to be "modern." A flapper dressed in a short dress would appear on a package of the 1920s, and probably would be replaced when longer dress styles returned in the 1930s. Some trademarks such as the Quaker Oats man or Morton's Salt girl have been updated many times and these changes in labels can be identified.

The country store at the Village Crossroads of the Farmers' Museum, New York State Historical Association, Cooperstown, New York. A reconstruction of a nineteenth-century store.

A typical grocery store from the World War I era. This store was in Cleveland, Ohio. Notice how packaged goods are seen in quantity.

CANNED FRUIT   FINE TEAS   COFFEES   EXTRACTS   FRESH BREAD   SERVES   DESSERTS

IN THE LIGHT
of its Record of Cures take
HOOD'S Sarsaparilla.

Art Nouveau styles influenced this Hood's Sarsaparilla poster dated 1896.

Paper labels were more elaborate in style and printing technique during the nineteenth century. The raised, embossed label of the mid-nineteenth century, often found on needle cases or fabric bolts, lost favor by the 1920s because of high costs. Printing techniques changed and the labels and signs went from stencils and printing to lithograph and mezzotint and finally to the more modern methods we use today.

Sometimes an attractive woman in an advertisement was considered a work of art to be hung on a wall. This ad for Anheuser-Busch beer uses a subtle approach. The poster, probably made to be hung in a bar, shows Liberty holding a beer glass. The barrel at the right has the brand trademark on it but no name appears. This sign probably dates from 1893 and the World's Columbian Exposition.

By 1900 the "look" of advertising had changed. This 1901 sign was a realistic picture of a man hanging a sign for Ferry's seeds.

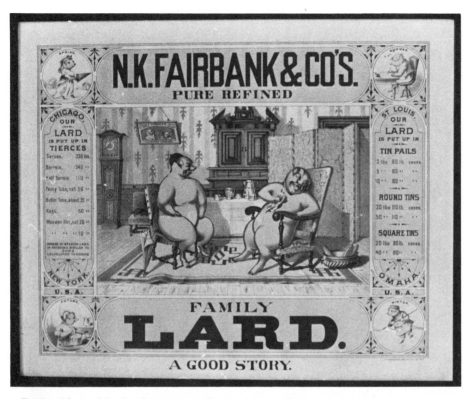

Fairbank's lard had a famous pig family in the 1890s. Notice the Renaissance Revival dining room piece and the decorative borders using designs similar to those found on the furniture of the period. The sign was done by a Cincinnati lithographer working at the turn of the century.

The typical Victorian house during cleaning time was used for the Sapolio products. Later they developed a famous advertising campaign based on cleaning a whale. Notice the 1875 furniture and drapery treatment.

The advertising bus and the border design help date the Chief Two Moon Bitter Oil in the 1930s. This cardboard sign was 36 inches long by 18 inches high, probably made for a store window display.

Know the Brand Logos

Many well-known companies with advertising memorabilia going back to the nineteenth century had early advertising with a monetary and historic value, but the well-known brands lead the lists. This listing gives the dates, history, and change of "look" for the major brands wanted by collectors.

Buster Brown

Buster Brown, a boy in Lord Fauntleroy clothes, and his dog, Tige, first appeared in Richard Fenton Outcault's cartoon strip in 1902. In 1903 these comic figures were sold to merchants at the St. Louis World's Fair Exposition for use as trademarks. It did not take long before there were packages and products bearing the name "Buster Brown" and the likeness of Buster Brown and his dog, Tige. Over the years these have included soap, toothbrushes, soft drinks, whiskey, coffee, cake, cookies, flour, apples, leggings, cigars, silverware, shaving mugs, garters, dolls, hats, belts, horseshoes, gum, watches, spoons, candy, sweaters, hosiery, knitwear, puzzles, toys, rings, wallets, and shoes. The name Buster Brown and the likeness of the boy and his dog are still in use as trademarks by Brown Shoe Company, a division of Brown Group, Inc., on children's shoes and by Buster Brown Textiles, Inc. on other items of children's wearing apparel. Advertising items with the Buster Brown trademarks are still being made. The ones most valued by collectors are the Buster Brown shoe ads of past years.

The logo for Buster Brown shoes.

Coca-Cola

Coca-Cola was first served in 1886 in Atlanta, Georgia. John S. Pemberton, a pharmacist, originated the syrup and sold it to other nearby pharmacists. The Coke syrup was first mixed with plain water, but early in 1887 Willis Venable used carbonated water and the new product became an instant success. Coca-Cola was heavily advertised from the beginning through point-of-sale signs, newspaper advertisements, and sampling coupons that were good for one drink.

The bottles, tin trays, calendars, tin advertising signs, and hanging leaded glass lamps are the most sought-after items. There is nothing printed with the words "Coca-Cola" that is not saved. Glasses, gum wrappers, knives, razor blades, cigar bands, toys, dolls, bottle openers, ice picks, paperweights, ashtrays, cigarette lighters, sheet music, fabrics, tin plates, advertising cards, key chains, clocks, fans, thimbles, sewing kits, T-shirts, and other items are among the thousands of Coke collectibles.

The trademark "Coca-Cola" in script was patented in 1893. It is still used. "Coke" was registered in 1945.

"Coke" trademark 1945

The Coca-Cola ads favored attractive women and the distinctive trademark. This 1899 tin sign pictured Hilda Clark, an actress.

The annual Coca-Cola tray has remained popular. This is Betty, the 1914 tray.

Cracker Jack

Frederick William Rueckheim started selling popcorn in Chicago, Illinois, in 1872. A molasses mixture was added in 1896 and the popcorn named Cracker Jack. A prize was added to each box in 1912. The type of box and the design of the package have changed many times over the years. Today, collectors want the packaging materials, advertising, and the prizes that were given in the early boxes.

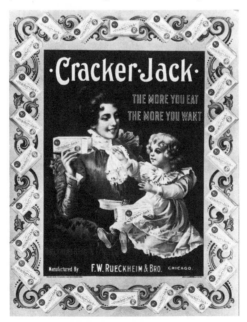

Cracker Jack boy, 1925

A 1900 Cracker Jack advertisement, offering the product, which at that time was sold without the toy.

1955

1940

1940

1935

1930

1956

1925

1959   1960

1970

1910

The Cracker Jack boxes in use since 1910. Notice the change in appearance of the Cracker Jack boy.

The sailor trademark helps date all Cracker Jack products. This is the 1925 package.

Cracker Jack boy, c. 1960–present

Betty Crocker—General Mills

Betty Crocker is a trademark that was first used by the Washburn Crosby Company. The name was created to be used on letters asking for help with problems in cooking. "Crocker" came from the director of the company, William Crocker, and also from the name of the first Minneapolis flour mill. "Betty" was a nice-sounding name. The signature was that of an employee who won the contest held to find the best signature. In 1924 Betty Crocker became a voice on the radio. In 1936 a picture was painted to represent Betty Crocker to the public. This image has been updated regularly. Betty Crocker is a symbol used by General Mills.

Betty Crocker is another trademark that has been updated with the times. See the six faces of Betty Crocker, in use from 1936 to 1980.

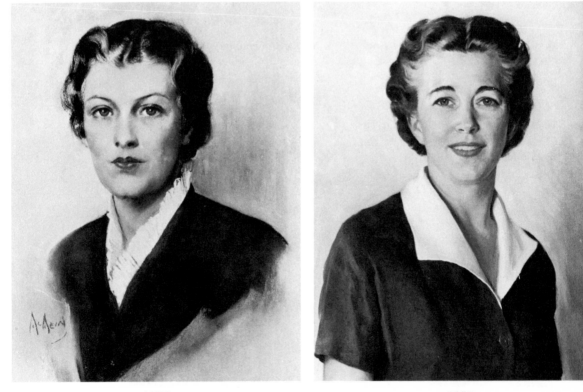

1936   **1955**

1965

1968

1972

1980

Dr Pepper

Dr Pepper is well known for its unusual advertising, and its early examples are much in demand. In 1885 the drink was originated by Charles Courtice Alderton, named by W. B. Morrison, and perfected by R. S. Lazenby, a Waco, Texas, beverage chemist. The "Dr Pepper" logo has changed from script to printed letters. The company removed the period from "Dr." in 1950.

1885

1891

c. 1905

1905; Waco, Texas

1905; Dallas, Texas

1929

1950

1961

1950–present

"Drink Dr. Pepper" was the slogan in 1910 when this advertising poster was issued. Notice the words King of Beverages in the tail of the r, part of the trademark.

Hires Root Beer

Charles E. Hires opened a drugstore in Philadelphia during the 1870s. He was on a vacation when he was served a delicious temperance tea. He learned how to make it, using an assortment of roots and herbs until he finally produced an improved version of the drink. It was named "Root Beer" to attract the workingman.

The drink was served in his store and sold commercially. Many soda fountains were selling drinks similar to Hires's in the early 1900s. He sold his extract syrup product through grocery stores. In 1905 Mr. Hires decided to sell his syrup to the soda fountains. He began advertising and his first promotion item was a Mettlach mug picturing the Hires boy. Other mugs, mirrors, trays, signs, lamps, and additional items came later.

There have been attempts to date Hires memorabilia from changes in the trademark wording (Hires, Hires' or Hire's; Root Beer or Rootbeer), but variations do not follow a consistent pattern. The apostrophe (Hires') seems to have been used only from 1892 to 1914.

One of the earliest and most famous Hires advertising symbols was the Hires boy. Between 1891 and 1906 he was shown wearing a dress and a

Hires' Boy in bib, used about 1891–1906

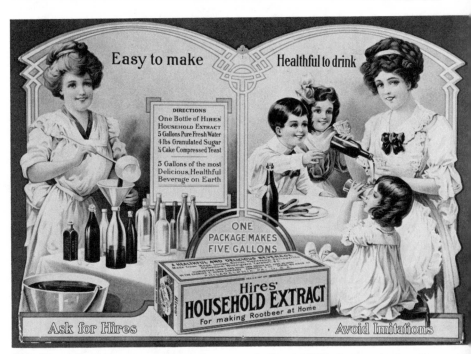

This Hires' Root Beer counter card was used about 1892. It gives instructions for making Hires' Root Beer at home.

bib or a bolero-style jacket; from 1907 to 1914 he wore a bathrobe; and from 1915 to 1926 he wore a dinner jacket.

H. J. Heinz

Henry Heinz worked as a young boy in his father's brickworks and as a produce salesman in Shappsburg, Pennsylvania. He started making horse-radish, which he sold in glass bottles to the local stores. The successful salesman finally joined with L. C. Noble to form the Anchor Brand Food Company in 1869. In 1872, the name was changed to Heinz, Noble and Company. The company did well, but in 1875 there was a depression and the firm went bankrupt. Through an agreement with his relatives, the F. and J. Heinz Company was established in 1876. H. J. Heinz Company became the company name in 1888.

Henry J. Heinz had always believed in advertising and the term "57 varieties" was part of the slogan that was chosen for its advertising effect. It was not because there were fifty-seven products. The company continued to grow, and expanded to all parts of the world.

Thousands of cans, bottles, signs, and giveaway trinkets, advertising cards, and other Heinz advertising materials can still be found.

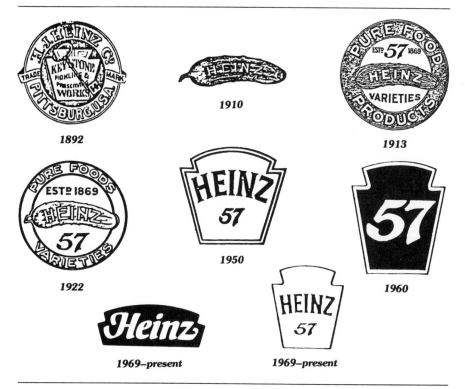

1892

1910

1913

1922

1950

1960

1969–present

1969–present

Ivory Soap

Procter & Gamble was founded by brothers-in-law William Procter and James Gamble in 1837. They made soap and candles in Cincinnati, Ohio. The company trademark started to develop around 1851. It began with a cross painted on boxes of candles to help identify the crates. Later someone changed the cross to a star inside a circle, possibly because the product was Star Candles. William Procter added thirteen stars and the moon in 1859. The moon and star mark continued to be updated.

Ivory soap was marketed in 1879. It was named for a line in the Forty-fifth Psalm, "All thy garments smell of myrrh and aloes and cassia out of the ivory palaces whereby they have made thee glad." Harley Procter, son of William, saw the possibilities in selling a floating soap that was "99 44/100% pure." The soap was heavily advertised and became a classic success. It was a soap that was white at a time when most were yellow or brown; it was wrapped when most were sold in unwrapped slabs; and it was mild. The package has been updated at intervals for more than a hundred years.

This crude cross, painted by a wharf hand on a wooden box of Star candles around 1851, was the beginning of the "Moon and Stars."

By 1902, the trademark, still basically the same, displayed some of the "gingerbread" frills typical of the turn of the century.

In time, the cross developed into this encircled star—still merely part of the rivermen's shipping "sign language."

Around 1920 the trademark became simpler—still, however, there was no fundamental change from the original design.

The first standard trademark adopted by the company was this roughly drawn crescent enclosing thirteen stars.

In 1930 a sculptor was commissioned by P&G to design today's version of the "Moon and Stars." P&G was gradually phasing out the symbol by the early 1990s.

The 1882 model "Moon and Stars" had been refined and registered in the U.S. Patent Office.

The changing trademark and package design of Ivory soap. The moon and star logo changed from a simple cross to a star in a circle to a drawing of thirteen stars and the man in the moon.

Morton Salt

The name "Morton Salt Company" was first used in 1910 when Joy Morton reorganized a salt company under that name. In 1911 the Morton girl with the umbrella and package of salt was used in an ad. With it came the slogan, "When it Rains it Pours." The first package to have the trademark was sold in 1914, in a blue round box. The Morton girl has been updated many times to be sure the package looks contemporary. In 1948, the company also changed its name on advertisements and packages from "Morton's Salt" to "Morton Salt." The company became Morton International, Inc., in 1965 and is now part of Morton-Norwich.

| 1914 | 1921 | 1933 |

The Morton Salt box and its changes. The company says the words "Morton's Salt" became "Morton Salt" before 1941.

| 1941 | 1956 | 1968 |

Moxie

Moxie was first served in 1876. Dr. Augustin Thompson of Salem, Massachusetts, developed the liquid as a concentrated nerve food to be taken by the teaspoon. It was called Moxie Nerve Food and was served in a drink with carbonated soda during the late 1880s.

Moxie was bottled in a series of bottles, including a glass labeled version, a Hutchinson stopper type, and several shapes of bottles with crown caps. Moxie was one of the main soft drink firms in the United States from the early 1900s to the 1920s. It is still being produced.

Many types of Moxie collectibles are to be found, including trays, bottles, tin signs, glasses, and small giveaway items.

Nabisco

After a series of price wars and marketing battles several large midwestern and eastern baking companies decided to merge and form the National Biscuit Company. Their first joint product was a soda cracker

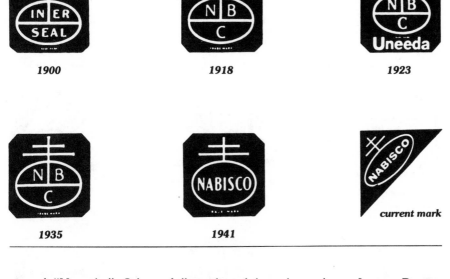

named "Uneeda." Others followed and brands such as Lorna Doone Shortbread, Fig Newtons Cakes, Zu Zu Ginger Snaps, Butter Thin Biscuits, Cream of Wheat, and Shredded Wheat were offered and advertised. All of these old items are collected today.

Pepsi-Cola

Pepsi-Cola, the drink and the name, were invented by Caleb D. Bradham, a New Bern, North Carolina, druggist. His customers called it Brad's Drink, but Bradham decided Pepsi-Cola would catch on faster.

He bought the rights to an existing registration for "Pep-Kola," drew up his own trademark in calligraphy, and registered it at the patent office on June 16, 1903. He said he had been using the name since 1898.

A somewhat simplified version was registered on August 7, 1906.

On September 14, 1937, the Pepsi-Cola Company registered yet another variant, this time framed within a hexagonal border. Labels in use bore the legend "A Sparkling Beverage."

No registration date is shown for the modernized logo placed between two curved areas within an oval. Apparently it came into use about 1950. Nor is there a registration shown for the simulated cap logo, which apparently was also introduced about 1950.

The name in shortened form as "Pepsi" was used as early as 1911. In 1966, a logo with the shortened name in block lettering was registered. Both names are still in use.

Some Pepsi-Cola items have been reproduced. The firm made a copy

June 16, 1903

August 7, 1906

September 14, 1937

paper label, used after September 14, 1937

paper label, used after 1950. Notice the simplified form of Pepsi-Cola

Bottle cap, used after 1950

1962–1969

PEPSI circle logo image

used 1963, registered 1973

used 1970, registered 1973

of a turn-of-the-century oval metal tray in 1973. It was 13 inches long and made by modern methods that will not fool the collector. It also reproduced some soda fountains, salt and pepper shakers, mirrors, wooden beverage cases, and ceramic syrup dispensers.

Planters Peanuts

Amedeo Obici and Mario Peruzzi started the Planters Nut and Chocolate Company in 1906 in Wilkes-Barre, Pennsylvania. Obici had been roasting and selling peanuts to stores but now he bought several roasters, hired eight employees, and rented a building. The company made Burgomaster Brand blanched and salted peanuts to be sold in bags. This was a novel idea at the time. Blue tin cans and vacuum jars of the Planters

1961–present
(registered 1965)
Mr. Peanut ®

1913–1961
(registered 1918)

salted nuts were also sold to the stores. Mr. Peanut, the peanut figure with monocle and top hat was adopted as a trademark in 1916, and Planters's national advertising began in 1918. The company was acquired by Standard Brands, Inc., in 1961.

Many jars, cans, dishes, and figures showing Mr. Peanut items are still being made by the company. All Mr. Peanut memorabilia is collectible. The glass jars with Mr. Peanut or a large molded peanut were reproduced in Italy in the 1970s and in Korea and Japan in the 1980s.

Quaker Oats

Henry Seymour and William Heston started an oatmeal milling company in Ravenna, Ohio, in the 1870s. It was sold soon after but the Quaker man continued in use as a trademark. The Quaker Mill Company used the symbol in 1877, when it was registered as the first trademark for a breakfast cereal.

The Quaker Oats Company made many products. One of their trademarks was Aunt Jemima, a symbol first used by the Pearl Milling Company in the 1890s and later by the R. T. Davis Milling Company and Quaker Oats after 1926.

Advertising materials using either of these symbols or any other Quaker Oats products, such as Mother's Oats, are in demand today.

| 1877 | 1895 | before 1971 / QUAKER / 1971 |

Royal Crown Cola

1965

1936

Claude A. Hatcher of the Union Bottling Works of Columbus, Georgia, started making Royal Crown Ginger Ale in 1905. The company, renamed Chero-Cola Company, began making a cola drink in 1912. The firm began issuing franchises to bottlers to make Chero-Cola, Royal Crown Ginger Ale, and Melo, a fruit-flavored drink. The drink Nehi was added in 1924 and it was later publicized with the trademark of a girl's leg. The drink was so popular that the firm changed its name to the Nehi Corporation in 1928. Royal Crown Cola was first introduced in 1934. Once again the most popular drink of its line won the name game and the corporation became the Royal Crown Cola Company in 1959. The firm had many advertising gimmicks for each of their products.

STORE COLLECTIBLES: DATES AND FIRSTS, JUST FOR FUN

Teabag tags	First teabag appeared in 1904. Lipton Tea put the first advertising tag on a bag, in 1919.
Pencil sharpener	First patented in America in 1901. There were some made earlier but not patented.
Printed matchbook label	Oldest known, "Percussion Matches Manufactured by P. Truesdell, Warsaw, New York. Warranted New Yorker Print." Made from 1855 to 1857.
Cigarette and cigar lighter	First cigar lighter, patented in 1871. In 1872 commercially rolled cigarettes appeared, used cigar lighter.
Cigarette cards	In 1885 Allen and Ginter of Richmond, Virginia, issued ten cigarettes in a box plus a picture card for five cents.
Paper advertising fans	Paper fans were made in the eighteenth century. A Crystal Palace exhibition in New York in 1853 used advertising fans
Paper napkins	First paper napkins, plain tissue paper squares, at Chicago World's Fair in 1893. First printed paper napkin appeared in 1898.
Earliest known U.S. advertising wall calendar	An 1863 calendar advertising medicine for John L. Hunnewell of Boston, Massachusetts.
Cash register	Invented in 1884 by John and James Ritty.
Paper bags	Paper bags appeared in Europe in the seventeenth century and in the United States in the nineteenth century. In 1852 Frances Wolle of Bethlehem, Pennsylvania, invented a machine that made bags. By 1884, the Union Bag & Paper Company was making brown bags with flat bottoms and pleated sides.
Folding box with marked scoring	1879, Robert Gain, Brooklyn, New York.

Tin Cans

Collectibles and antiques can be part of the decorative arts of a period or part of history. In this era of disposable containers and throwaways, it seems inevitable that collectors should look back at the history of an industry and try to save a limited number of survivors. The tin containers used in America for the past 150 years are part of the container and advertising story.

History of Canning

Tin cans, or canisters as they were first known, became important because Napoleon's army had to eat. The problem of feeding a large moving body of men was the key to victory in war, and realizing this, Napoleon offered a reward to the person who could develop a safe, tasty way to preserve food for long periods of time. Nicolas Appert received the money for his method of canning in 1795. His meat and vegetables were stored in glass jars. Breakage was a problem, so most manufacturers soon switched to tin cans. Peter Durand patented an iron-coated tin can with soldered cover in 1810. He canned food for the British army in 1813. Today food is put in steel coated with tin.

The first known metal containers for food or tobacco were used in England about 1780. Snuff was sold in small lead drums marked with engraved paper labels. Large metal drums were used to store varnish by the early nineteenth century. A two-pound can of carrots that was packed in London in 1824 was opened for study in 1936 and the contents were found edible.

Thomas Huntley started packing biscuits in tins about 1830 when his brother, a tinsmith, developed a safe package for shipping biscuits.

Before safety matches were invented (1855), matches sometimes ignited in a pocket. Many "hot seats" were saved after 1845 when matches were packed in tins.

The tin can did not come into commercial use in the United States until 1819. Ezra Dagget and Thomas Kensett patented their containers in 1825. After a few years of manufacturing, Mr. Kensett moved to the Baltimore, Maryland, area and canned fruits, oysters, tomatoes, and other foodstuffs in his patented can.

William Underwood of London, England, came to Boston in 1821 and sold pickles, sauces, and other foods in glass jars and in tin cans. By 1835 he was offering canned tomatoes, which had been believed poisonous. He also canned deviled ham and milk.

Burnham and Merill of Portland, Maine, canned food in 1842. Gail Borden canned condensed milk and milk products in 1856.

EARLY TIN CAN MANUFACTURERS

Manufacturer and Location	First Date of Manufacture	Date Closed
UNITED STATES		
American Can Co. Maywood, Illinois	1901	Present

Manufacturer and Location	First Date of Manufacture	Date Closed
American Stopper Co. Brooklyn, New York		Sold to American Can, 1905
Ginna and Company New York, New York		Sold to American Can, 1901 Dismantled prior to 1903
Hasker and Marcus Manufacturing Company Richmond, Virginia	1891	Sold to American Can, 1901
S. A. Ilsley and Company Brooklyn, New York	1865	Sold to American Can, 1901
Somers Bros. Brooklyn, New York	1869	Sold to American Can, 1901
Tindeco Baltimore, Maryland	1900	

ENGLAND

Barclay & Fry London	Late 1890s	
Barringer, Wallis & Manners Mansfield	1892	Part of the Metal Box Group
Hudson Scott & Sons Carlisle	1876	Part of the Metal Box Group
Huntley, Boorne & Stevens Reading	1837	Part of Associated Biscuit Manufacturing Ltd.
Tin Plate Decorating Co. South Wales	1862	

Tins of Special Interest

A few of the early lithographed American-made tin containers have the name of the company as part of the design. The name is usually printed in very small letters near a seam or near the bottom of the can.

The first firm to make containers lithographed directly on the metal was Somers Brothers of Brooklyn, New York. Daniel, Joe, and Guy Somers were making tins by 1869. It took until 1879 for the lithograph process to be developed. A patent was issued and cans are known with the patent dates 1878, 1879, or 1880. The printing process was successful and the elaborately designed cans were favored by many firms. Today some of the cans show crazing because the paint that was applied was thick and has shrunk slightly. The firm went out of business in 1901. Collectors favor Somers tins, and prices are higher than for many other similar containers.

Other early tin manufacturers who printed their names on the containers include the American Can Company, American Stopper Company, Ginna and Company, Hasker and Marcus Manufacturing Company, and S. A. Ilsley and Company.

The Civil War brought a surge in the canning industry in America. Van Camp started packing pork and beans in 1861; Libby McNeil started in 1872. Anderson and Campbell of Camden, New Jersey, began packing over two hundred food items, starting in 1869. (The firm became Joseph Campbell Preserve Company in 1892, and was the forerunner of the Campbell Soup Company of today.) Schepps coconut products were sold in cans during the 1890s. Many types of spices were also offered in tins. Food was not the only product to be offered in the new tin cans: in 1866 Dr. Israel Lyon used the first metal box for his tooth powder. Tobacco products such as snuff, pipe tobacco, cigars, and later cigarettes were offered in tin cans.

Most tin collectors today specialize, but the most popular areas seem to be beer, tobacco, tea canisters, and coffee cans, with the figural cans following close behind. Containers for talcum powder, food, gunpowder, and other items interest special collectors. The value of all tin containers is judged by the same criteria. Rarity and condition are always the most important factors. If the can has a three-dimensional shape it has extra value, with the roly-poly particularly prized. An animal pictured on the container is always considered a plus. If a bottle or a lady is pictured, add more to the value. Nude female figures have always had a special interest.

Some collectors want cans made for Log Cabin syrup or Planters Peanuts or made by such companies as Ginna, Somers, or American Can Company. Tobacco collectors sometimes specialize in tins made for one company, such as Scotten Dillon. Beer can collectors want examples from each company.

Baking Powder, Spice, Mustard, Yeast

Phosphate baking powder was first sold in the United States by the Rumford Chemical Works in 1857. Horsfords self-rising bread preparation, a self-rising flour for pancakes, and Rumford Yeast were also made about the time of the Civil War. Baking powder was first marketed in glass, but after 1880 metal cans with paper labels were used. Fiber cans were used for a short time around 1900. Baking powder tins were made with a completely removable lift-off lid. Royal Company made cans as early as 1868. Fiber cans were used on and off after 1934. Other early baking powder tins include (the earliest is a can made by Ginna and Company, c. 1885) Amazon, c. 1900; Andrews & Company, c. 1890; Arm & Hammer, c. 1867; Calumet, c. 1814; Charm, c. 1900; Clabber Girl, 1899; Cleveland's, c. 1880; Climax, c. 1890; Cowbrand, 1876; Crescent, c. 1900; Czar, c. 1900; Davis & Davis, c. 1900; De Land and Company, c. 1890; Dr. Price's, c. 1900; Gillet's, c. 1900; Gold Label, c. 1900; Grant's, c. 1900; Hanfords, c. 1890; Hecker's, c. 1900; Horsfords, c. 1880; Lewis, c. 1900; Pearl, c. 1900; Pioneer, c. 1900; Pure Gold, c. 1880; Redhead's, c. 1900; Royal, c. 1867; Rumford, c. 1895; Snow Flake, c. 1900.

All types of spices were put in tins soon after the Civil War. Large store bins held spices in bulk and small tins held them in ounces. The earliest examples were Japanned and stenciled; later, lithographed designs and paper labels were used. Many of the spices were packaged for wholesale grocers and labeled with the company name. Early cans had full lift-off lids. The spoon-lift top first appeared in the 1930s. Some cans for spices were for Eagle Spice Company, 1870–1892; Emmett Spice Company, before 1896; Forbes Spice Company, 1853–1880; John Hancock and Sons, 1865–1904; Heeker Spice Company, 1899–1919; Justice Spice Mills, 1892–1895; McFadden Spice Company, 1904–1941; Millar Spice Company, 1880–1905; Slades Spice, 1888–1935; Steinwinder-Stoffregan Spices, 1894–1934; Thompson and Taylor Spice, 1883–1920; Watkins, c. 1880–present; and Woolson Spice Company, 1880.

Some of the companies that sold spices were national brands and their products were sold in all parts of the country. McCormick and Company, 1889, had many labels, including Bee Brand, Silver Medal, Clover Brand (1895), Banquet Brand (1902), Clover Blossom Brand (1905), Green Seal (1909). Stickney and Poor's was established in 1815; Colburns in 1857; Durkee in 1857; Glidden, 1917.

Mustard was another well-packaged product. It was sold in tins and other containers from the 1860s on. Westmoreland Glass made milk glass mustard holders for sale in the stores. Pottery mustard containers are also known. Companies packing mustard include Colburns, c. 1870; Colmans, c. 1860; and Kenns, c. 1875.

Beer Cans

The newest rage in can collecting is the beer can. The first successful can to hold beer without damaging the flavor was made in 1935. The G. Krueger Brewing Company of Newark, New Jersey, began selling beer in cans. The can was made by the American Can Company, which had been trying since 1931 to develop a can lining that would protect the beer's flavor. It was a flat-topped can. Pabst marketed its beer in a can by July 1935. That same year Schlitz decided to use a cone-top can, or crown-sealed-top can. It looked like a bottle and could be opened without an opener. It could also be filled using the existing filling equipment at the plant. Others soon started selling beer in cans. From 1935 to 1950 the cone top was popular.

The aluminum can was first made in 1950, and the lift-top aluminum can in the late 1950s, the tab top in 1962. The tin-free steel can was used after 1965. These cans were cemented, not soldered. In the late 1970s the two-piece can—a shaped body and a top—was made.

The serious beer can collector prefers cans that have been opened from the bottom, leaving the top tab in position. Cans that can be dated by a special design, short-lived brands, and cone tops are the most popular.

Cans should be in good condition, with little or no rust or dents. Cans can be protected with wax or spray polish but some purist collectors will still argue about this. Some collectors will buy only cans without protective coating.

Biscuit Boxes

The first biscuit tins were made in England during the 1830s. Thomas Huntley, a baker, had his brother Joseph, a tinsmith, make some boxes to ship biscuits by stagecoach. They founded a firm that is still working. A method of transfer printing directly on tinplate was patented by Benjamin George about 1860. The Huntley and Palmers' biscuits were packaged in tin with paper labels, but by 1868 printed tins were made. The words "by appointment" appear on Huntley and Palmers' tins after 1885.

This marbleized pedestal was a Huntley and Palmers box, used with green marble and a brown center in 1909, and with brown marble and a green center in 1910.

Some of the most elaborate boxes ever made to hold store products were the English biscuit boxes. This windmill box was used by Huntley and Palmers about 1924. The log cabin was used by several companies about 1912.

"Literature" is the theme of this Huntley and Palmers box made in 1901. Several versions of this box, shaped like a bundle of books, were made. This box had marbleized paper for each book and titles such as "Shakespeare" and "Self Help."

Direct printing on tin by lithography was patented by Barclay and Fry in 1875. This method made decorations that were more lasting.

Elaborately shaped and decorated biscuit tins were made in quantity by the early 1880s. The designs often reflected the styles of the times or special events. The tins continued to be made after the 1930s, when simpler shapes were used. After World War II the fancy tins almost completely disappeared because of the high cost.

All sorts of biscuit tins were made. The Art Nouveau influence can be noticed in the tins made during the late 1890s. Novelty tins shaped like games or toys were popular after 1918.

English firms using the tins include John Buchanan and Brothers Confectioners; William Crawford and Sons, Ltd; W. Dunmore and Sons; Huntley and Palmers; W. R. Jacob and Company; MacKenzie and MacKenzie; McVitie and Price, Ltd.; Meredith and Drew, Ltd.; Peek Frean and Company.

Cleanser

The first commercial scouring powder made in the United States was Sapolio, in 1869. Sand or bath brick were used before that time.

Sapolio was sold in cardboard packages. Several types of sifter-top cans appeared as early as 1905. The newest cans have holes that are punched out; earlier ones had separate tops that turned. Well-known cleansers include Bab-O, c. 1843; Bon Ami, 1884; Borax, c. 1905; Kitchen Klenzer, c. 1910; Old Dutch Cleanser, 1906; and Sapolio, 1869.

Coffee Cans

Coffee has been a popular drink since the eighteenth century. Originally, green beans were sold, and the consumer had to roast and grind them before making the beverage. By the nineteenth century there were stores that roasted and ground coffee. The first coffee was sold in paper bags and soon after it could be purchased in tin containers. Large store containers with colorful lithographed labels appeared in 1870. Large and small lithographed rectangular tins or paper-labeled cans were used for a pound of coffee. Early cans were made in all sizes and shapes, but by the 1920s the can manufacturers tried to standardize the package. A rectangular or cylindrical package was used in standard one-, two-, or three-pound sizes. The vacuum-packed can was first used about 1900.

Labels before 1906 (the year of the Pure Food and Drug Act) could include the words "Java" or "Mocha." After 1906 claims had to be true. For example, medical claims were not permitted. Careful reading of the label should help date it as before or after 1906.

All of these cans can best be dated by the design techniques, the general tin shape, and the age of the company. Early cans were stenciled or hand-painted on a Japanned tin (an orange black background made of

Sometimes a coffee can was made with no brand name. This one shows scenes of Boston, Massachusetts.

asphalt). Later designs and labels were hand-painted, or applied with decals, or lithographed on the colored tin.

Food Cans

The earliest cans were made by hand. Isaac and Nathan Winslow of Portland, Maine, sold handmade cans in 1842. The can had a small hole in the top, and when sealed, it was sealed with a soldered disk. A workman could make about six cans an hour.

The cans were partially shaped by machine in 1847. By 1858 the method of manufacturing was more mechanized and a single workman could make 1,000 cans a day. By 1883 automation had speeded up production to about 2,500 cans per hour. These cans were made with a small hole in the top and a soldered closure.

Pickaninny Brand Peanut Butter was sold in a small pail with appropriate pictures as part of the design. This package was in use in the 1920s.

The paper label for cans was developed in the 1850s. This salmon label is from the 1940s. You can date labels like this from the size, the directions for use, and the design elements.

The type of can that we use today was made in 1898. It has crimped ends, a soldered lock-seam body, and a seam on the side that can be felt. Some of the earlier handmade cans are smooth at the joints. Cans with a baked varnish interior that appears golden in color were first made in 1903. Cans were labeled with printed or engraved labels or with tin-soldered metal labels in the early nineteenth century. The oldest known food can label in America is a steel engraving of tomatoes by Rechbow and Larne of New York, dating from the mid-nineteenth century. Some containers had embossed or raised designs. The method of printing on the metal can started about 1850. Lithography was done directly into the tin about 1875, when the process was developed by Robert Barclay of England.

Gunpowder

The gunpowder flask is probably the earliest tin container used in America that can still be collected. A gunpowder can with the paper label "Kentucky Rifle Gunpowder Hazard Powder Co. founded 1843" can be found in the Bella C. Laundauer Collection at the Metropolitan Museum of Art, New York City. The early tins had paper or stenciled labels. Later the tins were either printed with a lithographed design or had a paper label.

Tea

Tea was a popular eighteenth-century drink and it was considered so valuable it was stored in tea caddies that were often kept locked. Tea caddies were made of porcelain, silver, or for the less well-to-do, Japanned tin. Caddies were made with a flat or domed top and the style continued into the commercial packages used in the stores. Tea was sold loose from bins for years. With the advent of commercial tin containers for coffee came similar containers for tea. Store bins were known by the Civil War; the type of tea was usually written on the bin. Bins often had a cylinder that revolved so the storekeeper could indicate which tea was in stock. Names of tea like Gunpowder, Orange Pekoe, and Oolong can be found on the containers.

Talcum Powder

The talcum powder sprinkle-top can has become a specialized area in collecting. Mr. Mennen started it with his sprinkle-top can in 1883. These cans can be dated by the baby on the side. The child seems to be better-looking in later years.

Many other firms marketed talcum powders in sprinkle-top cans of varying design. A screw top was used about 1910. Tins held many other types of products such as tooth powder (especially Dr. Lyon's, a brand started in 1886).

Tobacco Cans

The majority of cans collected under this name were made to hold pipe tobacco. There were some tins that held chewing plugs, snuffs, cigars, or cigarettes. Store dispensing or display containers as well as packages were made. Tobacco was sold in cloth or paper bags until 1880, when tobacco tins were made. Stoneware and glass jars were also used.

Dan Patch, the famous horse, even had a brand of tobacco named for him. This bright yellow tin is favored by collectors because of the picture of an animal. It is a bit lower in price than some others that are not as attractive because the supply is ample. A large group of these tins was discovered in storage in the 1960s.

There are several ways to date a tobacco tin. Examine the method of decoration, the design elements, and the lettering. Check on any name and try to trace the age of the tobacco company or the manufacturing company that made the can. Tax stamps can be of some help but they are not always as useful as they would seem. The stamp will help to determine the date the tin was sold, but it could be several years after it was made. A

Tobacco cans came in many sizes and shapes. These are all lithographed tobacco containers.

1901 stamp could be in use until June 1902, the 1902 stamp to June 1910, a 1909 stamp to October 1917. The 1917 stamp was used until February 1919, the 1919 stamp until November 1921, the 1921 stamp to June 1924. In 1924 a stamp was issued that was good until February 1926; the 1926 stamp was used for many years, until November 1951; and the 1951 stamp was in effect until December 1965. The law for tax on tobacco and snuff was repealed in 1966. There were tax stamps in use at least as early as 1864. These are not dated with a year and they must be recognized by the designs.

Roly-Poly

The name "roly-poly" may be a recent idea but the famous tobacco tins have been popular with collectors for many years. One of the early books written about tin containers named them "roly-poly" even though the tins were marked "This Brownie Tin comes in different designs, get a collection." The tins were made in six different designs, with each design depicting a person. The figures are now named the "Storekeeper," "Dutchman," "Man from Scotland Yard," "Mammy," "Singing Waiter," and "Satisfied Customer." The four tobacco brands that used these tins were Dixie Queen, Mayo's, Red Indian, and U.S. Marine. It might be thought that there would be twenty-four varieties of this tin but six are still missing. The Dutchman, Man from Scotland Yard, and Satisfied Customer do not seem to have been used by Red Indian or U.S. Marine brand tobacco.

The tins were patented and made by the Tin Decorating Company, of Baltimore, Maryland. The patents date from 1912 or 1913.

Probably the most famous tobacco tin made, the roly-poly. The gentleman with the pipe is called the Storekeeper, the other is the Singing Waiter.

There are a few differences in the designs used by the four companies. The brand name is on all of the cans in the front or back. The Storekeeper is carrying Red Indian tobacco in his pocket for that brand, just cigars for the other companies. There are at least two versions of the Mammy and at least two of the Storekeeper. The rarest of the roly-polies is the Man from Scotland Yard, but all are considered prize examples of tin containers.

Three of the roly-polies were reproduced in 1980.

Care and Cleaning

There are differences of opinion on how to care for the containers. The purist will say, Don't do anything to the tin: don't clean it, don't wax it, and most important don't repaint it. The average collector will usually want to do some repairing or maintenance. Do as little to the tin as possible. It is

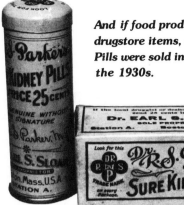

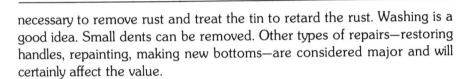

And if food product containers aren't interesting enough, try drugstore items, another collectors' field. Dr. Parker's Kidney Pills were sold in a tin in a box for only twenty-five cents in the 1930s.

necessary to remove rust and treat the tin to retard the rust. Washing is a good idea. Small dents can be removed. Other types of repairs—restoring handles, repainting, making new bottoms—are considered major and will certainly affect the value.

Cleaning

Each type of tin needs a special type of cleaner. Always test a small unseen area at the back of the tin before cleaning. First wash the tin with clear warm water to remove any loose dirt. Be sure to dry it thoroughly. It may be best to place it in a warm oven for a few minutes to assure complete drying. Rust spots should be removed. Use garnet paper or a wet silicon paper to rub off the rust. A rubber eraser will sometimes remove the loose rust. A clever rust remover is 0000 steel wool dipped in kerosene. For desperate cases oxalic acid or naval jelly will work. Then treat with a rust preventer. Do not use any of these methods on the painted part of the can. Cleaning the printed part on a can requires extreme care. Many types of tins are printed on unprimed tin and the design will rub off with little effort. Do not clean. You may want to protect the finish with a spray wax. Tins made with transfer labels can be washed with a sponge or soft cloth and pure soapsuds.

Never use a detergent. Lithographed cans can be cleaned by using a damp sponge and soapsuds. If the color is dull and the design very dirty, there is a dangerous and not recommended way to try to restore a "new" look. Use a liquid cleaner and mix a strong solution; lightly rub the painted design, and you will remove part of the paint. Too much cleaner or too much rubbing could be disastrous and remove all the paint. Careful cleaning can sometimes renew the color and appearance.

After the tin is clean be sure that it is dry by wiping it, let it stand a day or so, or place it in a warm oven for a few minutes to remove all moisture. Rust is the greatest foe of the tin container collector.

Some collectors color in the scratches and remove the dents with a rubber hammer. Beer can collectors are especially prone to repairing cans by replacing the tops or bottoms with parts of other cans. If the can is useless without repairs it is permissible, but a repaired can is worth much less than an original whole can.

You may want to wax the tin container after it is cleaned. Do not use lacquer or varnish: they discolor in time. Most collectors will not buy a lacquered can unless there is no other way to get a particular example.

If the tin has a paper label, wipe off the dirt and, again if desperate, try a very gentle wipe with a liquid cleaner. Glue any loose parts and spray with a nonyellowing varnish or acrylic. This is permissible and much safer than using a wax on a paper label.

TIN CONTAINER COLLECTOR'S DICTIONARY

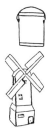

Bail-handled Pail: The pail is a round container with a lift-off lid. It was sold filled to the customer. Most were about 7 by 17 inches in circumference. See Round Canister.

Biscuit Tin: A large variety of tins in special shapes were made to hold English biscuits or cookies. These were three-dimensional representations of vases, chests, clocks, books, and other objects. See section on biscuit tins.

Box: Small container for tobacco or other material that does not fit the other definitions.

Canister: Cylindrical tin made to be reused in the kitchen to hold flour or sugar. It had no handle, and was sometimes marked with the word "flour" on one side, and had the "tobacco ad" on the other.

Cigar Tin: These containers were made to hold cigars and are therefore sized 7 by 6 by 4 inches.

Coffee Pail: A reusable tin that held coffee but was later used for milk. It was about 10 by 7 by 23 inches, cylindrical, with a round removable lid and often had a bail handle.

Concave Pocket Tin: See Upright Pocket Tin.

Cream Pail: A few types of tobacco were sold in containers that could be reused as cream pails. They were cylindrical, about 9 by 13 inches in circumference, with a lift lid and a handle.

Fire Extinguisher: A tin, about 22 by 6½ inches in circumference, that was filled with chemicals to put out a fire.

Flat Fifty: A flat tin made to hold fifty cigarettes. The top lid is lifted up. Corners not usually rounded.

Flat Pocket Tin: Tobacco, pipe tobacco, or cut plug tobacco was sold to the store customer in these tins, roughly 3 to 4 inches by 3½ by ½ by 2 inches. Corners often rounded so they could be carried without tearing pockets.

Food Tin: Any tin of a variety of sizes and shapes that held foodstuffs for resale. Pepper, mustard, tea, coffee, baking soda, cocoa, yeast, spices, marshmallows, canned fruits, vegetables, and meats were sold in these tins.

4 by 6: A container, usually for tobacco, that is 4 inches from front to rear, 6 inches long.

Gunpowder Tin: Gunpowder, to be used in rifles, was sold in tins. Most of the tins were about 6 by 9 inches with a small round screw cap. There were also larger barrel-shaped gunpowder tins.

Humidor: Tobacco was sold to store customers in this tin, roughly rectangular in shape, often with rounded corners. The top usually is oval, about 5 by 4 by 6 inches. It was pictured in ads from 1910 to 1915.

Lunch Box: Handleless. See Humidor.

Lunch Box: A container, filled with one pound of tobacco, sold to the customer. It was made to be reused as a lunch box. The tins were about 4 to 6 inches by 5 to 8 inches by 4 to 10 inches, usually rectangular in shape. The lunch box has a pair of bail handles and hinged lid, or a leather handle, or occasionally a wire handle. The entire lid of the box lifts off; it is not hinged.

Milk Pail: See Cream Pail.

Peanut Butter Pail: A small tin shaped like a sand pail, about 7 by 14 inches in circumference, to be reused by children as a toy. It has a bail handle. Peanut butter, mincemeat, coconut, and other foods came in pails. These date from about 1880.

Roly-Poly: The roly-poly tin held tobacco for the customer. It is 7 by 19 inches in circumference at its widest part. The body pulled apart. It was made in a variety of styles.

Round Canister: A container sold filled with one pound of tobacco, similar in size and shape to the bail-handled pail but with a lift-off lid and no handle.

Spice Bin: A slant top, hinged lift-off container about 10 by 8 by 9 inches. Usually decorated with little obvious advertising so the container could be used in a kitchen at home.

Store Bin: These containers were made to hold tobacco, tea, coffee, or other materials of the store. The loose contents or small packages stored inside were for sale. There are several types of bins. The slant-top container or bin is about 12 by 14 by 18 inches. It has a hinged lid. Some store containers have lift-off lids. The tea or coffee bin often had a front opening with a lift lid.

Store Bin, Coffee: See also Store Bin. These containers were made to be set on the floor of the store. The hinged lid lifted near the top or perhaps rolled backward so coffee could be scooped from the inside. These large bins are about 28 by 14 by 20 inches.

Talcum Powder: The tin containers for home use of talcum powder had an adjustable screw-on sprinkle top.

Tea Container: A tin, about 6 by 3 inches square, made to hold tea at the table. It had a round lift-off lid and was shaped very much like earlier tea canisters made of pottery or porcelain.

2 by 8 (pie-shaped): A flat, round tin, 2 inches high and 8 inches in diameter, that held one pound of tobacco. The entire top is a lift-off lid.

Upright Pocket Tin: This tin held smoking tobacco. The tin is about 4 by 3 by 1 inches, with rounded corners. It opens with a removable lid, or one hinged from the top. The concave pocket tin was shaped on one side so it could be more easily held in a pocket.

BIBLIOGRAPHY

Coca-Cola

Munsey, Cecil. *The Illustrated Guide to the Collectibles of Coca-Cola.* New York: Hawthorn Books, 1972.

Munsey, Cecil and Petretti, Allan. *Official Coca-Cola Collectibles Price Guide.* 1980–81 ed. Hackensack, New Jersey: Nostalgia Publishing Co., 1980.

Weinberger, Marty and Don. *Coca-Cola Trays from Mexico & Canada.* Willow Grove, Pennsylvania: Privately printed, 1979.

Club: Cola Clan, 3965 Pikes Peak, Memphis, Tennessee 38108

Cracker Jack

Russo, James D. *Cracker Jack Collecting for Fun and Profit.* Cincinnati: MLR, 1976.

Dr Pepper

Ellis, Harry E. *Dr Pepper, King of Beverages.* Dallas: Dr Pepper Co., 1979.

Planters Peanuts

Reddock, Richard D. and Barbara. *Planters Peanuts Advertising & Collectibles.* Des Moines: Wallace-Homestead, 1978.
Publication: Peanut Pals, P.O. Box 4465, Alabama 35802

Tin Containers

Bragdon, Charles. *Metal Decorating from Start to Finishes.* Freeport, Maine: Bond Wheelwright Co., 1961.
Clark, Hyla. *The Tin Can Book.* New York: New American Library, 1977.
Clemens, Kaye. *Tobacco and Food Tins: A Price Guide.* Vol. I. Kansas City, Missouri: Privately printed, 1973.
Corley, T.A.B. *Huntley & Palmers of Reading, 1822–1972: Quaker Enterprise Biscuits.* London: Hutchinson Publishing Group, 1972.
Davis, Alec. *Package & Print: The Development of Container and Label Design.* New York: Clarkson N. Potter, 1968.
Franklin, M. J. *British Biscuit Tins, 1868–1939.* London: New Cavendish Books, 1979.
Griffith, David. *Decorative Printed Tins.* New York: Chelsea House, 1979.
Herscher, Georges. *L'Art et les Biscuits (Art & Biscuits).* Paris: Chene, 1978.
Johnson, Laurence A. *Over the Counter and on the Shelf: Country Storekeeping in America, 1620–1920.* Rutland, Vermont: Charles E. Tuttle, 1961.
Pettit, Ernest L. *The Book of Collectible Tin Containers with Price Guide.* Wynantskill, New York: Privately printed, 1967.
———. *Collectible Tin Containers with Price Guide.* Book 2. Wynantskill, New York: Privately printed, 1970.
Rawlins, Chris. *English Biscuit Advertising and Tins: Illustrated Price Guide.* Kermit, Texas: Collector's Weekly, 1974.
Tin Container Collectors' Association. *TCCA Directory/Index, 1975.* Denver: Privately printed, 1975.
———. *A Pictorial History of the Metal Can from Its Earliest Beginnings to the Present Day.* Denver: Privately printed, 1973.
Yena, Louise. *The Handbook of Antique Coffee and Tea Collectibles: A Price Guide.* Vol. I. San Antonio: Privately printed, 1972.
Club: Tin Container Collectors' Association, P.O. Box 4555, Denver, Colorado 80204

Beer Cans

Anderson, Will. *The Beer Book: An Illustrated Guide to American Breweriana.* Princeton: The Pyne Press, 1973.
The Beer Can Collectors of America. *The Beer Can: A Complete Guide to Beer Can Collecting.* Matteson, Illinois: Great Lakes Living Press, 1976.
———. *Guide to United States Beer Cans.* Matteson, Illinois: Great Lakes Living Press, 1975.
Dabbs, Robert L. and Harris, David S. *World Wide Beer Can Collector's Guide.* Des Moines: Wallace-Homestead, 1974.

Harris, David S. *World Wide Beer Can Collector's Guide.* Vol. II. Des Moines: Wallace-Homestead, 1975.

Toepfer, Thomas. *American Beer Can Encyclopedia.* Gas City, Indiana: L-W Promotions, 1976.

———. *Beginner's Guide Beer Cans.* Gas City, Indiana: L-W Promotions, 1975.

———. *Obsolete Beer Cans with Current Values.* Vol. I. Privately printed, 1975.

———. *Obsolete Beer Cans with Current Values.* Vol. II. Gas City, Indiana: L-W Promotions, 1976.

Universal Beer Can Guide and Handbook. Appleton, Wisconsin: Midland Litho Print, 1975.

Clubs: Beer Can Collectors of America, 747 Merus Ct., Fenton, Missouri 63026; National Association of Breweriana, Willson Memorial Drive, Chassell, Michigan 49916; World Wide Beer Can Collectors, P.O. Box 1852, Independence, Missouri 64055

Publication: The Beer Can Advisor, P.O. Box 146, South Beloit, Illinois 61080

15

Paper, Metal, and Miscellaneous

Some collectors have discovered areas that other collectors are ignoring. It is these adventuresome souls who inspire the more timid collector to buy in uncharted areas. Ten years ago it was the first beer can collector, the Coca-Cola collector, or the Heisey or Depression glass collector who was buying what others threw away. Collecting the "as yet" not popular items is one way to amass a collection at a modest cost. At the beginning, it's always a guess as to whether they will ever be important collectors' items. Will historians ever search them out as they are now searching for early advertising and paper ephemera? Are they trash and not important, attractive, or useful enough to be saved?

Postcards

The first postcard that was legally mailed was sent in Austria in 1869. Postcards could not be mailed in the United States until 1873. It is said that the first picture was printed on a card mailed in Europe between 1871 and 1879 and it was probably not until 1893 that the first picture postcard was mailed in the United States.

You can be an expert and recognize old cards with little effort. Pre-1900 cards were often drawn by an artist. Color lithographed cards were popular until about 1914.

Dies were sometimes used to emboss cards, and raised designs such as flowers were preferred. Photographs or pictures printed in black and white or sepia were used on cards in the early 1900s. Comic cards became popular during the 1920s.

Postcard picturing a group of cats by the famous cat artist Louis Wain. It was printed by Raphael Tuck and Sons.

Hand-colored postcards in the 1920–1930 period had a linenlike textured surface. Color film was in use after 1935 and it gave the postcard a professional modern picture.

Postcards were made from a variety of materials. Some of the earliest cards were made in odd shapes—the outline of a beer stein or a bouquet of flowers. Government regulations soon stopped the odd shapes, and the size and shape of the card was determined by law.

Birchbark, leather, feathers, fur, peat moss, mother-of-pearl, celluloid, real hair, fabrics, wood, and paper were used for cards. Unusual cards called "mechanicals" were made. Some used a metal spring for the tail of a donkey; others had a double card that squeaked when pressed, or a girl who winked when the flaps of the card were moved. Foldout cards, see-through or hold-to-the-light cards, and puzzle cards were also popular. The majority of cards that were made and sent were scenic views, greetings, or comics.

Manufacturers and artists gained fame for their designs and production of cards. Names like Raphael Tuck, Ellen Clapsaddle, Bertha Corbett, Howard Chandler Christy, Lance Thackerey, Gene Carr, and Frances

This was the 1920s version of a very daring bathing beauty, pictured on a postcard.

Brundeye add to the value. The general rules for postcard values are many. The most expensive are the very early (pre-1898) cards, woven silk cards, and those from the World's Columbian Exposition of 1893. Cards made of strange materials such as birchbark or aluminum and those that either move or have unusual add-on features like hair are more in demand. Postcards picturing coins, stamps, early planes, special sets, fire equipment, advertising, or early autos sell well.

The more ordinary scenic view, glossy photographs, and color-wash cards are the least expensive.

Cards should always be carefully stored in boxes or albums. Don't mount a card with any form of glue or tape. Be sure to keep framed cards out of direct sunlight, as they will fade.

Dating Postcards   Sometimes you can date a postcard if you know when the postal rates changed. Postcard collectors should keep this table handy.

1872	1 cent	1959	3 cents	1978	10 cents
1917	2 cents	1963	4 cents	1981	12 cents
1919	1 cent	1968	5 cents	1981	13 cents
1925	2 cents	1971	6 cents	1985	14 cents
1928	1 cent	1973	8 cents	1988	15 cents
1952	2 cents	1975	7 cents	1991	19 cents
		1976	9 cents		

Cigar Box Labels

Wooden cigar boxes, paper labels, and cigar bands were made from the early nineteenth century when cigars first became popular. The best wooden cigar boxes were made of cedar. The brand name was die-stamped into the wooden top. Paper labels were used on the sides and inside the top lid. The boxes and labels were even collected in Victorian times. The boxes were always useful for holding small items.

There were nearly twenty thousand different brands of American cigars by 1870, and labels were needed for each. Early cigar box labels were made using a stone lithography process. As many as twenty colors were used on a single label. The designs were often embossed and decorated with gold highlights.

Cigar bands are equally collectible, and it has been said that they were invented around 1900. Glass ashtrays decorated with cigar bands are fun to collect.

Fruit Crate Art

These two orange crate labels are typical of the 1920s designs.

Old fruit crate labels once identified wooden crates of oranges, lemons, apples, and pears. Orange growers in California began using colored lithographed labels on their wooden crates during the 1880s and soon growers of other fruits followed suit. Each grower tried to outdo the other in the color and appeal of his individual label. There were over two thousand different brand labels for oranges alone by 1930.

Landscapes and seascapes, Spanish señoritas and Indian princesses, knights and matadors, birds and horses, Cupids and Santas, were all used on labels. Early designs tended to be romantic and sentimental. A 1918 study showed that it was more important to attract the wholesale jobber than the housewife, and designs became bolder and more masculine. The ladies on labels became more seductive.

Early labels were produced by using a stone lithography process that required a separate stone for each color of ink used in the design. Five inks could be combined to make as many as fifty colors. The heavy stones were replaced by engraved metal plates in the 1930s.

Cigar box labels were masterpieces of the printing art. Colorful stone lithographs were used, often with raised gold lettering and embossing. The subjects of the labels seem to have little to do with tobacco. Some men playing checkers, the Christy girl playing golf, and Honest Abe are typical subjects. ⟶

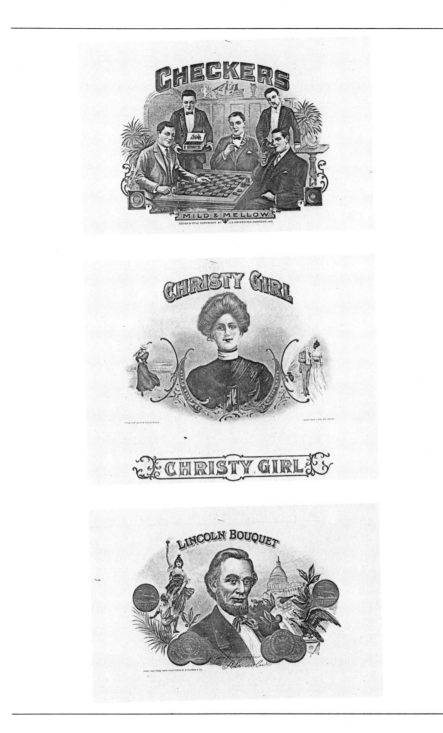

The end of the label era came with World War II, when many cardboard cartons were substituted for the old wooden crates. A simple two-color stamp on the cardboard was much cheaper and more efficient than the paper labels. Most of the unused labels were thrown away or destroyed, but enough of them were stored in warehouses and printing plants to spark a collecting craze during the 1970s.

Collecting orange crate labels gained a new respectability in February 1976, when a show of old orange crate labels opened at the De Young Museum in San Francisco.

Matchbox Labels

Matchbox labels came into use around 1827 with the invention of the friction match. The first label on a matchbox was strictly utilitarian. The design was black and white and had directions on how to use the new invention.

By 1830, N. Jones & Company of England produced a crude, pale green, pictorial label of an Englishman and a Highlander smoking, with two serpents breathing flames to add interest.

Early manufacturers found the labels were good selling devices; and by 1880, people began collecting them. Some of the best labels came from Italy, Belgium, Spain, and Australia. The oldest labels featured royalty, important people, and buildings, but by the end of the 1800s animals and birds were extremely popular.

Sports, flowers, geography, and personalities were also favorites with collectors. Many famous Japanese works of art have been used on labels.

Labels commemorating particular events were wanted because they usually had a limited issue and were on sale for only a certain period of time. For example, a flood disaster in Johnstown, Pennsylvania, in 1936 prompted a commemorative matchbox label that campaigned for more and better dams.

The oldest known United States printed matchbox label was produced by P. Truesdell of Warsaw, New York. The Truesdell matches were made only from 1855 to 1857. Safety matches were invented in 1855, and many labels after that date are printed with those words.

There are no official label catalogs, and the prices depend mainly on the individual collector and personal tastes. Labels often come in a number of variations. One variety may be common and another may be worth much more because of its rarity. If the label is worn, dirty, or torn, the price drops.

Typical matchbox labels of the 1920s.

Labels that were made to wrap around three sides of the box are valueless, no matter how old, if they are cut apart. Beginners are advised not to pay high prices for labels before becoming familiar with what is available. Remember, there are forgeries in the matchbox label field as in other collecting fields.

If matchbox labels are hard to find, there are always the matchbooks. Book matches were patented by a U.S. attorney in 1892. The first matchbook issued by the Diamond Match Company as an advertisement was for the Mendelssohn Opera Company. By 1896, book matches were made in volume.

Bookmarks

The earliest bookmarks were made of parchment, cloth, or leather from the time when printing was first done with movable type. Others were made of woven silk ribbon, stiff paper or thin cardboard, Celluloid, wood, silver, other metals, tortoiseshell, as well as other materials.

Bookmarks made before 1850 are scarce, but you can find examples that were made between 1885 and 1920. L. Prang and Company (Louis Prang) started producing lithographed bookmarks as well as greeting cards in Roxbury, Massachusetts, by 1869. The cards pictured Bible texts or events in literature, or flowers. They sold for ten dollars a set.

The "Ribbon Period" of bookmarks was from 1850 to 1880. Woven silk bookmarks were made by the Thomas Stevens firm in Coventry, England, after 1860. They were called Stevensgraphs and most of them were rectangular ribbons ranging up to 8 inches in length, with tassels at either end.

The "Victorian Advertising Period" from 1880 to 1901 produced markers made of stiff paper or cardboard. They were advertisements for products such as soap, ladies' corsets and garments, popular foods, and quack medicines. Some even had calendars on the reverse side.

The "Pre–World War I Period" covered the years 1901 to 1914. Insurance companies and publishers informed the public of their services through bookmarks.

From 1914 to the present time is considered the "Publicity and Greetings Period." Nonprofit-making enterprises used bookmarks to promote the war effort or to urge people to save money during both world wars.

Modern bookmarks are often made with religious verses or clever sayings.

A typical printed paper bookmark, made about 1910, advertising baking powder.

Book Jackets (Dust Jackets)

Paper book jackets are the latest type of paper ephemera to interest collectors who would like to assemble a collection of commercial art at little cost.

Plain paper jackets protected books as early as 1833, but pictorial jackets did not appear until the turn of the century.

Some of the best-known names in commercial art have designed covers: Francis Meynell, Edward McKnight Kauffer, and Rex Whistler in the 1920s; R. H. Macartney and Harold Jones in the 1930s; Paul Nash and H. M. Brock in the 1940s; Cecil Beaton, Philip Gough, Lynton Lamb, and Edward Ardizzone in the 1950s.

An International Book Jacket Exhibition was held at the Victoria and Albert Museum in 1947, and the Metropolitan Museum of Art has a collection.

Tips: Used book sales have books of little current value with outstanding jackets. Discard the book if you must, but preserve the jacket and record the publication date inside. Look for artist identification on the cover or inside the flap; study books on commercial art for important names.

Bookplates

Collectors secretly went about stealing bookplates by slashing books in antiques shops during the early 1900s. Bookplate collecting is popular today, but has not quite returned to its former peak of interest.

Bookplates date back five hundred years to when they were first used in medieval libraries. These bookplates were first made in about 1400, when the art of woodcutting was developed. Early designs were usually of mythological characters, ships, landscapes, and wreaths. Later, in England, they tended to heraldic designs.

The earliest dated French plate was 1529, and an English bookplate appeared in 1574. In the seventeenth century, Samuel Pepys, the famous diarist, used a bookplate for his library.

In America, the earliest known bookplate, dated 1642, was by Steven Day of Cambridge, Massachusetts. Designs in the United States were usually landscapes and motifs from myth or fiction. Personalized plates pictured the book owner, his library, or even his home.

There are now very large collections in the Metropolitan Museum of Art and the Library of Congress. The greatest number of bookplates is in the Pearson-Lowenhaupt Collection at Yale University.

Most advanced collectors specialize in design, country, or age. There are collections of mottoes, humor plates, poetic plates, and animal plates.

Copperplate engraving of inscriptions was popular and many plates instructed book borrowers to return the book. One even read, "Bookkeeping taught in one lesson. Don't lend them."

Bookplates that belonged to famous people is another category. The George Washington armorial plate is one to watch out for—it has been counterfeited. A Paul Revere bookplate would be very expensive today; in 1904, one was sold for $165 in London. Rudyard Kipling, Charles Dickens, Daniel Webster, and Eugene Field all had their own bookplates.

Mr. Sticht was a famous bookplate designer; David Castle had a specialized library about Australian exploration. Both bookplates were drawn by Sticht in the early 1900s.

Bookplates designed by noted artists is another major category for collectors. Women's plates of the eighteenth century are considered desirable, since few women owned libraries and had plates.

Some new bookplates are very collectible. Many castaway books have plates that can be removed by steaming; otherwise, the rule is—don't ruin a book by cutting out the plate.

Most collectors get their bookplates from other hobbyists. Bookplates may be kept in binders or albums attached with philatelic hinges or photo corners.

Sheet Music

The history of illustrated sheet music goes back to the fifteenth century, when music was often hand-decorated with letters. Today's collectors want sheet music starting with the 1820s. Most of the lithographed vignettes and covers were made on the East Coast. Many early songs had been written in England, but by the 1830s American sheet music with typically American illustrations was produced.

In general, the smaller the picture on the title page, the older the sheet music. By the 1870s, a full picture with title in decorative type was the fashion. Most of these title pages or covers were lithographed. Color was added in the 1840s. Chromolithographs were first used in 1843. The look of the sheet music changed in the early 1900s, and color and designs were made that included the title as part of the art. Photographs were often part of the cover. Sheet music was printed on pages measuring 13½ by 10½ inches before 1917. During World War I, four sizes were made: regular (13½ by 10½ inches), 10 by 7 inches, 4 by 5 inches, and 12 by 9 inches. After 1920, most sheet music was published on sheets measuring 12 by 9 inches.

Often sheet music can be dated by the subject of the illustration. This telephone and the song date from about 1910.

Collectors feel that the best covers were made before the 1930s. Look for work by artists or firms such as Winslow Homer, Currier and Ives, Louis Prang, and Sarony. The best-known firms to specialize in sheet music are John H. Bufford (Boston), William Sharp (Philadelphia), B. W. Thayer (Boston), Robert Cooke (Boston), Endicott (New York), Penniman (Baltimore), Sinclair (Philadelphia), and Endicott and Swett (Baltimore).

Desirable twentieth-century artists include Norman Rockwell, James Montgomery Flagg, Archie Gunn, Hamilton, Alexander King, Starmer, Albert Barbelle, Andre Detakacs, Pfeiffer, John Frew, Frederick S. Manning, Gene Buck, and Whohlman.

Sheet music should be in good condition with all pages intact. Be sure the music is the proper size, not cut down, after 1920, to fit a piano bench. You can dust the music and try to remove pencil marks and smudges with an art gum eraser. Transparent tape permanently damages any paper and lowers the value. Value is determined by age, popularity, rarity, condition, fame of artist, and category. Often music picturing special categories such as automobiles or political events bring more money than earlier, more artistic covers.

An easy way to date sheet music is by the copyright date that is used on all music.

Japanese Woodblock Prints

Japanese woodblock prints were produced in quantity during the seventeenth, eighteenth, and nineteenth centuries. They were examples of a popular art form called *ukiyo-e*, or pictures of the "floating world" of everyday existence. Typical subjects were landscapes, family life, actors, courtesans, and wrestlers.

The making of a finished print required the work of four men: a publisher who decided to offer a print and provided the money and materials, and hired the necessary workmen; an artist who drew a design on transparent paper, then took it to an engraver who pasted the picture to a wooden block and cut the wood between the lines to produce a block with the artist's lines in relief. After a series of steps the artist and engraver made a separate block for each color to be used in the final print. These

The portrait of Ushiwakamaru with a sword from the 36 Chrysanthemums series, aiban *(13 by 9 inches).*

blocks were taken to the fourth man, a printer who printed each color in turn on the paper to produce the multicolored picture.

An edition from a set of blocks was limited to about two hundred but many editions were made from the same blocks.

Prices for Japanese woodblock prints are influenced by subject, artist, and condition. A print that has been glued to a mat or faded by sunlight is of little value.

Woodblock print of a woman by Yoshitoshi, ōban (15 by 10 inches) tate-e (vertical print).

Care of Prints

To keep unframed prints in good condition, store them in a dry, dark place; air them every six months to prevent mildew and insect damage. If prints are framed, use pure rag matboard, and do not let the prints touch the glass. Do not hang prints in bright sunlight.

Woodblock print of a pilgrim and a barber by Kuniyoshi, ōban tate-e.

Ballooning in America, a Japanese print by Yoshitora. This is typical of the unusual Oriental style of portraying Europeans with European clothes and Japanese features.

A famous scene of Edo by Hiroshige, ōban yoko-e (horizontal print).

Major Artists

The big names to look for in Japanese woodblock prints are Utamaro (1753–1806), known for his prints of beautiful women; Hokusai (1760–1849) and Hiroshige (1797–1858), known for landscapes; Kiyonobu (1664–1729) and Toyokuni (1769–1825), who specialized in theater prints; and Harunobu (1725–1770), who perfected full-color prints.

WOODBLOCK PRINT ARTISTS

Buncho	1726–c.1792	(Toyokuni III)	1786–1865
Choshun	1673–1753	Kuniyoshi	1797–1861
Eiri, Fl.*	1793–1802	Masanobu	1686?–1764?
Eishi	1756–1815	Moronobu	1618?–1694
Harunobu	1725–1770	Sharaku, Fl.	1794–1795
Hiroshige	1797–1858	Shigemasa	1739–1820
Hokusai	1760–1849	Shigenaga	1697?–1756?
Kaigetsudo, Fl.	1704–1716?	Shuncho, Fl.	1772–1800
Kitao Masanobu	1761–1816	Shunei	1762–1819
Kiyochika	1847–1915	Shunman	1757–1820
Kiyohiro	1718?–1776?	Shunsho	1726–1792
Kiyomasu I	1694–1716?	Sukenobu	1671–1751
Kiyomitsu	1735–1785	Toyohiro	1763?–1828
Kiyonaga	1752–1815	Toyokuni	1769–1825
Kiyonobu I	1664–1729	Toyonobu	1711–1785
Kiyonobu II	1702–1752?	Utamaro	1753–1806
Koryusai, Fl.	1765–1780	Yoshitora	1840–1870
Kunisada		Yoshitoshi	1839–1892

Confusion can arise because the prints are signed in Japanese; because some artists used more than one name; and because students of a famous artist sometimes adopted his name. When in doubt, consult an expert.

A GUIDE TO WOODBLOCK TERMINOLOGY

The terminology used in describing Japanese woodblock prints in auction catalogs and shops can be confusing: Signatures *ga, fude, hitsu,* or *zu* following an artist's name means "drawn by" or "painted by."

---

* Fl. means working dates.

Subject Designations

Bijin-ga: Prints of women.

Fukei-ga: Prints of landscapes.

Nagasaki-e (Also Yokahama-e and Nambam): Prints of foreigners and foreign life.

Shibai-e: Theater prints, Kabuki actors.

Shun-ga: "Spring pictures," or erotic prints.

Sumo-e: Prints of sumo wrestlers.

Surimono: Prints that relate to the seasons; used as greeting cards.

Uki-e: Prints using Western-style perspective.

Ukiyo-e: General term for pictures of everyday existence.

Color Designations

Beni-e: A *hand-colored* print using *beni,* a rose red color.

Benizuri-e: A *printed* picture, introduced in the 1740s, using *beni* color; later a two-color print using red and green or other colors.

Nishiki-e: A full-color print, introduced in 1764.

Sumizuri-e: A black and white "ink-printed picture."

Tan-e: A hand-colored print using *tan,* a red lead color.

Urushi-e: A "lacquer picture," in which glue and brass bits were added to the paint in imitation of lacquerware.

Aluminum Antiques

It is hard to believe that at one time aluminum sold for about one-third the cost of gold. It sold for more than the cost of silver between the 1850s and 1870s. It was during this time that chemists first learned how to refine bauxite in order to get aluminum. The amounts were small and it was expensive. Aluminum was used for jewelry, serving dishes, combs, coins, small picture frames, card cases, and other small pieces. A commercial method of smelting aluminum was invented in 1914 and then the metal was able to be used for inexpensive novelties. Aluminum cookware was popular by the 1930s. The early novelties and the hand-hammered giftwares of the 1940s are the aluminum items of greatest interest. Wendell August Forge, still working in Grove City, Pennsylvania, and Kensington, Inc., making pieces until World War II in New Kensington, Pennsylvania, are the most important of the United States makers.

Trademark of Wendell August Forge.

Chase Chrome

Another metal line of interest to some collectors is the Chase chrome made by the Chase Brass and Copper Company of Waterbury, Connecticut, from 1930 to 1942. The serving trays, electric warmers, candlesticks, trays, vases, smoking stands, lamps, bowls, and boxes were designed in the Art Deco style.

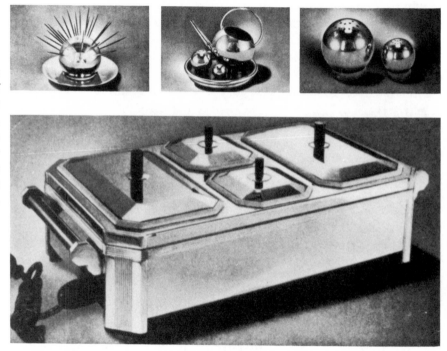

From the Chase Chrome catalog of 1936, from left to right: a cocktail ball, a pancake and corn set, salt and pepper spheres, and an electric buffet server.

Frankart

Frankart, Inc., of New York, New York, made a line of green metal pieces in the Art Deco style during the 1920s and 1930s. Max le Verrier of France made nude figures, using a white metal with a greenish patina that resembled bronze. They sold so well that several American makers began making similar, but less expensive, figures. They were called "greenies" and were typical of the Deco period. The nude ladies held ashtrays or lamps; but stylized gazelles, doves, and other animals were also popular. Pieces were marked "Frankart, Inc." on the base. Similar wares were made by Nu-Art.

Doorknobs

A popular television show of the 1970s featured a slightly eccentric aunt who was also a confused witch who collected doorknobs. It was considered a joke that she would take the hardware from the door and leave the home with a problem. However, there are many serious doorknob collectors. They want the brass and glass hardware that was popular during the late nineteenth and early twentieth centuries. It was in 1876, for the Centennial Exposition, or so the story goes, that hardware was first designed to reflect the decor of the building. By 1900 catalogs offered hardware in Greek, Roman, Gothic, Renaissance, Louis XIV, Rococo, Colonial, Art Nouveau, and other styles. Hardware could be purchased in iron, tin, copper, brass, bronze, silver, and even gold. Knobs were also made in pressed or cut glass, painted porcelain, pottery, or wood. A monogram or emblem could even be placed on handles that were made to order. Some important manufacturers were Russell and Erwin Manufacturing Company, P & F Corbin and Company, Yale & Town Manufacturing Company, Reading Hardware Company, and Sargent & Company. Most collectors find the knobs in secondhand shops or in demolished building sites.

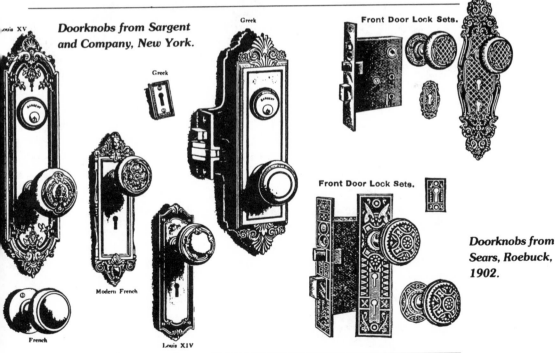

Doorknobs from Sargent and Company, New York.

Greek

Greek

Front Door Lock Sets.

Front Door Lock Sets.

Louis XV

Modern French

French

Louis XIV

Doorknobs from Sears, Roebuck, 1902.

Shellwork

Shellwork has a long history. Elaborate floral bouquets, figures, and pictures were made in the eighteenth and early nineteenth centuries, when shellwork was an elegant parlor pastime for "genteel" ladies.

"A Present from Barbados" is spelled out in shells in this "sailor's valentine."

"Sailor's valentines," of specially framed shell groupings, were made as souvenirs for travelers to the West Indies and other islands. Today's bargains are trinket boxes, pincushions, and souvenir items that came into vogue around 1850. Most were made of cardboard covered with plaster of Paris, then decorated with shells, marbleized paper, lithographed scenes, fabric, or mirrors. They took the form of cottages, shoes, miniature furniture, and other imaginative shapes. Shell-decorated souvenirs are still being made but differ in style and construction from the old ones.

Christmas Tree Antiques

The first decorated Christmas trees in America may have been a display in Bethlehem, Pennsylvania (1747), Easton, Pennsylvania (1816), Philadelphia, Pennsylvania (1819), Lancaster, Pennsylvania (1821), York, Pennsylvania (1823), Harrisburg, Pennsylvania (1823), Boston, Massachusetts (1832), St. Clair County, Illinois (1833), Circleville, Ohio (1838), Williamsburg, Virginia (1842), Farmington, Iowa (1845), Wooster, Ohio (1847), or Cleveland, Ohio (in a church, 1851). The records are imperfect and each area claims a "first tree." The early trees were decorated with paper cornucopias, gilded eggcups or nuts, apples, small dolls, cookies, seed pods, pinecones, ribbons, and candles. Homemade cloth ornaments and paper chains were used by the 1880s. The first glass ornaments were imported from Germany about 1860 and were manufactured in the United States by the early 1870s. Small mirrored or tin reflectors were offered for sale by the 1880s. Silver-foil icicles were made by 1878, lead-foil icicles appeared in the 1920s, Mylar icicles in the 1950s. Angel's hair was made by 1880. Electric lights were first used on a Christmas tree in New York City in 1882.

Collectors did not become serious about old Christmas ornaments until the mid-1970s. Before that time, old Christmas ornaments sold for less than one dollar, and they were usually found in attic or garage sales. The earliest commercial ornaments to be found date from the 1870s. German tin or tin-and-lead castings were made in geometric shapes. Some were colored and some had added cut glass. Wax ornaments were also made in Germany at the same time. They were usually angels with paper-and-ribbon clothes and wings. The "Dresden" ornaments of 1880–1910 are most desired by collectors. They were made of silver- and gold-embossed cardboard in a variety of shapes including animals, fish, toys, furniture, and people. Fragile glass ornaments were available in quantity from Germany by 1880. They were made in shapes ranging from angel heads to potatoes. It was not until 1939 that the first machine-made lacquered glass ornaments were made.

Other Christmas tree decorations included chromolithographed pictures of angels, Santa Claus, and ornaments that were imported from Germany until 1914.

Papier-mâché candy containers for hanging on trees were made in Germany by 1900.

Glass holders for candles and tin-clip holders for candles were used during the nineteenth century. The first electric Christmas lights were used by Thomas Edison in 1882. By 1901, General Electric was selling a string of lights for twelve dollars, which was more than a week's wages for the average worker. Figural bulbs were first introduced from Austria in 1909. Shortly after, they were made in Germany, Japan, and the United States. Character bulbs became an important part of Christmas decorations by the 1920s. Hundreds of styles were made, including comic figures, vegeta-

Santa Claus looks a bit less jolly in this papier-mâché figure made in the 1920s. He is 14 inches high.

bles, animals, autos, birds, and, of course, Santa Claus. Bubble lights were first made in the 1940s, twinkle bulbs in the 1950s, plastic bulbs by 1955. The cool lamp made for plastic trees was first sold in 1958.

If you plan to use the bulbs you collect, always check that the cords are not frayed. Old wiring can be a fire hazard.

There are other Christmas antiques. The first card was sent in England in 1843, or possibly as early as 1839; the first American card was made by Louis Prang in 1873. Christmas seals were first used in 1904. The first Christmas plate was made by Bing and Grondahl of Denmark in 1895. The first Christmas spoons were made by Michelsen Silversmiths of Denmark in 1910. One can never tire of Christmas, but there are other holidays. Today, collectors are searching for Halloween candy holders, old masks, Easter eggs, Thanksgiving decorations, and hundreds of other holiday-related items.

Trunks

The history of old trunks is not always easy to discover. Most old trunks and sea chests that turn up in attics or house sales date from the nineteenth or early twentieth centuries. Only general guidelines can be given on dating and classifying trunks or chests.

Nineteenth-century sea chests were often handmade by the sailors who used them. Early chests had sloping sides to provide more stability on rolling ships. Most had flat tops, so they could be used as seats or worktables.

American sea chests were usually made of unpainted wood, but the inside lid was sometimes carved or painted. Sea chests with carved or painted exteriors were often of German or Dutch origin.

Reproduction sea chests are now on the market. Intricate, handmade ropework handles (beckets) were a typical feature of old sea chests. Reproductions usually have plainer handles.

Sailors who went to the Orient often brought brass-fitted camphorwood chests from Singapore. Reproductions of these camphorwood chests are being made in Korea, and are available in Oriental import shops.

Leather-covered trunks were popular for overland travel from the late eighteenth to mid-nineteenth centuries. The trunks were made of wood, covered with leather, and often decorated and reinforced with nailheads or studs. Tops were flat or slightly rounded. The interiors were commonly lined with old newspapers. Sometimes wallpaper, cloth, or paint was used. Handles were heavy leather or metal. The "Jenny Lind" trunk of the 1850s was a late example of this type. It had a flat top, rounded corners, and studded metal bands around the edges and center.

Trunks and Traveling Bags.

WE SELL TRUNKS AT ALL PRICES. We can suit you in style and quality. We want your order, because we can sell you GOOD TRUNKS AND BAGS CHEAPEST. In trunks and bags, as in most other kinds of merchandise, we recommend the medium and better grades, for they are cheapest in the end. **A dollar or two added to the price of a trunk may mean many years of additional usefulness. The particular reasons why we deserve careful consideration and your order, is because we protect you from high prices, from dishonest quality and workmanship.** While we sell the cheaper kinds as well as the better grades, each represents the best value of that kind at lowest possible prices. We do not offer one kind of trunk or bag at cost and then ask you to pay too much for another. **THERE IS INTEGRITY in trunks as in other merchandise.** They should be made to stand the wear and tear which they are sure to get from time to time.

OUR TRUNKS AND BAGS are made under careful supervision; every nail, rivet, clamp, hinge and lock is attached with the exactness and skill of thorough workmen. **THIS IS WHY WE WARRANT EVERY TRUNK AND BAG to be as represented and the best of its kind at the lowest possible price.**

If you do not see what you want, write to us for information and get our prices.

WHEN ORDERING duplicate keys, give catalogue number of trunk or bag, also number of letter on key or lock. Duplicate keys furnished at 5 cents each.

Trunks offered for sale by Sears, Roebuck and Company in 1902.

Crystallized or Fancy Metal Covered Trunks.

Cross Bar Slats, Iron Bottom.

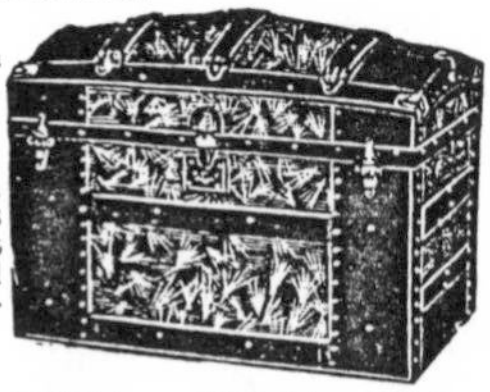

No. 33R5002 Very substantially made; barrel stave top, iron bound, cross bar slats on top, body slats, set up tray with covered bonnet box, iron bottom.

Length	Width	Height	Weight	Price
26 in.	14½ in.	17½ in.	27 lbs.	$1.65
28 in.	15½ in.	18½ in.	31 lbs,	1.95
30 in.	16½ in.	19½ in.	34 lbs.	2.10
32 in.	17½ in.	20½ in.	37 lbs.	2.40
34 in.	18½ in.	21½ in.	41 lbs.	2.65
36 in.	19½ in.	22½ in.	46 lbs.	2.90

Crystallized Metal Covered Trunks.

Flat Top.

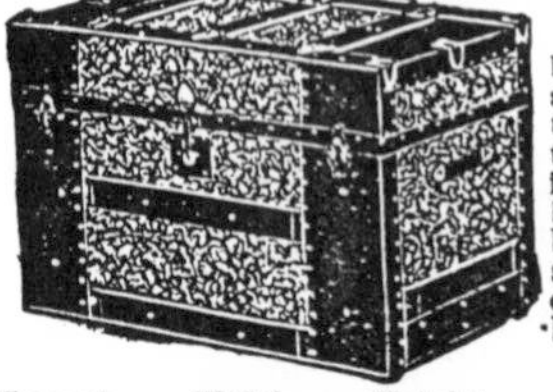

No. 33R5010
Will stand the hard knocks that any trunk is sure to receive. Flat top, large shape, iron bound, cross bar slats on top; long slats on body, set up tray with covered bonnet box. Iron bottom.

Length	Width	Height	Weight	Price
26 in.	14½ in.	17 in.	28 lbs.	$2.25
28 in.	15½ in.	18 in.	32 lbs.	2.50
30 in.	16½ in.	19 in.	35 lbs.	2.75
32 in.	17½ in.	20 in.	39 lbs.	3.00
34 in.	18½ in.	21 in.	43 lbs.	3.25
36 in.	19½ in.	22 in.	46 lbs.	3.50

GIVE CATALOGUE NUMBER IN FULL WHEN YOU WRITE YOUR ORDER

New Shape Up to Date Trunk, Cross Bar Slats, Iron Bottom.

No. 33R5020
Fancy metal covered, flat top, with front and back rounded, hardwood reverse bent slats, metal corner bumpers, clamps, bottom rollers, etc. Monitor lock and patent bar bolts, heavy strap hinges, tray, with bonnet box. Fall-in top and side compartments, all separately covered, and four slats on all sizes. Without a doubt this is the handiest and most substantial trunk ever built for our low price.

Monitor Lock.

Length	Width	Height	Weight	Price
28 in.	16 in.	18½ in.	34 lbs.	$3.20
30 in.	17 in.	19½ in.	39 lbs.	3.45
32 in.	18 in.	20½ in.	44 lbs.	3.90
34 in.	19 in.	21½ in.	51 lbs.	4.15
36 in.	20 in.	22½ in.	55 lbs.	4.40

Crystallized Metal Covered Trunk.

No. 33R5024
Cross bar slats, hinge tray, iron bottom, full finish, with parasol case. Barrel stave top, wide iron bound, five cross bar slats on top and upright on front, end slats, malleable iron corners and shoes, etc., stitched leather handles. Excelsior lock, patent bolts, fancy skeleton work, covered tray with bonnet box, parasol case and side compartment, fall-in top.

Length	Width	Height	Weight	Price
28 in.	16 in.	19½ in.	39 lbs.	$3.65
30 in.	17 in.	20½ in.	42 lbs.	3.95
32 in.	18 in.	21½ in.	47 lbs.	4.30
34 in.	19 in.	22½ in.	51 lbs.	4.70
36 in.	20 in.	23½ in.	58 lbs.	5.10
38 in.	21 in.	24½ in.	64 lbs.	5.60

EXTRA QUALITY CRYSTALLIZED METAL TRUNKS.

GREAT BARGAIN, $2.25 TRUNK.

No. 33R5014 Full finished cross bar slats, iron bottom, barrel stave top, cross bar slats on top, and upright on front, iron clamps, brass Monitor lock, patent bolts, rollers, hinges, etc.; covered tray with bonnet box and side compartments; fall-in top. This is a handsome trunk, very wide and high and extra well made.

Length	Width	Height	Weight	Price
26 in.	14½ in.	17½ in.	30 lbs.	$2.25
28 in.	15½ in.	18½ in.	33 lbs.	2.50
30 in.	16½ in.	19½ in.	37 lbs.	2.75
32 in.	17½ in.	20½ in.	41 lbs.	3.00
34 in.	18½ in.	21½ in.	46 lbs.	3.25
36 in.	19½ in.	22½ in.	50 lbs.	3.50

By 1895, trunks were covered with canvas or decorated sheet metal. They were available in flat top or high-rounded barrel-stave top styles, and corners were square or rounded. Most had iron bottoms and were iron-bound for extra security. Embossed metal coverings were used between 1870 and 1910.

By 1925, trunks were much more utilitarian. The covering was a "vulcanized fiber" or plain, undecorated metal. Tops were flat, and corners were reinforced with brass or iron angles.

While most American trunks were made of wood covered with various materials, many British trunks from the turn of the century were made of compressed cane. The cane was covered with leather or canvas.

Care and Refinishing of Trunks

Take the trunk outside and spray it with an insecticide. Close the lid and let the trunk stand for at least twenty-four hours.

If the trunk smells musty put a bar of scented soap inside, or spray with a room deodorant. If an odor remains, try a deodorant sold at marine supply houses that is made to take the damp smell from boats.

Next, wash the trunk inside and out with a half-and-half mixture of water and white vinegar. This will help neutralize odors too. Remove all hardware. Use a commercial rust remover on rusty metal pieces.

If your trunk is painted or covered with worn cloth or paper, it must be stripped. Don't destroy original labels. Use a commercial stripper to remove paint. Paper can be scraped off after sponging with warm water. A single-edge razor blade will take off leather.

Smooth the surface by sanding with a medium-grade sandpaper. Then wipe the trunk with paint thinner to give a clean surface for a new finish.

If you want to restore the trunk to its original condition, either stain or varnish a wooden trunk. Metal trunks should be painted.

BIBLIOGRAPHY

Bookmarks
Coysh, A. W. *Collecting Bookmarkers.* Devon, England: David & Charles, 1974.

Bookplates
Allen, Charles Dexter. *American Book-Plates: A Guide to Their Study with Examples.* New York: Hacker Art Books, 1894, reissued 1968.

Arellanes, Audrey Spencer. *Bookplates: A Selective Annotated Bibliography of the Periodical Literature*. Detroit: Gale Research, 1971.

Club: American Society of Bookplate Collectors and Designers, 1206 N. Stoneman Ave., Alhambra, California 91801

Chase Chrome

Koch, Gladys. *Chase Chrome*. Stanford: Privately printed, 1978.

Christmas Tree Ornaments

Rogers, Maggie and Hawkins, Judith. *The Glass Christmas Ornament: Old and New*. Forest Grove, Oregon: Timber Press, 1977.

Snyder, Phillip V. *The Christmas Tree Book*. New York: Viking, 1976.

Cigar Box Labels

Human, Tony. *Handbook of Cigar Boxes*. Elmira, New York: Arnot Art Museum, 1979.

Club: International Seal, Label and Cigar Band Society, 8915 E. Bellevue St., Tucson, Arizona 85715

Doorknobs

Eastwood, Maudie. *The Antique Doorknob*. Tillamook, Oregon: Privately printed, 1976.

Club: Doorknob Collectors, 221 2nd St. S.E., Waverly, Iowa 50677

Fruit Crate Art

Salkin, John and Gordon, Laurie. *Orange Crate Art*. New York: Warner Books, 1976.

Japanese Woodblock Prints

Michener, James. *The Floating World*. New York: Random House, 1954.

————. *Japanese Prints: From the Early Masters to the Modern*. Rutland, Vermont: Charles E. Tuttle, 1963.

Salmon, Patricia. *A Guide to Japanese Antiques*. New York: Van Nostrand Reinhold, 1976.

Stewart, Basil. *Guide to Japanese Prints & Their Subject Matter*. New York: Dover, 1979.

Matchbox Labels

Rendell, Joan. *Matchbox Labels*. New York: Praeger, 1968.

Paper

McCulloch, Lou W. *Paper Americana: A Collector's Guide*. San Diego: A. S. Barnes, 1980.

Clubs: Ephemera Society, 124 Elm St., Bennington, Vermont 05201; National Association of Paper and Advertising Collectibles, P.O. Box 471, Columbia, Pennsylvania 17512

Postcards

Holt, Tonie and Valmai. *Picture Postcards of the Golden Age: A Collector's Guide.* Folsom, Pennsylvania: Deltiologists of America, 1971.

Klamkin, Marian. *Picture Postcards.* New York: Dodd, Mead, 1974.

Miller, George and Dorothy. *Picture Postcards in the United States, 1893–1918.* New York: Clarkson N. Potter, 1976.

Range, Thomas E. *The Book of Postcard Collecting.* New York: Dutton, 1980.

Staff, Frank. *The Picture Postcard and Its Origins.* New York: Praeger, 1966.

Clubs: Deltiologists of America, 3709 Gradyville Rd., Newtown Square, Pennsylvania 19073; Post Card Club Federation, P.O. Box 27, Somerdale, New Jersey 08083

Publication: American Postcard Journal, P.O. Box 20, Syracuse, New York 13201

Sheet Music

Dichter, Harry and Shapiro, Elliott. *Handbook of Early American Sheet Music, 1768–1889.* New York: Dover, 1977.

Klamkin, Marian. *Old Sheet Music.* New York: Hawthorn Books, 1975.

Westin, Helen. *Introducing the Song Sheet.* New York: Thomas Nelson, 1976.

Publication: National Sheet Music Society Newsletter, 1597 Fair Park Ave., Los Angeles, California 90041

Trunks

Klamkin, Marian. *Marine Antiques.* New York: Dodd, Mead, 1975.

Labuda, Martin and Maryann. *Price & Identification Guide to Antique Trunks.* Cleveland: Antique Trunk Company, 1972.

Index